SUPER HUMAN
ENCYCLOPEDIA

SUPER
HUMAN
ENCYCLOPEDIA

DISCOVER THE AMAZING THINGS YOUR BODY CAN DO

Steve Parker

Chief editorial consultant
Professor Robert Winston

DK LONDON

Senior Editor
Janet Mohun

Project Art Editors
Alison Gardner, Clare Joyce,
Duncan Turner, Francis Wong

Editors
Wendy Horobin,
Ruth O'Rourke-Jones

US Editor
Jill Hamilton

Jacket Designer
Mark Cavanagh

Jacket Design
Development Manager
Sophia M.T.T

Jacket Editor
Maud Whatley

Pre-production Producer
Francesca Wardell

Senior Producer
Mary Slater

CONTENTS

DK INDIA

Senior Editor
Anita Kakar

Senior Art Editor
Devika Dwarkadas

Editor
Sumita Dey

Art Editors
Parul Gambhir,
Konica Juneja,
Vanya Mittal

Managing Editor
Rohan Sinha

Managing Art Editor
Sudakshina Basu

Production Manager
Pankaj Sharma

Senior DTP Designer
Neeraj Bhatia

Pre-production Manager
Balwant Singh

DTP Designers
Jaypal Singh Chauhan,
Syed Md. Farhan

Picture Researcher
Aditya Katyal

**LONDON, NEW YORK, MELBOURNE,
MUNICH, AND DELHI**

Managing Art Editor
Michelle Baxter

Art Director
Philip Ormerod

Publishers
Sarah Larter, Liz Wheeler

Associate Publishing Director
Liz Wheeler

Managing Editor
Angeles Gavira Guerrero

Publishing Director
Jonathan Metcalf

BODY FRAMEWORK

MISSION CONTROL

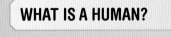

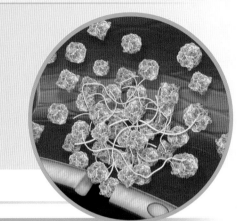

TOTALLY SENSATIONAL

POWER SYSTEMS

Illustrations	**Photography**
Peter Bull Studios	Ruth Jenkinson
Additional text	**Consultant**
Chris Woodford	Frances Ashcroft

First American Edition, 2014
Published in the United States by

DK Publishing
4th floor, 345 Hudson Street
New York, New York 10014

14 15 16 17 18 10 9 8 7 6 5 4 3 2 1
001—192974—Sept/2014

A catalog record for this book is available from the Library of Congress.

ISBN 978-1-4654-2445-7

Printed and bound in China by Leo Paper Products

Discover more at
www.dk.com

DK books are available at special discounts when purchased in bulk for sales promotions, premiums, fund-raising, or educational use. For details, contact: DK Publishing Special Markets, 345 Hudson Street, New York, New York 10014 or SpecialSales@dk.com.

FUEL AND WASTE

DEFENSE AND CONTROL

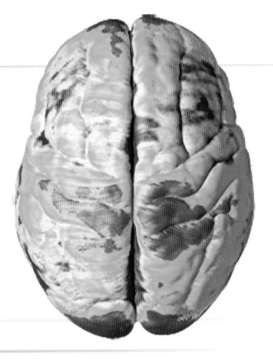

NEW LIFE AND GROWTH

FUTURE HUMANS

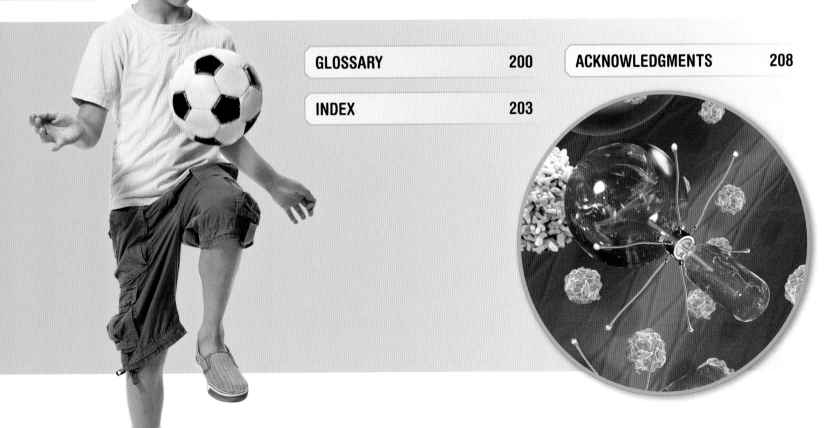

HUMAN PLANET
Where we live

Humans have adapted to almost every corner of planet Earth. From the coldest poles and steepest mountains to sweltering rain forests and scorching deserts, people survive and thrive. Of course, this is partly due to our cleverness and skill in making suitable clothing, suits, shelters, warming fires, cooling fans, and other inventions. But over thousands of years, the body itself has also adapted to enormously varied environments.

RAIN FORESTS

People living in tropical forests tend to have a smallish, slim stature and wear little clothing. They have sharp senses and the ability to remember forest tracks, plant uses, and signs of animals.

SPACE

Sealed in a spacesuit, with a supply of air to breathe, humans can even venture out into space. The suit also has temperature control, so it does not fry in the sun's glare or freeze in the shadows.

POLAR REGIONS

People with a broad physique tend to lose heat less quickly in cold conditions, especially when clothed in thick furs and skins of local animals that have also adapted to the snowy landscape.

MOUNTAINS

A broad chest, large lungs, and relatively more red blood cells allow mountain people to take in maximum oxygen from the thin air at altitude.

DESERTS

A slim body loses warmth more rapidly in hot conditions. Traditional loose robes allow air to circulate around the body for added cooling.

UNDERWATER

Divers can stay under for hours with the help of a scuba tank containing compressed air. This air is breathed in through a regulator that maintains air pressure at a safe level and supplies air as necessary.

ALL SHAPES AND SIZES
The same but different

There are so many human bodies in the world that counting them all would take more than 200 years! They all have the same main parts, such as skin, a heart, bones, and a brain. Yet they are all different. Each body is an individual person, outside and in. You have your own facial appearance, eye color, and hair style, and your own likes, dislikes, and memories. It is this endless variety that makes the human body truly fascinating.

"250 babies are born every minute"

All smiles

All these people are different in skin color, hair style, eye shape, cheek width, and many other features. Yet they all have something in common— they are smiling. Facial expressions such as anger, surprise, and pleasure are understood throughout most of the world.

ALMOST IDENTICAL

Identical twins look similar, especially when they are babies. But each develops small physical variations, from fingerprints to nose length and the shape of their smiles. As they grow up together, their characters become more individual too, with different favorite foods, fashions, and friends.

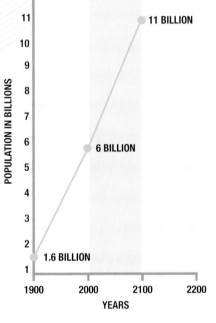

COMMON PROPORTIONS

The structure of the human body has been studied for thousands of years. This sketch, by Italian artist and anatomist Leonardo da Vinci, was drawn around 1490. On average, in relation to total height, the legs are one-half, the arms just over two-fifths, and the head one-eighth.

RAPID GROWTH

There are more people on Earth now than have ever lived in all the centuries before. For thousands of years humans numbered in the low millions, rising slowly to a billion by the 1800s. Since then it has grown rapidly to more than 7 billion today and is expected to reach 11 billion by the end of this century.

POPULATION IN BILLIONS

11 — 11 BILLION
10
9
8
7
6 — 6 BILLION
5
4
3
2
1 — 1.6 BILLION

1900   2000   2100   2200
YEARS

STATS AND FACTS

AVERAGE LIFESPAN

MEN — **65** years

WOMEN — **69** years

300 MILLION TONS (270 MILLION TONNES) The total weight of all humans on Earth = **800 ×** Empire State Building

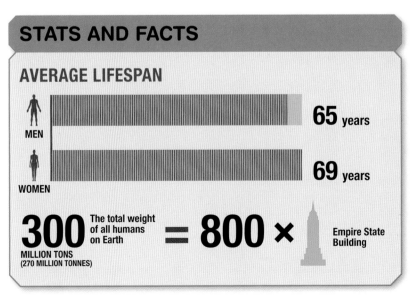

11

WHAT IS A HUMAN?

Body analysis

What would alien visitors to Earth think of its main large inhabitants? The human species, *Homo sapiens*, belongs to the animal group we call mammals, which are warm-blooded with hair or fur. Among mammals, we are included with the lemurs, monkeys, and apes in the group called primates. Within primates, our closest cousins are apes such as chimps and gorillas. But with our upright posture, amazing intelligence, and incredible language skills, we are unique.

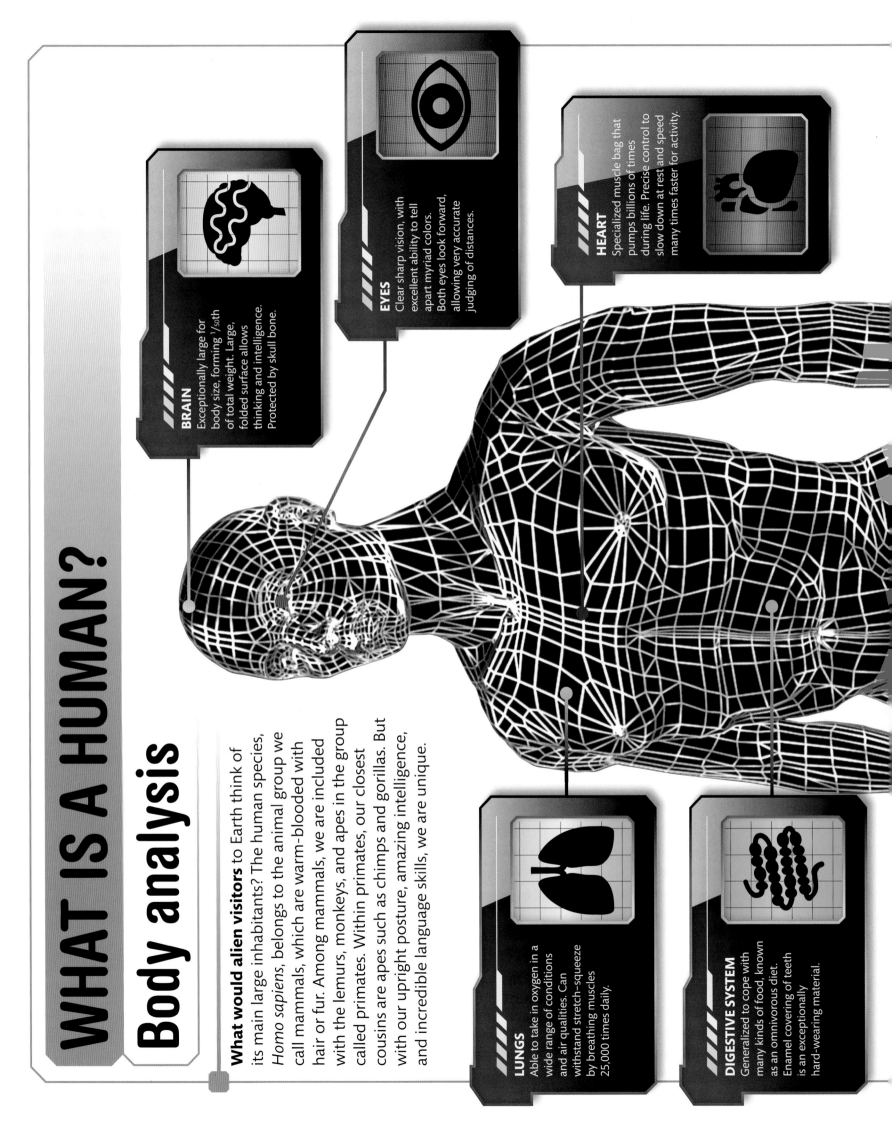

BRAIN
Exceptionally large for body size, forming 1/50th of total weight. Large, folded surface allows thinking and intelligence. Protected by skull bone.

EYES
Clear sharp vision, with excellent ability to tell apart myriad colors. Both eyes look forward, allowing very accurate judging of distances.

HEART
Specialized muscle bag that pumps billions of times during life. Precise control to slow down at rest and speed many times faster for activity.

LUNGS
Able to take in oxygen in a wide range of conditions and air qualities. Can withstand stretch–squeeze by breathing muscles 25,000 times daily.

DIGESTIVE SYSTEM
Generalized to cope with many kinds of food, known as an omnivorous diet. Enamel covering of teeth is an exceptionally hard-wearing material.

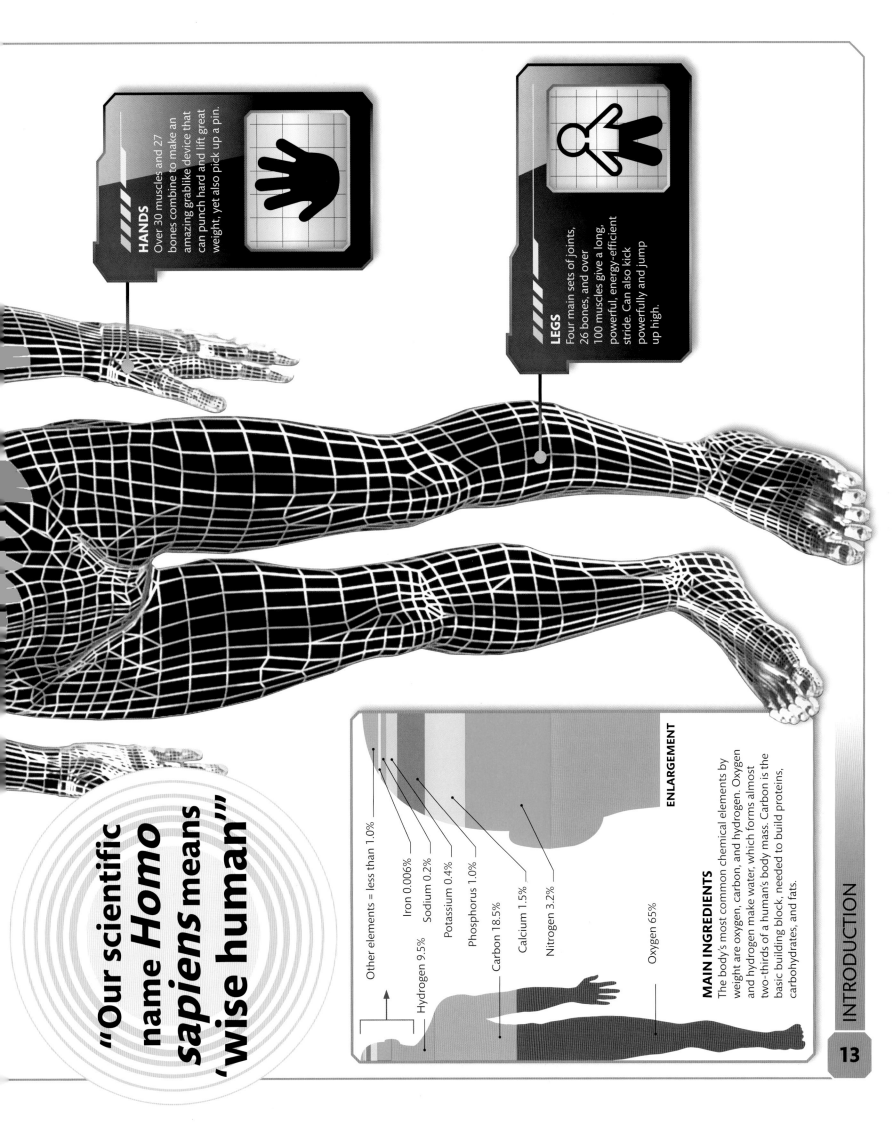

HANDS

Over 30 muscles and 27 bones combine to make an amazing grablike device that can punch hard and lift great weight, yet also pick up a pin.

LEGS

Four main sets of joints, 26 bones, and over 100 muscles give a long, powerful, energy-efficient stride. Can also kick powerfully and jump up high.

"Our scientific name *Homo sapiens* means 'wise human'"

Other elements = less than 1.0%

Iron 0.006%

Sodium 0.2%

Potassium 0.4%

Phosphorus 1.0%

Hydrogen 9.5%

Carbon 18.5%

Calcium 1.5%

Nitrogen 3.2%

Oxygen 65%

ENLARGEMENT

MAIN INGREDIENTS

The body's most common chemical elements by weight are oxygen, carbon, and hydrogen. Oxygen and hydrogen make water, which forms almost two-thirds of a human's body mass. Carbon is the basic building block, needed to build proteins, carbohydrates, and fats.

WORKING TOGETHER

Systems and organs

The body is a marvel of coordination—a massive team of more than 2,000 parts working together. The main parts, such as the liver, intestines, heart, lungs, and brain, are known as organs. Each organ, along with other smaller parts, is part of a larger system, which carries out a vital task to keep the body alive. All the systems rely on each other to work properly.

"Working together, body systems burn an average of 1,700 Calories a day for men"

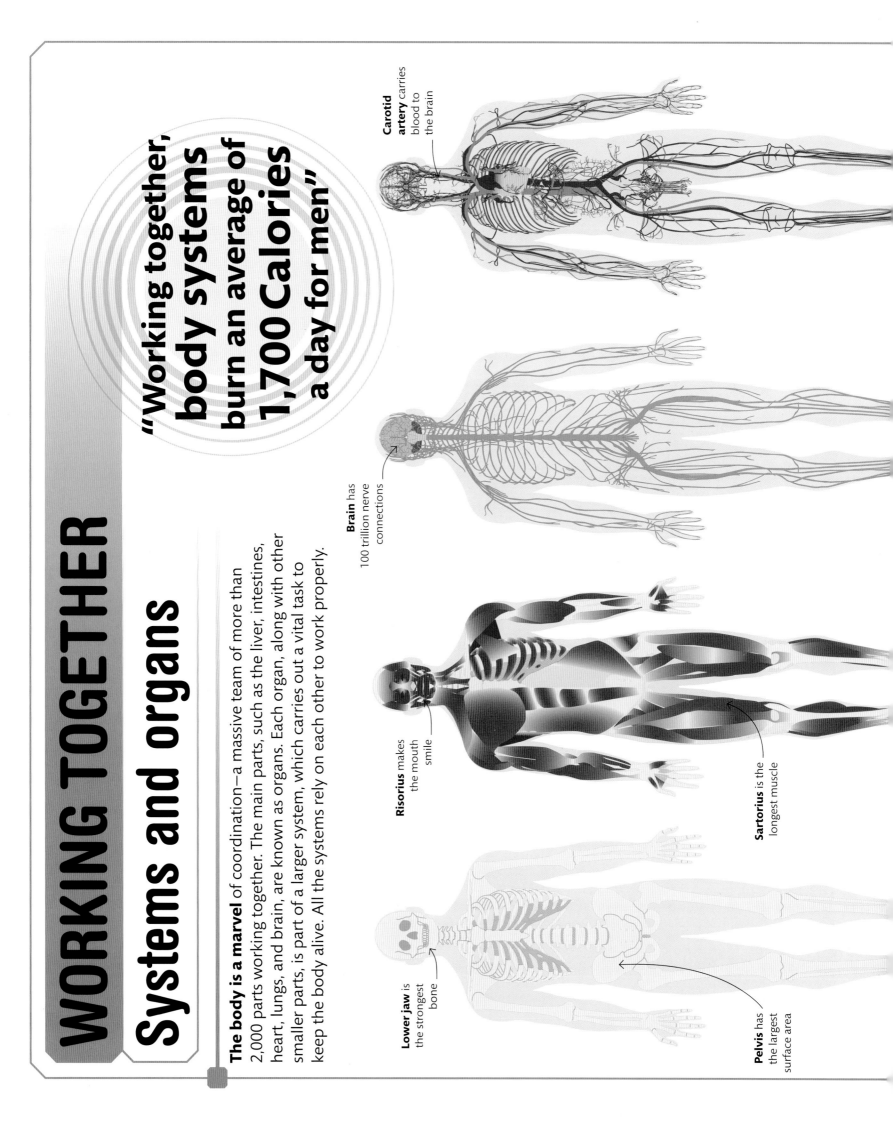

Carotid artery carries blood to the brain

Brain has 100 trillion nerve connections

Risorius makes the mouth smile

Sartorius is the longest muscle

Lower jaw is the strongest bone

Pelvis has the largest surface area

SKELETON

Bones form the skeletal system, to support and protect soft parts. Joints allow it to take up endless different positions, moved by the muscles.

Lungs contain about 1,560 miles (2,500 km) of airways

MUSCLES

There are over 640 muscles. Attached to bones, each muscle causes movements by pulling the bone into a new position. Muscles are controlled by nerves.

Largest lymph vessel is ¼ in (5 mm) wide

Small intestine is over 20 ft (6 m) long

NERVES

Nerves carry signals from the brain, which also receives data from sense organs such as the eyes and ears. The nervous system is nourished by blood.

Thymus gland produces hormones, which develop germ-fighting cells

Pancreas is in both digestive and endocrine systems

FEMALE

HEART AND BLOOD

The heart sends blood nonstop around our huge network of blood vessels. Blood carries oxygen from the lungs and nutrients from the digestive system.

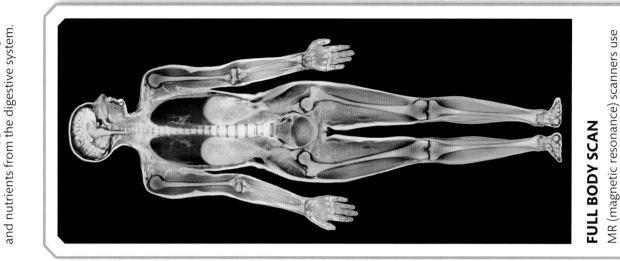

FULL BODY SCAN

MR (magnetic resonance) scanners use magnets and radio waves to picture the body's insides. Except for air in the lungs and gas in the intestines, there are no gaps. Parts are pressed close together—as one moves, so do the others.

LUNGS AND DIGESTION

Lungs take oxygen from the air, while the stomach and intestines absorb nutrients from food. Both depend on the immune system for protection.

LYMPH AND IMMUNITY

The lymphatic system transports lymph around its web of vessels. It is also home to the microdefenders of the immune system, which is under the control of hormones.

HORMONES

Glands of the endocrine system make many chemical messengers, or hormones. These control and coordinate other systems, such as skeletal growth.

INTRODUCTION

MINIATURE WORLD
Inside a cell

The body is a gigantic collection of billions of living units called cells. They are busy with hundreds of parts and processes inside, yet they are truly tiny in size. If a typical cell was as big as you, the whole body it was in would be 62 miles (100 km) tall—up to the edge of space! There are more than 200 different kinds of cells. Each has a distinctive shape, design, and inner parts, to do its specialized tasks.

PARTS OF A CELL

Just as the body has main parts called organs, each cell contains parts known as organelles. Most are made of sheets or membranes that are curved, bent, and folded into different shapes. Each organelle performs its own vital functions.

Nucleus is the control center, containing genetic material

Smooth endoplasmic reticulum does various jobs, mainly making and storing fat

DIVIDING CELLS

Body cells continually wear out. They also replace themselves by cell division. First, the genes are copied to give two sets. These sets then move apart, one into each end of the cell, and a furrow forms in the center. This furrow deepens and gradually pinches the cell into two.

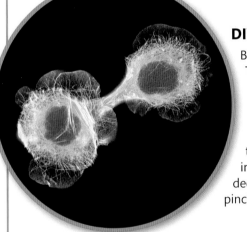

STEM CELLS

Every human starts as a cell—the fertilized egg. This divides to make general-purpose, or stem, cells. While not specialized for any particular tasks initially, stem cells have the ability to divide further into any kind of specialized cell type. The type of cell they grow into depends on the signals they receive.

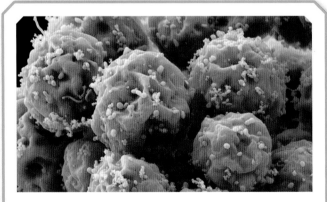

Cytoplasm is a jellylike fluid that fills the cell

Golgi body sorts and sends proteins to different parts of the cell

Centriole helps the cell divide

Rough endoplasmic reticulum makes proteins and stores and transports materials throughout the cell

TYPES OF BODY CELLS

Most specialized cells include all the basic cellular parts, such as a nucleus and mitochondria. But some parts may be larger and more numerous, depending on the cell's duties, such as making products, storage, or using energy. The cell's overall shape—long and thin, wide and rounded—also helps its function.

EPITHELIAL CELL
Shaped like bricks, blocks, or slabs, these make sheets that form coverings and linings of body parts.

SMOOTH MUSCLE CELL
Spindle-shaped, these cells can get shorter to make muscle contract.

LIGHT-SENSING CELL
The eye's rods and cone cells have light-sensing chemicals in one end and a nerve link at the other.

NERVE CELL
Thin, branching arms gather nerve signals and send them along the nerve fiber.

RED BLOOD CELL
Disk-shaped, it soaks up maximum oxygen to carry the highest amount possible in the bloodstream.

SPERM CELL
The head carries the father's genetic material. The tail lashes to swim toward the egg.

ADIPOSE FAT CELL
Most of the cell is filled with large blobs of fat—a valuable store of energy for tissues.

EGG CELL
This contains the mother's genetic material and large energy stores for early cell divisions.

Mitochondrion releases energy from glucose (sugar)

Lysosome contains substances called enzymes that break down any food the cell absorbs

Cell membrane is the outer covering and controls what goes in and out

Ribosome is where proteins are made

"Every human spends about one day as a single cell"

THE HUMAN CODE
DNA and genes

Every living body needs instructions on how to work as well as how to repair its old parts and build new ones. The instructions, genes, come in the form of chemical codes in the DNA (short for deoxyribonucleic acid). DNA is found in almost every cell in the body, as 46 coiled lengths known as chromosomes. In each kind of cell, some genes work while others are switched off. This is why cells are different and do varied tasks. When a cell divides, it copies its genes and passes them along to its offspring cells.

"Red blood cells are the only cells that do not contain DNA"

Humans have around 22,000 genes

Helix, or corkscrew, shape

Supporting chain of ribose sugars and phosphates

DNA SUPERHELIX

A length of DNA has a double-helix shape and resembles a long twisted ladder. This ladder's "rungs" are made up of four chemicals—adenine, cytosine, guanine, and thymine—called bases. The bases are always linked in pairs—adenine with thymine, and cytosine with guanine. A specific order of bases forms an instruction, called a gene, that controls a part of the body, such as skin or hair color.

GENES PASSED ON

A baby is created when an egg from the mother joins a sperm from the father. Both egg and sperm contain genes, so the baby has two sets, one from the mother and one from the father. This is why most children resemble both their parents.

BOY OR GIRL?

Two of the 46 chromosomes are known as sex chromosomes. One has an X shape; the other is shaped like a Y. Females have two Xs, XX, so a mother can only pass an X to her baby. Males have an X and Y, XY, so a father may pass on either. If the baby receives a Y from its father, it is XY—a boy. If it receives an X it is a girl, XX.

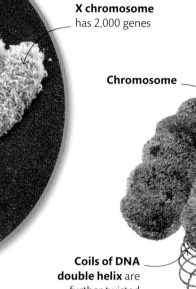

X chromosome
has 2,000 genes

Chromosome

Y chromosome
has more than 200 genes

Coils of DNA double helix are further twisted into a supercoil

Proteins act as spools for the DNA to wind around

The chemicals adenine and thymine pair up to create a rung, or base pair

Guanine and cytosine form the other base pair

HOW GENES WORK TOGETHER

The body has two complete sets of genes, one from each parent. That means we get two versions of every gene. These two versions may be different. For example, one of the genes that determines eye color may make blue eyes and the other brown. Which wins? Some genes are dominant and they beat the other ones, called recessive.

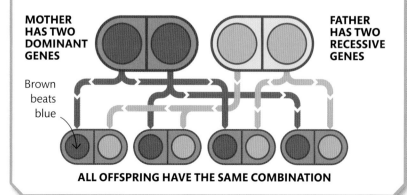

MOTHER HAS TWO DOMINANT GENES

FATHER HAS TWO RECESSIVE GENES

Brown beats blue

ALL OFFSPRING HAVE THE SAME COMBINATION

Tongue rolled into a tube

LOTS OF GENES

Recent discoveries about the body show that many features are controlled by several genes, rather than just one. Eye color, for example, is the result of two main genes plus at least six others, perhaps as many as 15. These genes do not work separately but affect each other in various ways. Tongue-rolling is another example where several genes are involved.

BODY FRAMEWORK

Stiff yet flexible, hard but soft, powerful yet delicate—bones, joints, and muscles are our all-action mobile framework. They are clothed in a tough coat of skin that is always worn yet never wears out.

BODY ARMOR
What skin does

Take a close look at your skin—almost everything you see is dead! Its outer layer, or epidermis, consists of dead cells that rub off and are replaced by new cells from below. This flexible, self-renewing layer protects us against dirt, germs, and injury. Deeper in the skin, the dermis is very much alive and provides our sense of touch.

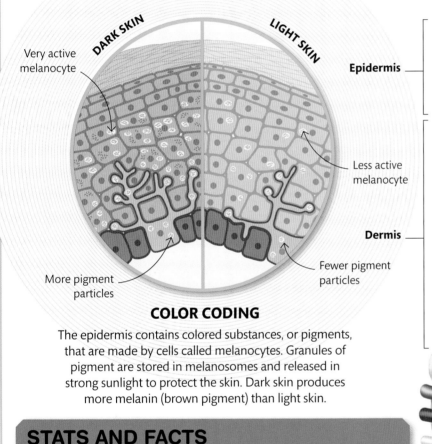

DARK SKIN

LIGHT SKIN

Very active melanocyte

Less active melanocyte

More pigment particles

Fewer pigment particles

COLOR CODING

The epidermis contains colored substances, or pigments, that are made by cells called melanocytes. Granules of pigment are stored in melanosomes and released in strong sunlight to protect the skin. Dark skin produces more melanin (brown pigment) than light skin.

STATS AND FACTS

SKIN THICKNESS

EYELID $\frac{1}{125}$ in (0.2 mm)

FOOT SOLE $\frac{1}{16}$ in (1.5 mm)

SKIN SHEDDING

50% of dust in your home is dead skin

SKIN RENEWAL TIME

27 DAYS

Hair shaft

Epidermis

Dermis

Touch and pressure nerve endings

Sweat gland
releases water to cool the skin

Hair root
grows in the hair follicle

BELOW THE SURFACE

The skin is made up of two layers, underpinned by an insulating layer of fat. Below the dead epidermal cells is a layer of fast-multiplying cells that gradually move up to renew the surface. The thicker dermis contains all the touch sensors, blood vessels, sweat glands, and hair roots.

FINGERPRINTS

The skin on your fingers, palms, soles, and toes is patterned with ridges and grooves that form curves, loops, whorls, and swirls. These ridges make it easier to grip small or smooth objects. Every finger has a different pattern, which can be pressed onto paper to provide a set of prints that are unique to you.

LOOP

WHORL

Scaly
upper skin

Sweat
duct

Multiplying
cells at base
of epidermis

THE SKIN IS THE LARGEST ORGAN OF THE HUMAN BODY

NATURAL OVERCOAT

This closeup view of the skin's surface shows how the flattened dead cells overlap like roof tiles. Made of tough keratin, they form a hard-wearing yet disposable protective barrier.

Small
vein

Small
artery

Subcutaneous
fat layer under
the dermis

"Your body sheds up to 50,000 flakes of skin every minute"

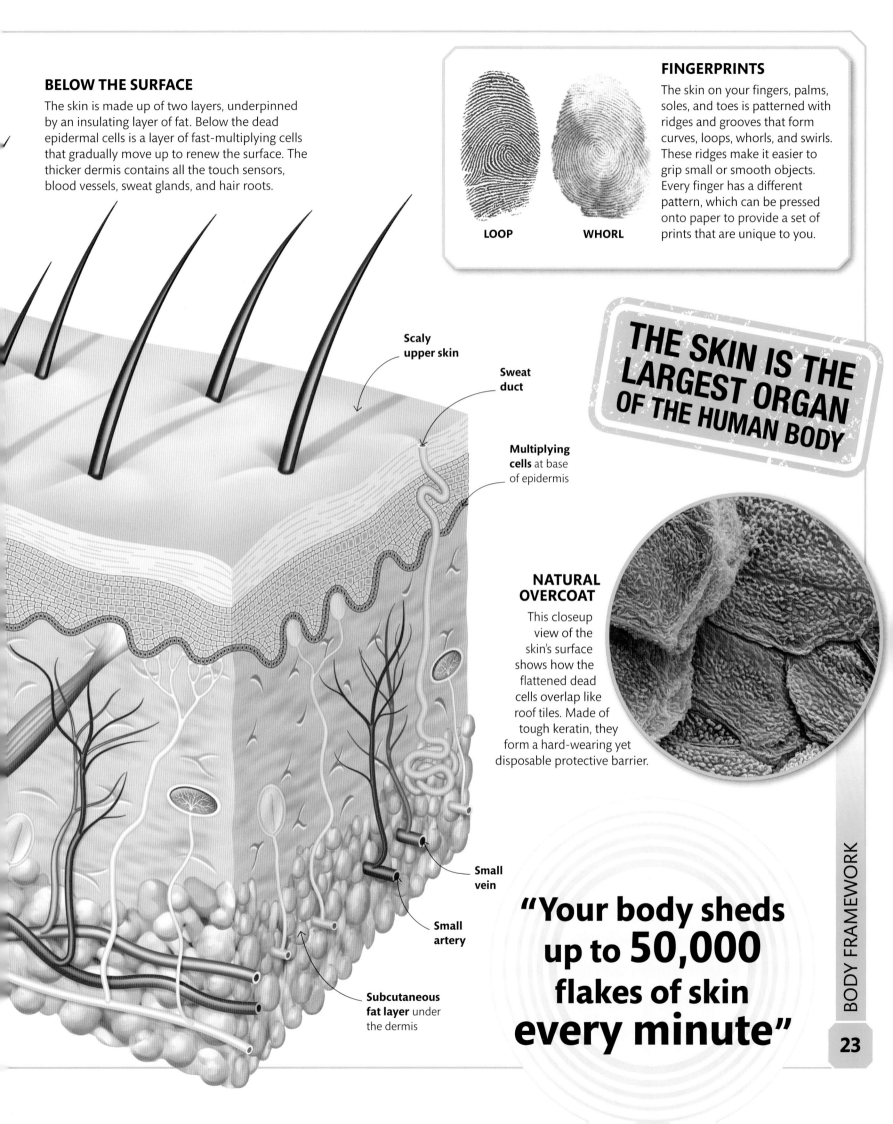

SWEAT AND SHIVER
Body temperature

The human body works best at a temperature of 98.6°F (37°C), give or take a degree. Cooler or warmer temperatures upset the delicate balance of the body's thousands of chemical processes, called metabolism. The skin, along with the muscles and tiny blood vessels just under the surface, plays a major role in keeping body temperature within these narrow limits.

Too hot

Deep in the brain, the temperature center monitors the blood. Above about 100.4°F (38°C), the sweat glands produce watery sweat. As the sweat evaporates, it draws heat from the skin and inner parts, and cools the body down.

Athletes sweat easily because they have a more efficient body thermostat

We sweat 3 pints (1.5l) an hour in severe heat

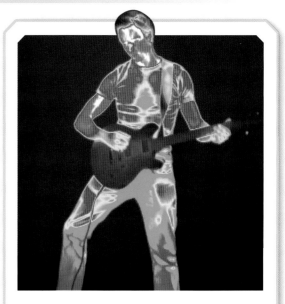

WHICH BITS ARE HOTTEST?

An infrared or heat-sensitive image shows the range of body surface temperatures, red being warmest and blue coolest. The head and extremities such as the ears and fingers have less fat, and cover a greater surface area for their volume or bulk, so they lose heat rapidly. The main body, with less surface area for its volume and a layer of insulating fat under the skin, stays warmer.

Sweat is mostly water but contains around 1% dissolved minerals

real- BERLIN-MARATHON 2005
25. September

adidas

real-

A

"Shivering can burn about 400 calories per hour"

TEMPERATURE REGULATION

A tiny cluster of cells in a fingertip-size part of the brain, the hypothalamus, detect the warmth of blood flowing past. They also receive messages from the skin, then send out nerve signals to control sweating, shivering, and other processes to regulate temperature.

Hypothalamus

Too cold

When the brain detects a fall in body temperature below around 97.7°F (36.5°C), it takes action to retain heat within the body. The muscles contract fast, or shiver, to produce extra heat, and the blood is kept away from the body's surface, where it would lose heat.

A hat reduces heat loss from the head

Shivering for 10 minutes can use as many calories as an hour of exercise

GOOSEBUMPS

Each body hair has a tiny muscle that can contract to pull the hair more upright. When many hairs do this, small skin mounds, called goosebumps, appear. The hairs trap warm air near the skin, providing insulation.

Layered clothes help trap heat against the body

ICY PLUNGE
Survival strategy

Gasp! A human body plunging into icy water instantly starts battling to survive. Panting allows the lungs to gulp in air for extra oxygen—also needed if the body goes under. The heart rate slows by as much as one-fifth, saving energy and reducing blood flow to the limbs to reduce heat loss. Small blood vessels narrow in the hands and feet, then arms and legs, also slowing heat loss. This keeps most of the blood, with its energy and oxygen, going to the brain and other vital organs.

STATS AND FACTS

SURVIVING IN COLD WATER

32–39°F (0–4°C)
20–40 MINUTES

| −40 | −30 | −20 | −10 | 0 | 10 | 20 | 30 | 40 | 50 |

LESS THAN 32°F (0°C)
10–20 MINUTES

39–50°F (4–10°C)
1–2 HOURS

POLAR SWIM

Farthest distance swum nonstop in polar waters

427 miles
(687 km)
in 9 days

POLAR BEAR

0.6 miles
(1 km)
in 18 minutes

HUMAN

Ice bath

Cold water rapidly affects your ability to swim, because movement lowers your body temperature. Survival time in icy water is 10–20 minutes, depending on physical fitness and thickness of under-skin fat.

"**Cold water** takes away body heat **30 times faster** than **cold air**"

FINISHING TOUCHES
Hair and nails

Hair and nails are almost entirely dead—otherwise, trimming them would hurt! Both grow and lengthen from their roots in the skin. They are made from squashed-together dead cells that contain the same tough protein as the outer layer of the skin—keratin. There are many different types of hairs, including long scalp hairs on the head, face and body hairs, underarm hairs, eyebrows, eyelashes, and thicker facial hair in men. Each type has its own thickness, growing speed, and life cycle.

"The **middle fingernail** grows the **fastest**, and the **thumbnail**, the **slowest**"

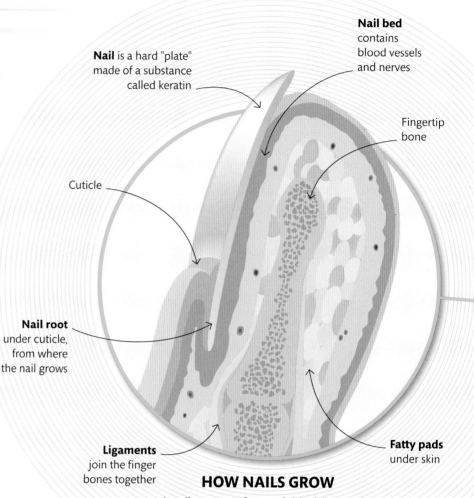

Nail is a hard "plate" made of a substance called keratin

Nail bed contains blood vessels and nerves

Cuticle

Fingertip bone

Nail root under cuticle, from where the nail grows

Ligaments join the finger bones together

Fatty pads under skin

HOW NAILS GROW

A nail emerges from a fold of skin under the cuticle, which is the layer of cells that produces keratin. Cells in the nail root fill with keratin, harden and die, and move slowly along the fleshy nail bed that lies beneath.

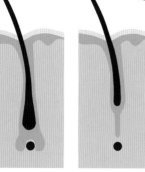

GROWTH   **TRANSITION**   **RESTING**   **GROWTH**

THE LIFE OF A HAIR

Each head hair has a limited life. Its growth phase lasts 2-6 years, so most hairs never grow longer than 3 ft (1 m)—hair grows about $1/100$ in a day. It then goes through a period of transition that lasts 10-14 days, when the follicle shrinks. A resting phase of 4-6 weeks follows, during which growth stops and the hair falls out. Gradually, the follicle recovers and a new hair grows.

The inside of the forearm has short, thin hairs that may be rubbed away by clothing

CURLY OR STRAIGHT

The color and waviness of scalp hairs is mainly due to genes inherited from parents. In cross-section, curly hairs tend to be oval or elongated, while straight hairs are rounded or circular. Brown-haired people usually have around 100,000 hairs on their heads, blondes have about 120,000 hairs, and redheads have 90,000 or fewer.

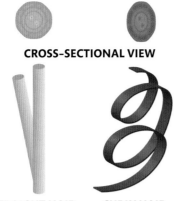

CROSS-SECTIONAL VIEW

STRAIGHT HAIR   **CURLY HAIR**

HAIRY ALL OVER

You have hair almost everywhere except your lips, the palms of your hands, and the soles of your feet. However, some are too tiny or too thin to see without a magnifier. Each hair grows from a deep pouchlike pocket in the skin, called a hair follicle.

Scalp hairs protect the skin and brain from knocks, sunburn, and extreme temperatures

Eyebrows divert sweat and water from the eyes

Eyelashes are relatively thick and swish floating dust away from the eyes

Lower eyelid has 70–80 lashes, upper eyelid has 90–120

Facial hair is lighter, thinner, and shorter in women than men, due to genes and female hormones

The longest recorded hair is 18 ft (5.6 m)

WE LOSE 80–100 SCALP HAIRS A DAY

CUTTING EDGE

Nailing it

Unlike hairs, which grow, die, and fall out, nails grow day after day, year after year. They help scratch off dirt and pests such as fleas, ease itches, and pick up tiny objects. A nail is also a hard plate that protects the soft fingertip under it, and helps us sense how hard the tip is pressing. But as a nail lengthens, it collects dirt and germs, and it may snag and break. Any pain is felt in the sensitive patch of skin under the nail, called the nail bed, since the nail itself is dead.

STATS AND FACTS

AVERAGE NAIL THICKNESS

1.5 mm
Toenail

0.5 mm
Fingernail

LONGEST SINGLE NAIL

4½ ft (1.3 m)

A fingernail grows ½ in (1 cm) every 100 days

WATER CONTENT OF NAILS

10-15 PERCENT

Tangled talons

Uncut nails tend to curve and curl because of tiny differences in the growth rates of the left and right side of a nail, and also of its upper and lower surfaces. Nails grow faster on the hand you use the most.

"Nails grow **faster** in **summer** than in **winter**"

BODY SUPPORT
Skeleton

Far from being dry, white, and dead, your skeleton—all the bones put together—is one-quarter water, pinkish white in color, and an active part of the body. Not only does the skeleton prevent you from collapsing into a heap of meat, it is a movable frame that helps you stand, walk, run, jump, lift, and push. It also protects organs such as the brain, spinal cord, heart, and lungs. The skeleton contains vital stores of key minerals, and every second it makes millions of new blood cells.

Wrist contains eight small bones for flexibility

Skull protects the brain

Ulna is one of two forearm bones

Radius works with the ulna to allow the forearm to rotate

Sternum (breastbone) links the ribs

Cartilage connects the ribs to the sternum

Lumbar vertebrae support the weight of the upper body

Humerus anchors the upper arm muscles

Clavicle (collarbone) is the only horizontal bone in the body

Scapula (shoulder blade) is the base for the arm muscles

Ribs are arranged in 12 pairs

Pelvis (hipbone) anchors the hip and leg muscles

TINIEST BONE

Located deep within the ear, the stirrup is just the size of this O. Yet it allows us to hear music, speech, and other sounds by passing on their vibrations.

Actual size is 1/10 in (2.5 mm)

YOUR SKELETON HAS 206 BONES

FLEXIBLE SPINE

The skeleton's central column of bones, or vertebrae, makes up the spinal column. Each joint between the bones moves only a small amount, but the movement adds up along the entire spine so that you can bend almost double.

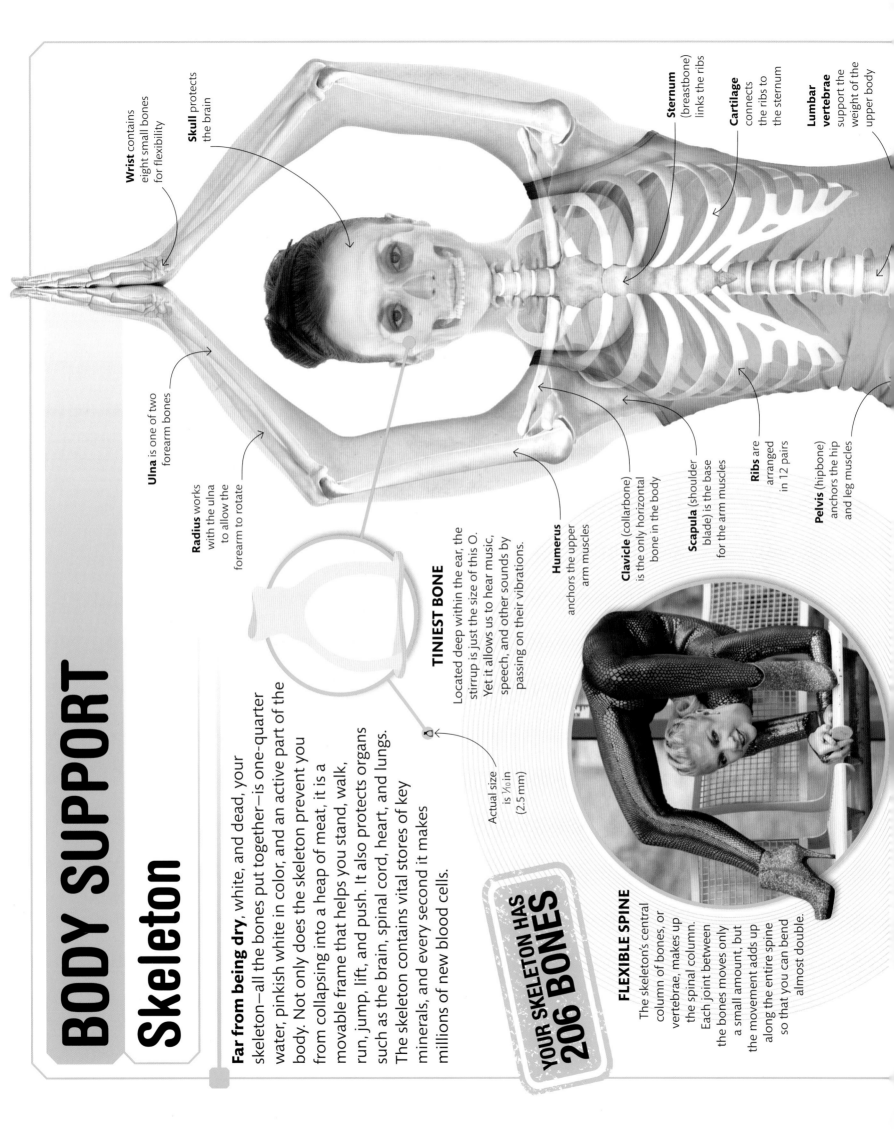

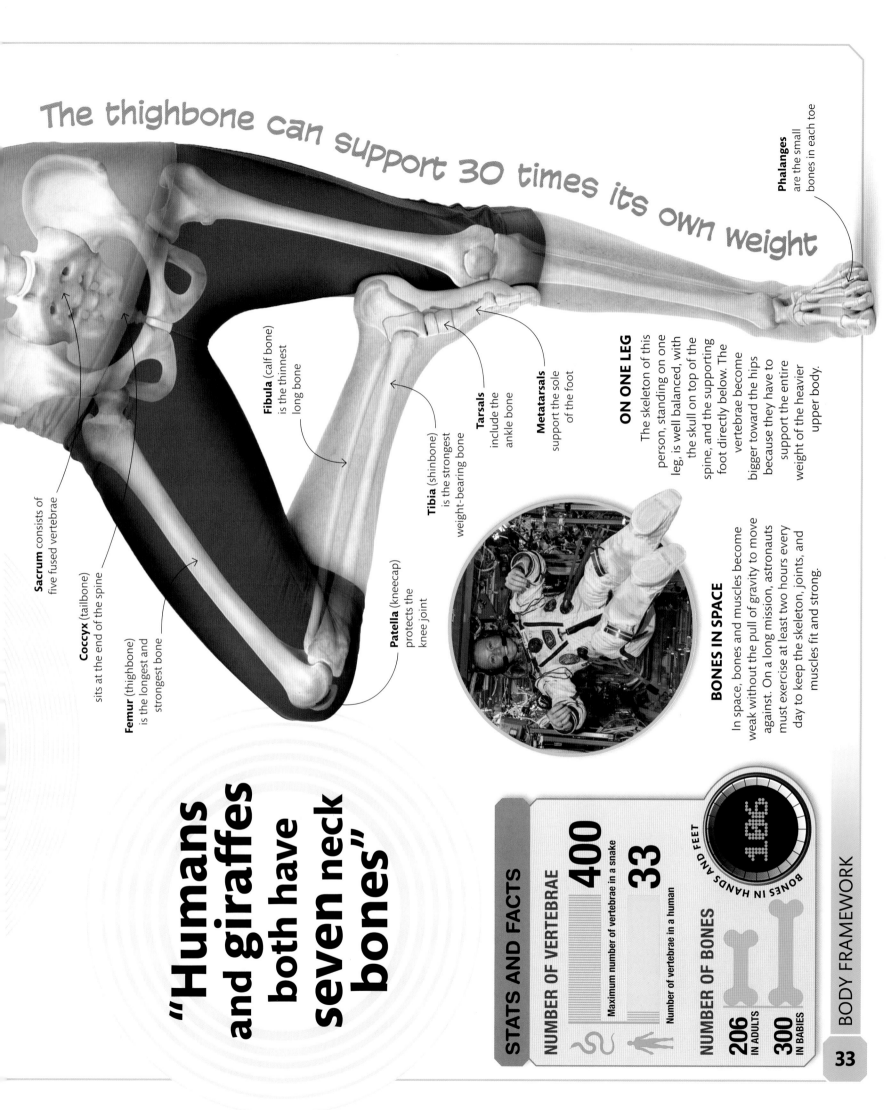

The thighbone can support 30 times its own weight

Phalanges are the small bones in each toe

Sacrum consists of five fused vertebrae

Coccyx (tailbone) sits at the end of the spine

Femur (thighbone) is the longest and strongest bone

Fibula (calf bone) is the thinnest long bone

Tibia (shinbone) is the strongest weight-bearing bone

Patella (kneecap) protects the knee joint

Tarsals include the ankle bone

Metatarsals support the sole of the foot

ON ONE LEG

The skeleton of this person, standing on one leg, is well balanced, with the skull on top of the spine, and the supporting foot directly below. The vertebrae become bigger toward the hips because they have to support the entire weight of the heavier upper body.

BONES IN SPACE

In space, bones and muscles become weak without the pull of gravity to move against. On a long mission, astronauts must exercise at least two hours every day to keep the skeleton, joints, and muscles fit and strong.

"Humans and giraffes both have seven neck bones"

STATS AND FACTS

NUMBER OF VERTEBRAE

400
Maximum number of vertebrae in a snake

33
Number of vertebrae in a human

NUMBER OF BONES

206 IN ADULTS

300 IN BABIES

BONES IN HANDS AND FEET

SUPER LEVERS

Record leaps

The human skeleton is a marvel of engineering that uses many of the same mechanical principles as a machine. Muscles that move limb bones are attached near joints. When such a muscle contracts a small distance, it moves the other end of the bone, like a lever, by five to ten times more. This movement is passed to the next bone of the limb, further increasing the motion. Athletes make use of this multilever effect to propel their bodies over incredible distances at amazing speeds.

STATS AND FACTS

HIGH JUMP RECORD

7⁹/₁₀ ft
(2.4 m)
MEN

7 ft
(2.05m)
WOMEN

CHAMPION LONG JUMPER

33 ft/sec
(10 m/sec) Long-jump speed at takeoff

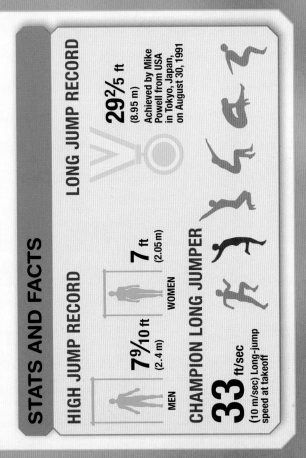

LONG JUMP RECORD

29²/₅ ft
(8.95 m)
Achieved by Mike Powell from USA in Tokyo, Japan, on August 30, 1991

"An average **neuron** connects with **7,000** others but some have over **200,000** connections"

BRAIN BUILDERS

Nerve net

The brain's billions of multishaped nerve cells, or neurons, have tentacle-like strands, called dendrites, all around them. Some neurons in the brain's outer layer, the cortex, have more than 10,000 multibranched dendrites, which connect to 200,000 other neurons. Nerve signals representing sights, sounds, thoughts, emotions, and movements travel in endless different ways through this giant network, which has trillions of connections, yet folds up neatly inside the head.

STATS AND FACTS

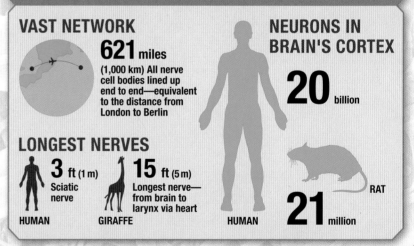

VAST NETWORK

621 miles (1,000 km) All nerve cell bodies lined up end to end—equivalent to the distance from London to Berlin

NEURONS IN BRAIN'S CORTEX

20 billion

LONGEST NERVES

3 ft (1 m) Sciatic nerve
HUMAN

15 ft (5 m) Longest nerve— from brain to larynx via heart
GIRAFFE

HUMAN

RAT

21 million

PROCESSING POWER
The brain

Soft, pale, wrinkly, and unmoving, the brain doesn't look very impressive. Yet it controls almost every move the body makes and is the site of our thoughts, feelings, and memories. Because it is so essential to us, it is well protected inside the skull's hard dome, surrounded by cushioning fluids and layers of tissue called meninges. Its biggest part, taking up three-quarters of its bulk, is the cerebrum whose surface is covered with grooves and bulges.

"The brain is a million times more efficient than a computer of a similar size"

Cerebrum
is folded to fit inside the skull

Corpus callosum
is a bundle of nerve fibers that links the two halves of the brain

Thalamus
relays nerve signals to the cerebrum

Hypothalamus
controls temperature, hunger, and many automatic processes

Pituitary gland
regulates hormones

Brain stem
connects the spinal cord with the brain

Cerebellum
is responsible for balance and posture

AT A GLANCE

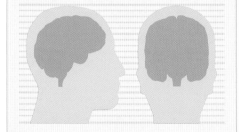

- **SIZE** Average adult brain: weight 3 lb (1.4 kg); width 6 in (14 cm); length 7 in (17 cm); height 4 in (9.5 cm)

- **LOCATION** Almost fills the top half of the skull

- **FUNCTION** Gets data, takes decisions, stores memories, controls movements and emotions

INSIDE THE BRAIN

The cerebrum is divided into two halves. The left half links to the right side of the body, and the right half to the left side. If unfolded, it would cover the area of a pillowcase.

Front area

This region is involved with the tasks of planning, reason, memories, and personality.

Motor area

Controls and coordinates muscle movements.

Sensory area

Deals with touch sensations from the skin, mouth, and tongue.

Sight area

The back of the brain handles vision and makes sense of what you see.

Speech and hearing areas

These control speaking, hearing, and understanding words.

Lower side lobes

This area deals with memory, information retrieval, and emotions.

Brain stem
The brain stem takes care of breathing, heartbeat, digestion, and other vital processes.

Cerebellum
The cerebellum ensures that movements are smoothly coordinated.

BRAIN FUNCTION

The cerebrum looks similar all over, but various areas are specialized for conscious tasks such as hearing, speech, movement, touch, and sight. The lower parts of the brain control more basic, automatic life processes, such as breathing.

Nerve pathways extend to all areas of the brain

NERVE TRACTS

This scan shows how bundles of nerve fibers spread from the lower brain to all parts of the cerebrum. They then branch out into billions of individual nerve cells that control everything you do.

STATS AND FACTS

BRAIN WEIGHTS

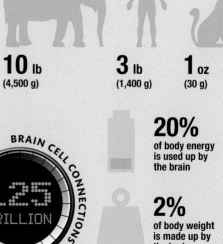

10 lb (4,500 g)

3 lb (1,400 g)

1 oz (30 g)

BRAIN CELL CONNECTIONS

125 TRILLION

20% of body energy is used up by the brain

2% of body weight is made up by the brain

LIVING DANGEROUSLY

The teen brain

On the outside, the brain looks similar all through life. But its trillions of microconnections are constantly changing, especially in the early years. Some parts of the brain develop faster than others. The parts that seek new thrills and exciting events develop faster than those that think through situations and avoid danger. The teenage years are a time when this mismatched development may affect the brain's natural balance for a while, until care and common sense take over again.

STATS AND FACTS

NEURONS IN THE BRAIN

CHIMP	**7** BILLION
ELEPHANT	**23** BILLION
HUMAN	**100** BILLION

LIGHTBULB MOMENT
10–20 WATTS
The power produced by a brain—enough to light up a low-energy bulb

PROPORTION OF FAT IN BRAIN
58 PERCENT

Defying gravity

Suspended in midair, arms thrown to his side, this young stunt biker throws caution to the winds. As different parts of the brain develop with age, we tend to make safer choices rather than take risks.

"**Older teenagers** are almost **twice** as likely to **take risks** than anyone else"

ACTION STATIONS
Making moves

Some body movements, such as heartbeats and breathing, happen day and night. These internal actions are mostly involuntary, or controlled by automatic parts of the brain, so the conscious mind does not need to think about them. Voluntary movements are controlled by the conscious mind's decisions. Their instructions begin as thousands of nerve messages in the motor area at the top of the brain. The messages speed to other brain parts, especially the small, wrinkled cerebellum at the lower rear, and finally race along nerves to the muscles.

CONCENTRATION

The brain's awareness can focus entirely on one movement or motor task, such as playing an instrument. Closing the eyes shuts off sight, and various brain parts, such as the thalamus, filter out other unwanted nerve signals.

ON YOUR MARK, GET SET, GO!

While crouched at the start line, a sprinter plans her first surge forward, with muscles tense and ready. As soon as the starting gun is heard, a well-practiced sequence of muscle actions powers the body away from the blocks.

Nerves in foot
send messages about its position against starting block

Nerve messages
travel to the brain

Hearing area
anticipates start sound

Front cortex
prepares to signal muscles

Visual area
prepares to scan track

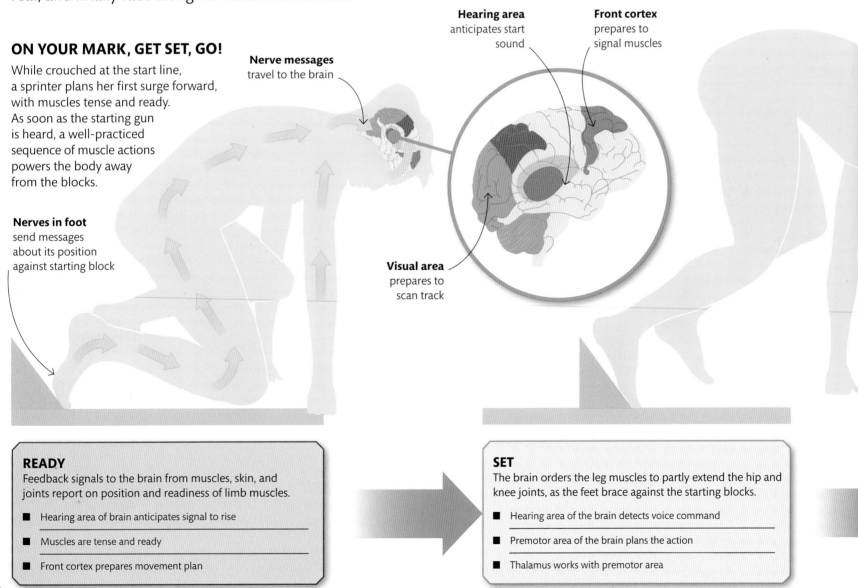

READY
Feedback signals to the brain from muscles, skin, and joints report on position and readiness of limb muscles.

■ Hearing area of brain anticipates signal to rise

■ Muscles are tense and ready

■ Front cortex prepares movement plan

SET
The brain orders the leg muscles to partly extend the hip and knee joints, as the feet brace against the starting blocks.

■ Hearing area of the brain detects voice command

■ Premotor area of the brain plans the action

■ Thalamus works with premotor area

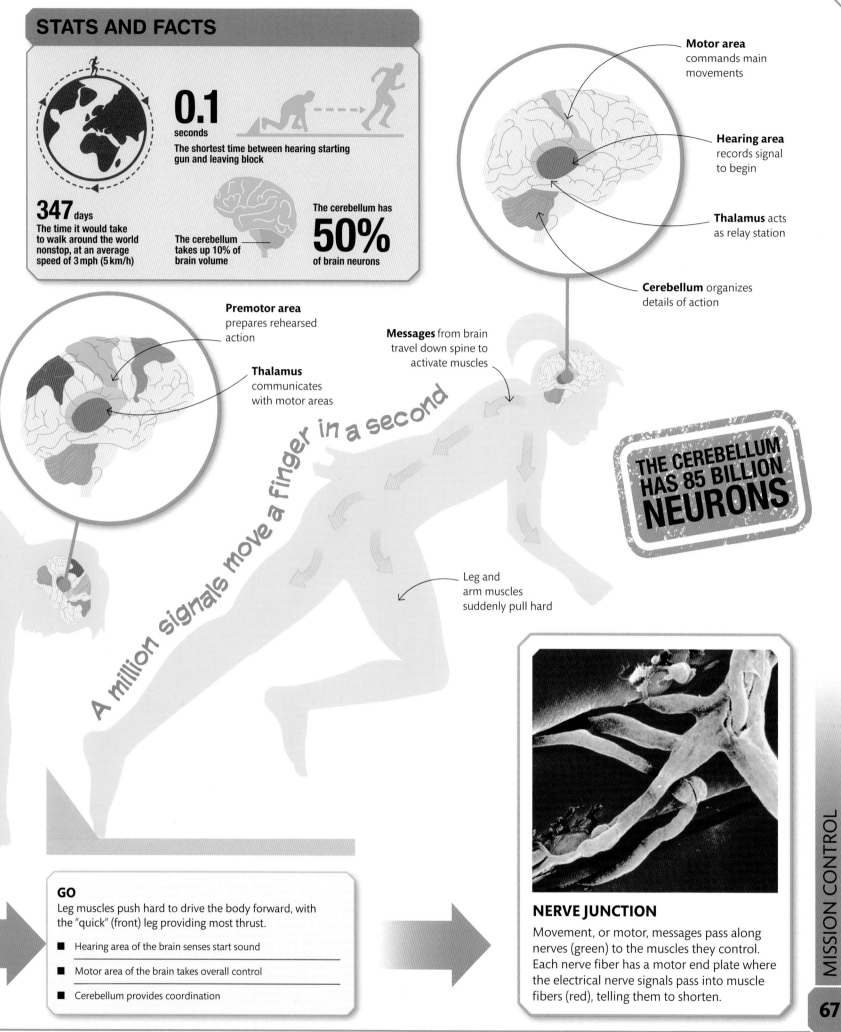

0.1
seconds
The shortest time between hearing starting gun and leaving block

347 days
The time it would take to walk around the world nonstop, at an average speed of 3 mph (5 km/h)

The cerebellum takes up 10% of brain volume

The cerebellum has **50%** of brain neurons

Motor area commands main movements

Hearing area records signal to begin

Thalamus acts as relay station

Cerebellum organizes details of action

Premotor area prepares rehearsed action

Thalamus communicates with motor areas

Messages from brain travel down spine to activate muscles

A million signals move a finger in a second

THE CEREBELLUM HAS 85 BILLION NEURONS

Leg and arm muscles suddenly pull hard

GO

Leg muscles push hard to drive the body forward, with the "quick" (front) leg providing most thrust.

- Hearing area of the brain senses start sound
- Motor area of the brain takes overall control
- Cerebellum provides coordination

NERVE JUNCTION

Movement, or motor, messages pass along nerves (green) to the muscles they control. Each nerve fiber has a motor end plate where the electrical nerve signals pass into muscle fibers (red), telling them to shorten.

LIGHTNING STRIKE

Fast reactions

The human body can react to a sudden sensation with incredible speed and produce a forceful move, such as a push or a kick, in just one-fifth of a second. Smaller movements are even faster, with a blink lasting a tenth of a second. But even with practice, there are limits to reaction times. For nerve signals to go from eye to brain and then be processed takes at least one-twentieth of a second, while nerve messages from brain to foot muscles may take almost one-thirtieth of a second.

STATS AND FACTS

REACTION TIMES

Fastest punch, start to finish
0.2 sec

Kick reaction speed
115 ft/sec
(over 78 mph)

RESPONSE TO STIMULUS

SOUND **0.14** sec

SIGHT **0.18** sec

80%
Improved reaction time after practice

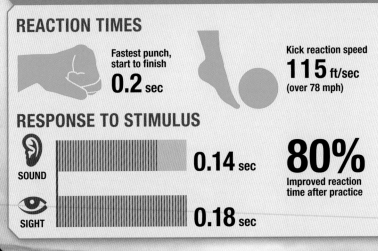

Capoeira acrobatics

Dance, music, and martial arts come together in capoeira. A combined game, sport, and competition from Brazil, it demands extreme speed in reactions and moves, such as kicks and leg sweeps.

LOOK OUT!
Reflex actions

Sometimes parts of the body move by themselves, without the thinking brain telling them. For instance, your eyes blink every few seconds. A tickly nose causes a sudden sneeze, while a sore throat prompts a cough. A loud noise makes you look around. Any feeling of pain triggers rapid action to stop it. These kinds of automatic actions are known as reflexes. They happen superfast and help the body stay safe and healthy—even when the brain is busy concentrating on something else. Only after the reflex action does the brain become aware of what has actually happened.

"The longest attack of hiccups lasted 68 years"

Brain not aware of problem yet

Signals arrive at spinal cord

PAIN REFLEX

The withdrawal reflex is one of the quickest reflexes. It pulls away, or withdraws, the affected body part from the source of pain or any unusual or unexpected sensation. The main reflex link is in the spinal cord. Nerve messages go to the brain a fraction of a second later.

Pain signals travel along nerve in arm

Skin sensors detect too much heat

BORED? TIRED? YAWN...

Yawns occur when tired, bored, stressed, worried—or when someone else yawns! There are many ideas about why we yawn, from getting more oxygen into the blood, or carbon dioxide out, to stretching face and throat muscles, even cooling the brain. But no one really knows.

1 Danger threatens
Too much heat, cold, pressure, or other discomfort could damage the body. So, when you unknowingly reach out toward a flame, skin sensors detect it and fire nerve signals along nerve fibers in the main nerves of the arm, direct to the spinal cord in the backbone. This can take as little as one-fiftieth of a second.

Candle flame

TYPES OF REFLEXES

Healthy reflexes show the nerve system is working well, so they are regularly tested at medical check-ups. The pupil reflex is the busiest. As the eye looks around at light and dark areas, a reflex link to the iris muscles (colored part) continuously adjusts the size of the pupil (hole), to keep the amount of light passing through the same. Another test is the knee jerk, when tapping just below the kneecap makes the lower leg kick up.

PUPIL WIDE OPEN

STATS AND FACTS

MOST PAINFUL BITES AND STINGS

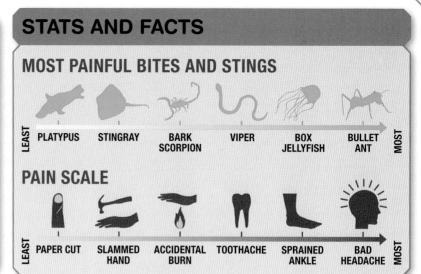

LEAST | PLATYPUS | STINGRAY | BARK SCORPION | VIPER | BOX JELLYFISH | BULLET ANT | MOST

PAIN SCALE

LEAST | PAPER CUT | SLAMMED HAND | ACCIDENTAL BURN | TOOTHACHE | SPRAINED ANKLE | BAD HEADACHE | MOST

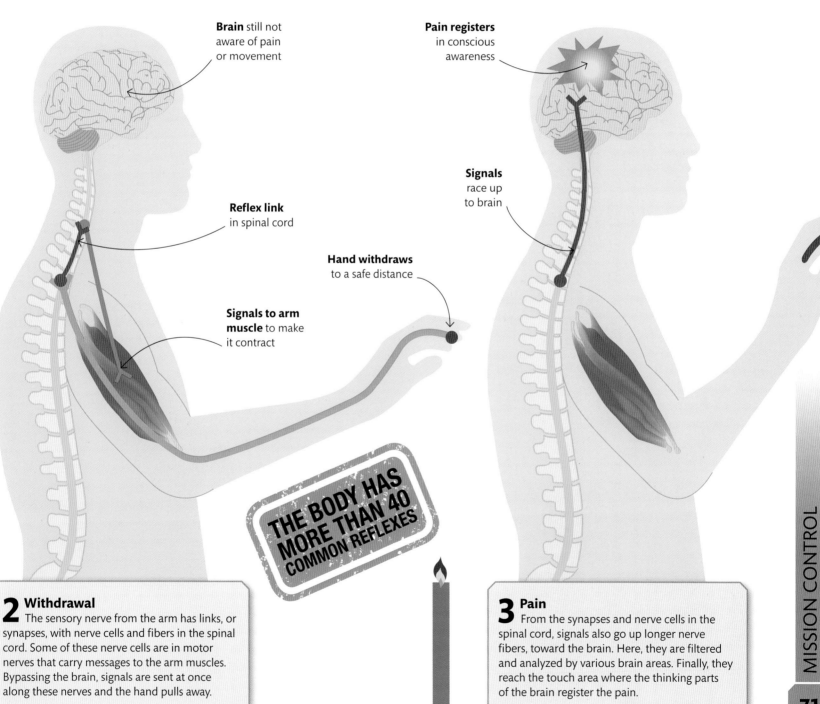

Brain still not aware of pain or movement

Reflex link in spinal cord

Signals to arm muscle to make it contract

Pain registers in conscious awareness

Signals race up to brain

Hand withdraws to a safe distance

THE BODY HAS MORE THAN 40 COMMON REFLEXES

2 Withdrawal

The sensory nerve from the arm has links, or synapses, with nerve cells and fibers in the spinal cord. Some of these nerve cells are in motor nerves that carry messages to the arm muscles. Bypassing the brain, signals are sent at once along these nerves and the hand pulls away.

3 Pain

From the synapses and nerve cells in the spinal cord, signals also go up longer nerve fibers, toward the brain. Here, they are filtered and analyzed by various brain areas. Finally, they reach the touch area where the thinking parts of the brain register the pain.

TOTAL RECALL
How memories are made

The brain is a giant storehouse of countless memories. But memories are not single items, each in a small place, and never changing. In fact, a memory is many patterns or pathways of nerve cell connections, spread around several parts of the brain, with links to other memories, events, and ideas. In this way, a thought, sensation, or movement can trigger one memory, which recalls another, and so on, like a chain reaction. Memories fade with time but recalling them often makes them stronger and last longer.

"As a digital store, the brain could hold the equivalent of **3 million hours of TV shows**"

HOW MEMORIES ARE FORMED

A memory is a new set of connections, or synapses, between neurons. Over time, as nerve signals pass between the neurons, they set up fresh connections. The more the pathways are used, the more established the memories become. If not recalled occasionally, they are forgotten as the connections weaken.

Neurons make new connections

Impulses to nerve cell

INPUT

New links reinforce learning and memory

Regular use strengthens memory links

CIRCUIT FORMATION

TASTE

TOUCH

SMELL

SOUND

SIGHT

MEMORY INPUTS

The brain usually remembers groups of information. Along with the value of a written number, it may store its shape, the ink, and even the paper color. For events such as vacations, memories retain a whole range of sights, sounds and other sensations. All five senses can feed a memory.

Links all over the brain

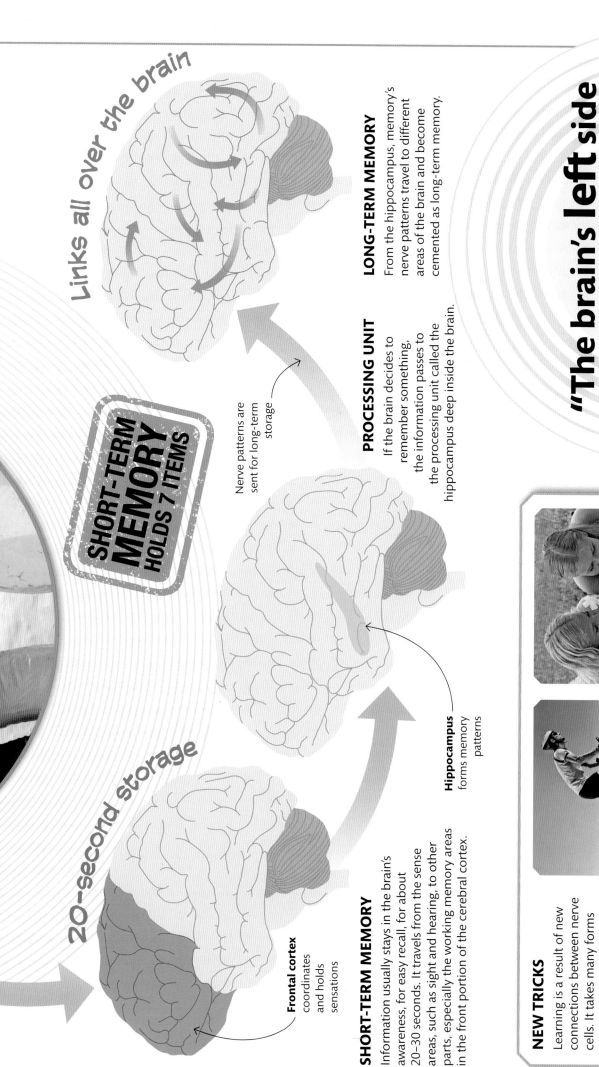

SHORT-TERM MEMORY
HOLDS 7 ITEMS

20-second storage

Frontal cortex coordinates and holds sensations

SHORT-TERM MEMORY

Information usually stays in the brain's awareness, for easy recall, for about 20–30 seconds. It travels from the sense areas, such as sight and hearing, to other parts, especially the working memory areas in the front portion of the cerebral cortex.

Nerve patterns are sent for long-term storage

Hippocampus forms memory patterns

PROCESSING UNIT

If the brain decides to remember something, the information passes to the processing unit called the hippocampus deep inside the brain.

LONG-TERM MEMORY

From the hippocampus, memory's nerve patterns travel to different areas of the brain and become cemented as long-term memory.

"The brain's left side is more involved in memories for words, the right side for pictures"

Practical skills
Riding a bicycle, doing up buttons, or writing your name gradually becomes automatic muscle movements.

Communication
You learn the meaning of words, numbers, symbols, and other information used to communicate.

NEW TRICKS

Learning is a result of new connections between nerve cells. It takes many forms and happens in different parts of the brain. A list of words or numbers is soon forgotten unless you recall it often, or you give the list items some meaning—such as a phrase for the colors of the rainbow, VIBGYOR. Another form of learning is for a practical skill, repeated until you can do it almost without thinking.

BRAIN DOWNTIME
While you sleep

At the end of a tiring day, the body relaxes into sleep. Its various parts—such as muscles and vessels—recover and carry out necessary repairs. But the brain, similar to an offline computer, remains busy with its own internal tasks and processes. These probably include organizing thoughts and filing memories, but exactly what happens during sleep is still a mystery.

"The **longest** a person has gone **without sleep** is **449** hours"

TIME TO GO SLOW

Almost every part of the body is affected by sleep, especially the heart, muscles, lungs, and the digestive system. The senses keep sending information about these areas to the lower parts of the brain, which monitor them, and, if necessary, wake you up.

Ears
The brain ignores familiar sounds such as a ticking clock, but becomes alert to a sudden, strange noise.

Nose
The brain's smell area registers background odors, but is aroused by possible danger such as smoke.

Lungs and heart
Breathing is shallower and each heartbeat pumps less blood, but the heart rates are much the same at rest as when awake.

Eyes
Eyelids remain closed and the eyes move relatively little, except during the REM (rapid eye movement) sleep period.

Mouth
Air flow may rattle the flap at the rear roof of the mouth, the soft palate, causing an annoying noise—snoring.

Digestive system
The churning, squirming movements of the stomach and intestines lessen during sleep, but chemical digestion—done by enzymes—continues.

SLEEP PATTERNS

A typical night's sleep is not the same throughout. The brain goes through several cycles of activity, including light, deep, and REM sleep. In light sleep, body processes are slow but waking is still easy. In deep sleep, systems slow down greatly and arousing the brain is more difficult. In REM sleep, the eyes flicker to and fro, breathing may speed up, and muscles can twitch. If woken at this time, the sleeper may remember dreaming.

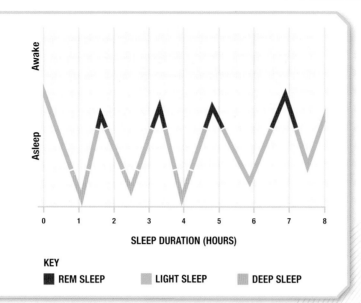

Awake

Asleep

0 1 2 3 4 5 6 7 8

SLEEP DURATION (HOURS)

KEY

■ REM SLEEP ■ LIGHT SLEEP ■ DEEP SLEEP

Muscles

Most muscles relax, although body position shifts several times to avoid squashing blood vessels and nerves.

DREAMING

Most dreams occur during REM sleep, although we only remember them if woken during or just after. Stress and worry seem to make dreams more frequent and disturbing. Sometimes they have links with life events, yet at other times they seem totally random.

Bladder

The kidneys produce less urine during sleep, so the bladder fills more slowly than when we are awake and active. But it is usually ready when we wake up!

STATS AND FACTS

TIME SPENT SLEEPING

		HOURS
NEWBORNS		16
PRE-SCHOOL		15
SCHOOL AGE		11
TEENAGERS		9
ADULTS		8

HOURS

CAT

20 HOURS

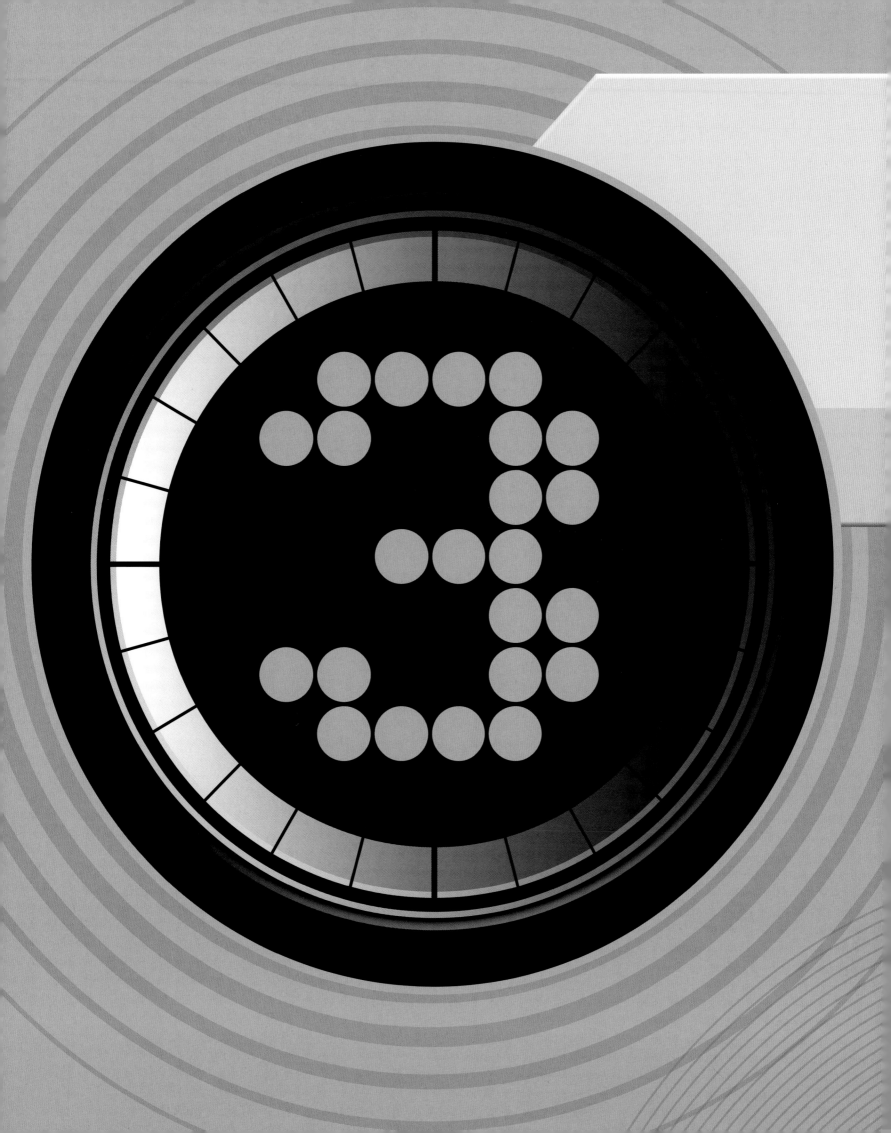

TOTALLY SENSATIONAL

Lightning flash, thunder roar, smell of fear, taste of success, even dreaded pain—the super senses track all events on, in, or around the body, and stream a never-ending torrent of information into the brain.

STAYING FOCUSED
The eyeball

Your amazing full-color, ever-moving view of the world comes into each eye through a hole hardly larger than this O, the pupil. Before light rays enter here, they pass through the sensitive front layer, or conjunctiva, and the rigid, domed cornea. After the pupil, the rays go through the lens and the vitreous humor—a glassy, jellylike fluid—filling the bulk of the eyeball. All these structures are clear or transparent. The rays finally shine onto the light-sensitive retina.

PARTS OF THE EYE

The eyeball has three layers–the white sclera, the delicate blood-rich choroid, and the retina lining the rear two-thirds. At the front, the tough sclera becomes the clear curve of the cornea. The filling of jellylike vitreous humor keeps the eye ball-shaped.

Sclera forms the tough outer layer, or white, of the eye

Conjunctiva is thin, sensitive, and covers the white of the eye

Cornea is dome-shaped to bend light rays

Iris contains muscles, and pigments that give the eye color

Object reflecting light rays

Pupil is the central hole in the iris that lets light through

Lens changes shape to focus

Ciliary body has muscles that pull or relax to change the shape of the lens

YOU CAN BLINK 5 TIMES IN A SECOND

Choroid supplies blood to retina and sclera

BLINKING

Eyes blink to wipe tear fluid across the delicate front surface and clear away dust and germs. A day's blinks added together would amount to 30–40 minutes with your eyes shut. Over a lifetime you blink half a billion times.

Upside-down image produced on retina

Optic nerve takes signals from the back of the eye to the visual cortex at the back of the brain

Blood vessels pass through optic nerve taking blood to and from the eye

Vitreous humour is a clear, jelly-like fluid that fills the eyeball

Retina is the inner light-detecting lining at the back of the eyeball

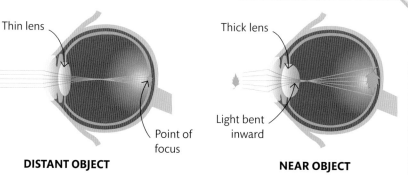

Thin lens

Thick lens

Point of focus

Light bent inward

DISTANT OBJECT

NEAR OBJECT

IN SHARP FOCUS

The eye bends, or focuses, light rays to form a clear, sharp image on the retina. The cornea does about two-thirds of this. The lens does the rest—changing shape for fine adjustment. Rays from a near object spread out more than those from a distant one. So the muscles around the lens have to adjust its shape, making it fatter to bend these rays more inward.

Lining up the target

The archer squints to get a clear, one-eyed view. Her eye muscles repeatedly move the eye just a millimeter to transfer focus from the arrow, a few centimeters away, to the target, 295 ft (90 m) away.

HAWKEYE
On target

The human eye is incredibly sensitive. In perfect darkness, it can detect a candle flame more than 6 miles (10 km) away! But such conditions are rare, because of light from the Moon, buildings, vehicles, and streetlights. The eye has extraordinary focusing powers, too. The muscle ring around each lens, the ciliary muscle, can alter the lens shape many times in a second. This enables you to switch focus from your hand to a distant target in less than one-tenth of a second.

STATS AND FACTS

DIAMETER OF EYEBALL

1/8 in
(4 mm)
SHREW

1 in
(24 mm)
HUMAN

11 in
(280 mm)
GIANT SQUID

RANGE OF VISION
2.25
MILLION LIGHT-YEARS
Distance to the Andromeda galaxy—the farthest the naked eye can see

EYE GROWTH AFTER BIRTH

2.0
PERCENT

"The bullseye of an archery target is only 5 in (122 mm) in diameter"

SEEING THE LIGHT
Fine detail and color

The human eye is one of the best of all mammal eyes at seeing colors and fine details. Light rays are detected by the eyeball's inner lining, the retina, which is thinner than the paper of this page and the size of two thumbnails. Here, millions of light-sensitive cells, when struck by rays of different brightness and color, send billions of nerve signals to the brain.

CAPTURING AN IMAGE

Light rays arrive at the eye in a continuous stream, with an endless variety of different colors and brightness. After being focused by the cornea and lens, the light rays pass through the clear jelly in the eyeball to the retina. The retina's task is to detect variations in color, shape, and brightness at incredible speed—dozens of times a second.

Ganglion cell layer combines signals from bipolar cells

Lens

Retina

Light source

Optic nerve

1 Light rays from image enter the eye
Light rays hit the pigment layer at the back of the retina and then pass through the light-sensitive cells, called rods and cones. These convert the information from the light rays into nerve signals.

WE CAN SEE UP TO 10 MILLION COLORS WITH TRAINING

Bipolar cell layer gathers signals from rods and cones

Cone cell

Pigment layer at back of retina protects and feeds the other retina cells

Nerve fiber

Path of light rays that enter the eye

Fibers come together as optic nerve

Nerve signals

Rod cell

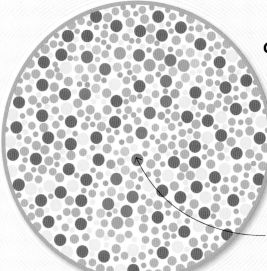

COLOR VISION PROBLEMS

Can you see a number here? Most eyes can see 2–5 million different colors and hues. But others do not see the normal range of colors, due to an inherited condition, faulty development, injury, or disease. For example, there may be only two kinds of working cone cells rather than three.

Color test
Those with red–green color blindness will not be able to distinguish the number in green from the red dots around it.

MIXING COLOR

There are three types of cone cell in our eyes that are sensitive to red light, green light, or blue light. Colors mix to produce a variety of different colors; for example, green and red produce yellow. So yellow light affects both red-sensitive and green-sensitive cones, but not as much as pure red for red cones or green for green ones.

Secondary colors are where primary colors mix

Yellow, a secondary color, is a mix of red and green

White, a mix of all three primary colors

Primary colors of light are red, green, and blue

COLOR WHEEL

Three types of cone cell provide detailed color information about the central part of the image

2 Cones and rods
Cone cells are most numerous in a small patch of the retina, the fovea. They need bright light to detect fine details and colors. Rod cells occur over most of the retina. They work well in dim light, but do not see colors.

Final image in color with greatest detail at center

3 In the mind's eye
The detailed color information given by the closely packed cones and the broader information, in shades of gray, from the rods is gathered by bipolar cells. Ganglion cells then combine the signals from the bipolar cells and transmit them through the optic nerve to the brain, to give a full-color, overall image.

Rod cells provide information about the entire view but only in shades of gray

READY TO FIRE

Rods and cones

Zooming into the retina of the eye reveals millions of rod and cone cells, standing like people in a gigantic crowd. Each is ready to fire nerve signals when enough light of the right color and intensity shines on it. Human eyes have cones for red, green, and blue light. Cones are tiny—about 100 cones on top of each other would be as high as this letter I—while rods are slightly slimmer and taller. In the whole retina there are 20 times more rods than cones.

STATS AND FACTS

TYPES OF CONE CELLS

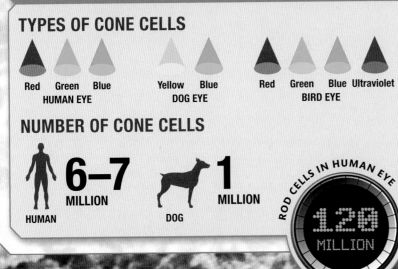

Red   Green   Blue
HUMAN EYE

Yellow   Blue
DOG EYE

Red   Green   Blue   Ultraviolet
BIRD EYE

NUMBER OF CONE CELLS

6–7 MILLION
HUMAN

1 MILLION
DOG

ROD CELLS IN HUMAN EYE
120 MILLION

Sight 'n' seeing

Shown here are rods (in green) and cones (in blue), 5,000 times their actual size. Rods and cones are packed into the retina at the back of the eye, from where they send signals to the brain.

"It takes **100 times** more light energy to make a **cone cell** generate nerve signals than a **rod**"

KEEP IT IN PERSPECTIVE
3D vision

Unlike a horse or a whale, which has eyes on the side of its head, both of a human's eyes face forward and see almost the same scene, but from slightly different angles. Just open and close each eye in turn to test this out. Comparing these two views in the brain, and using clues such as size, color, and blur, gives us a tremendous ability to judge depth and distance, and see in glorious three dimensions (3D)—height, width, and depth.

WORKING OUT A SCENE

This city street scene has all the components to help our eyes and brain create a complete image. Things like subtle changes in color, differences in size, and receding lines all contribute to the visual clues.

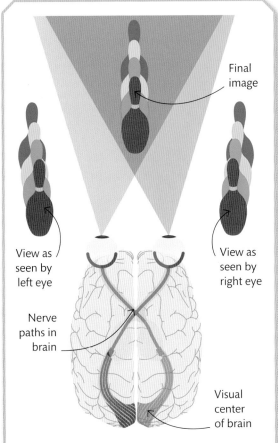

Final image

View as seen by left eye

View as seen by right eye

Nerve paths in brain

Visual center of brain

BINOCULAR VISION

Each eye sees a scene from its own angle. The vision center of the brain compares the left half of the left eye's view with the left half from the right eye, and similarly for the right halves. The more the two views of an object differ, the closer it is. This is known as binocular or two-eye vision.

ACTUAL SIZE

We know the real sizes of objects such as people, cars, trucks, and various animals. Checking their size in a scene such as a busy street allows us to guess how far away they are.

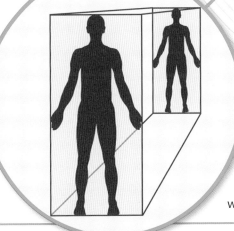

RELATIVE SIZE

Comparing the sizes of similar objects helps us estimate their distance from us. If there are two similar vehicles or people in view, for example, and one is twice as big as the other, we assume it is much closer.

COLOR, FADE, AND SHADOW

The same color will look different the farther away it is. It will get paler and more faded. Also, the distant view is hazier and more blurred—sometimes due to dust particles in the air. Our brain learns this, which helps us judge distance.

"**Good eyesight** can **detect** movements of less than **3 ft** (1 m) at a **distance** of **328 ft** (100 m)"

PARALLEL AND PARALLAX

Lines that are the same distance apart seem to come closer together as they go off into the distance. Also, shifting the head from side to side makes near objects move more than far ones. This is called parallax.

PLAYING WITH PERSPECTIVE

A two-dimensional (2D) image can look 3D using features such as perspective and shadows. Playing with these can produce an optical illusion. This does not trick the eyes, which record the scene. Instead, it fools the brain as it tries to turn 2D into 3D.

CROWDED AREAS MAKE OBJECTS LOOK NEARER

EYE FOCUS AND ANGLE

The brain detects the eye's lens becoming thicker to focus on near objects, and thinner for distant ones (see pp. 78-79). Both eyes swivel inward to look at nearer things.

COMPLETE CONTROL
Total focus

"The human eye can see a **bright flash** of only **4 ms** (**¹⁄₂₅₀ of a second**)"

Our two forward-facing eyes, each looking at a slightly different angle, let us judge distances more accurately than almost any other animal. As an object approaches it triggers more cells in the retina. Muscles adjust the lens to maintain a sharp focus. Both eyes move to look directly at the object, their muscles reacting to length changes of just 0.2 mm. Processing all this information, in some cases up to 100 times per second, allows humans to track motion in incredible detail.

STATS AND FACTS

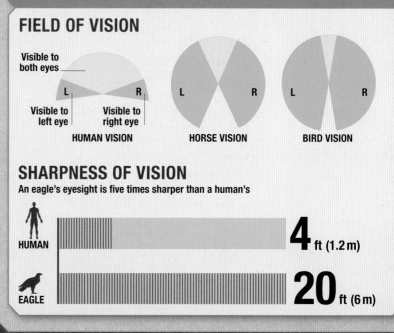

FIELD OF VISION

Visible to both eyes

Visible to left eye

Visible to right eye

L   R

HUMAN VISION

L   R

HORSE VISION

L   R

BIRD VISION

SHARPNESS OF VISION
An eagle's eyesight is five times sharper than a human's

HUMAN — **4** ft (1.2 m)

EAGLE — **20** ft (6 m)

Set to serve

Once it reaches the top of its travel, the tennis ball starts to fall faster and faster. At the precise moment, the server must catch it in the racquet's "sweet spot" to smash it away at over 150 mph (240 km/h).

WIRED FOR SOUND
How ears work

Ears are much more than flaps on either side of the head. They hear an immense range of sounds, varying in volume from the faintest whisper to a jet's mighty roar, and in pitch from deep rumbling thunder to a high, shrill bird song. The ear even has its own built-in protection system. On hearing a very loud sound, within one-tenth of a second two tiny muscles pull on miniature bones deep in the middle ear. This reduces their vibration movements and protects the incredibly delicate inner ear from damage. The ears also contain parts that help maintain balance.

Pinna, skin covering of the ear flap

INTO THE EAR

Invisible sound waves in the air travel along the ear canal to the middle ear, where the eardrum changes them into patterns of very fast to-and-fro movements, or vibrations. These vibrations pass across the middle ear and into the inner ear, where the snail-shaped cochlea changes them into patterns of nerve signals. The signals speed a short distance along the cochlear nerve to the brain's hearing center.

Invisible sound waves in air

Springy cartilage inside ear flap

1 Collecting sound waves
The central area of the outer ear flap, called the pinna, is shaped like a funnel. It channels sound waves into the 1 in- (2.5 cm-) long, slightly curved ear canal. Small hairs and wax made by the canal lining trap dirt, germs, and even the occasional small bug.

STATS AND FACTS

HEARING RANGE CHANGE

Age	Frequency
10 YEARS	19,000 Hz
20 YEARS	17,000 Hz
40 YEARS	9,000 Hz
60 YEARS	5,000 Hz

If unrolled, the cochlea, which is about the size of a pea, would be

1¹/₄ in (31.5 mm)

Inside each cochlea, there are around

15,000

hairs, all of which could fit on the head of a pin

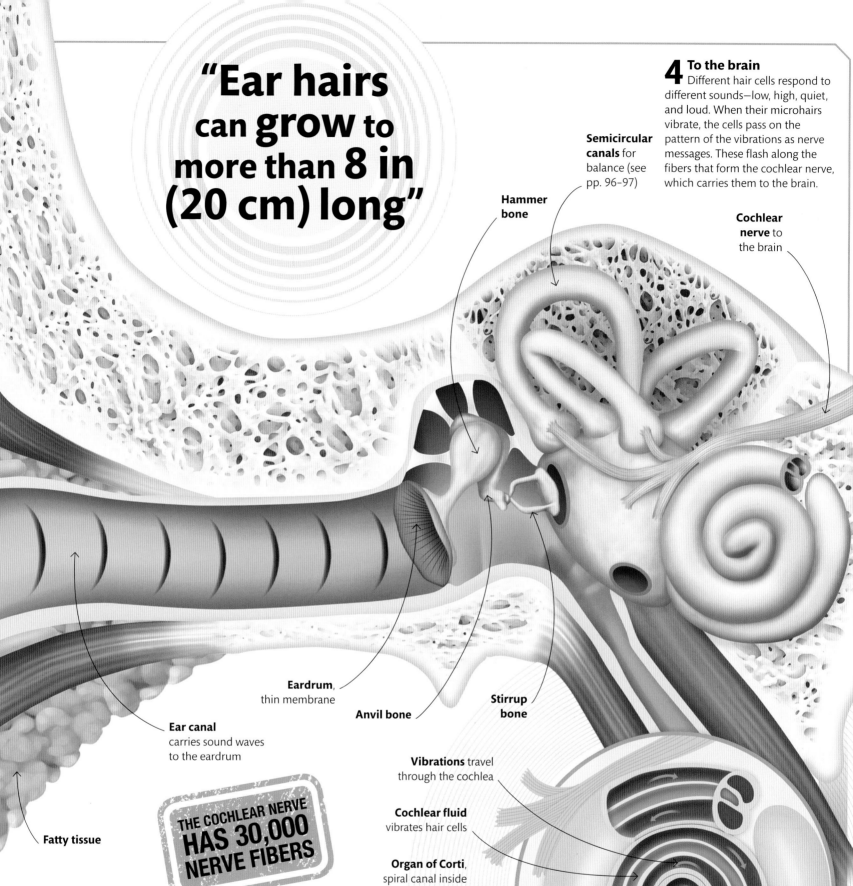

"Ear hairs can grow to more than 8 in (20 cm) long"

4 To the brain
Different hair cells respond to different sounds—low, high, quiet, and loud. When their microhairs vibrate, the cells pass on the pattern of the vibrations as nerve messages. These flash along the fibers that form the cochlear nerve, which carries them to the brain.

Semicircular canals for balance (see pp. 96–97)

Hammer bone

Cochlear nerve to the brain

Eardrum, thin membrane

Anvil bone

Stirrup bone

Ear canal carries sound waves to the eardrum

Vibrations travel through the cochlea

Cochlear fluid vibrates hair cells

Organ of Corti, spiral canal inside the cochlea

Fatty tissue

THE COCHLEAR NERVE **HAS 30,000 NERVE FIBERS**

2 Waves to vibrations
Sound waves bounce off the eardrum, which is a patch of thin skin the area of a little fingernail, and make it vibrate. These vibrations pass along a chain of three tiny linked bones, or the ear ossicles, called the hammer, anvil, and stirrup. The stirrup vibrates the cochlea and sets up ripples in the fluid inside it.

3 Inside the cochlea
Every second, the cochlea receives thousands of vibrations as ripples in its fluid. The vibrations from sound waves are concentrated as they pass from the eardrum to the tiny ear ossicles, making them around 20 times stronger than the original waves. These vibrations shake the microscopic hairs on the 15,000 hair cells lining the spiral canal inside the cochlea.

Good vibrations

Seen at 100,000 times their size, microhairs poke from the dished surface of a single outer hair cell. This is surrounded by ridges, and beyond are the similar downcurved surfaces of neighboring cells.

"An average **ear** produces enough **wax** in one year to **fill** an **egg cup**"

HAIRS THAT HEAR

Inside the cochlea

Deep in the ear, the cochlea—itself about the size of a pea—contains around 15,000 specialized microscopic hair cells. Each has a batch of even tinier microhairs called stereocilia on its surface. The hairs jut into a sticky fluid called endolymph and touch a jellylike sheet, both of which vibrate with sound. There are two sets of hair cells—inner and outer. The 3,000 inner cells do most of the hearing. Another 12,000 outer hair cells boost the vibrations to make hearing extra-sensitive.

STATS AND FACTS

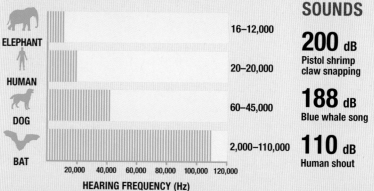

HEARING RANGE		ANIMAL SOUNDS
ELEPHANT	16–12,000	**200** dB Pistol shrimp claw snapping
HUMAN	20–20,000	**188** dB Blue whale song
DOG	60–45,000	**110** dB Human shout
BAT	2,000–110,000	

HEARING FREQUENCY (Hz): 20,000 40,000 60,000 80,000 100,000 120,000

BALANCING ACT

Staying upright

The unstable, two-legged human body has an astonishing split-second ability to stay upright and move without falling. Yet balance is not a single sense. It combines sensory information from the inner ears, skin, muscles, and joints. Every second they send thousands of messages to the brain, which monitors the information and sends out instructions to hundreds of muscles—usually automatically!

THE EAR'S BALANCE
**ORGANS ARE
PEA-SIZED**

Eyes judge horizontals and verticals, such as walls and floors

Cerebellum in the lower rear brain compares different inputs

HOW WE BALANCE

Balance is a continual process that relies on inputs from pressure sensors in the skin, stretch sensors inside body parts, fluid-filled canals and chambers deep in the ears, and even the eyes. The brain compares these inputs in the cerebellum, at the lower rear part of the brain, and structures called basal ganglia, which are deep in the brain's center.

Muscle sensors detect contraction

Sensors in the knee joint detect how much the knee is bent

Nerve from ear to brain

IN THE EAR

Five ear parts give balance information. Head movement makes liquid inside the three ear canals swish, bending the microhairs of hair cells, which send nerve signals to the brain. Hair cells in two chambers in the inner ear, the utricle and saccule, bend with gravity to show which way is down.

Utricle

Semicircular canals at right angles to each other so they detect movement across any angle

Microhairs of hair cells in jellylike blob, or cupula

Swishing liquid

DIZZINESS

Many sudden, fast-changing movements make the liquid in the inner ear slosh around, even after the motion stops and the eyes show the head is now still. The brain is confused by these conflicting messages, especially when the movements are unnatural—such as being thrown around and upside-down on a rollercoaster. It takes up to 30 seconds for the liquid's swishing to fade so that the brain can recover.

Touch receptors in skin respond to pressure on sole to detect leaning

Stretch sensors detect when the skin tightens

"Even standing still uses more than 300 muscles"

STATS AND FACTS

TIGHTROPE CROSSING

Fastest 328 ft (100 m) tightrope walk
45 seconds

Longest tightrope crossing by bicycle
235 ft
(71.6 m)

Most skips on a tightrope
1,323

Your body uses
50%
of its muscles to balance while standing still

Total volume of all inner ear fluid is less than
1/10 of a teaspoon

SUPER BALANCE

Sure-footed ride

Standing upright and well balanced, even on a steady surface, means over 300 muscles need to make tiny alterations many times each second. On a surface that moves suddenly and unpredictably, in a split second the challenge increases 100-fold. Balance sensors in the ears, muscles, joints, and skin fire constant streams of information into the brain—millions of signals per second! The brain continually decides on muscles to keep the body steady. Bend the back? Hold out an arm? Shift a foot?

STATS AND FACTS

STAYING ON BOARD

Longest surfing marathon
313 waves in
29 hours

Windsurfing record on a single wave
7 minutes **3** seconds

Longest surf on a continuous wave
3 hours **55** minutes

Most people on a surfboard **47**

Riding giants

Every wave is unique, with tiny variations in water speed, depth, current, angle of slope, and wind pressure. The surfer rides these unpredictable waves with the calculated slide of a foot.

"Training can **improve** balance by more than **10 times**"

TASTY!
How we taste food

Taste acts like a sentry to the digestive system. On one hand, it provides fantastic flavors that signal a delicious meal; on the other, it warns of bad or rotting foods that might poison the body. Like smell, taste is a chemosense—it detects the chemical substances that give flavors to food and drinks. Chewing releases these substances, which dissolve in saliva and seep into thousands of microstructures called taste buds. Here they touch taste receptor cells, which fire nerve signals to the brain.

Some papillae have tiny fingers that act like a rasp and help clean the tongue

Saliva carries dissolved substances into the taste pore

MIGHTY MUSCULAR

The tongue is almost all muscle, making it powerful and flexible. More than four-fifths of the taste buds lie on its upper surface, sides, and tip. There are also taste buds scattered on the inner lips, insides of the cheeks, roof of the mouth (palate), throat, and epiglottis.

Mucus-secreting glands help clean old tastes out of the pits between the papillae

A TONGUE PRINT IS AS UNIQUE AS A FINGERPRINT

1 Papillae
The tongue's upper surface is coated with hundreds of tiny lumps and bumps called papillae. Most of the taste buds are located around the sides of papillae, or in the gaps between them. Each taste bud is less 1mm across.

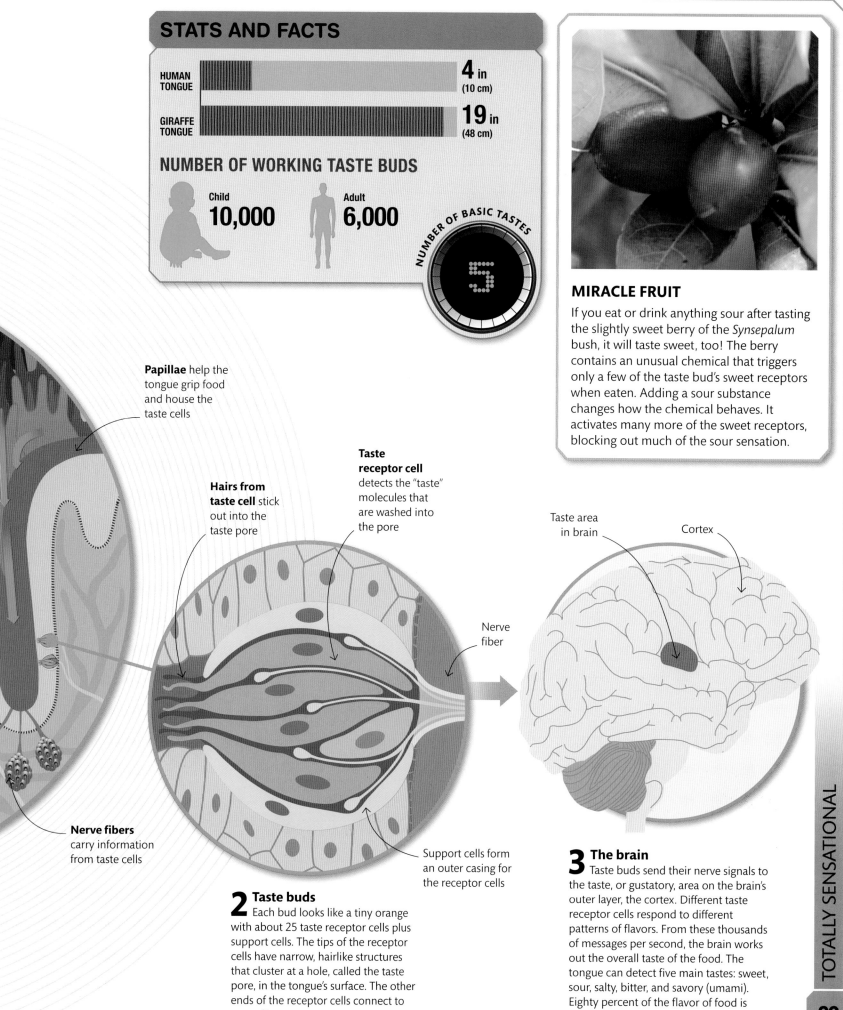

HUMAN TONGUE		**4** in (10 cm)
GIRAFFE TONGUE		**19** in (48 cm)

NUMBER OF WORKING TASTE BUDS

Child 10,000

Adult 6,000

NUMBER OF BASIC TASTES

5

MIRACLE FRUIT

If you eat or drink anything sour after tasting the slightly sweet berry of the *Synsepalum* bush, it will taste sweet, too! The berry contains an unusual chemical that triggers only a few of the taste bud's sweet receptors when eaten. Adding a sour substance changes how the chemical behaves. It activates many more of the sweet receptors, blocking out much of the sour sensation.

Papillae help the tongue grip food and house the taste cells

Hairs from taste cell stick out into the taste pore

Taste receptor cell detects the "taste" molecules that are washed into the pore

Taste area in brain

Cortex

Nerve fiber

Nerve fibers carry information from taste cells

Support cells form an outer casing for the receptor cells

2 Taste buds

Each bud looks like a tiny orange with about 25 taste receptor cells plus support cells. The tips of the receptor cells have narrow, hairlike structures that cluster at a hole, called the taste pore, in the tongue's surface. The other ends of the receptor cells connect to nerve fibers.

3 The brain

Taste buds send their nerve signals to the taste, or gustatory, area on the brain's outer layer, the cortex. Different taste receptor cells respond to different patterns of flavors. From these thousands of messages per second, the brain works out the overall taste of the food. The tongue can detect five main tastes: sweet, sour, salty, bitter, and savory (umami). Eighty percent of the flavor of food is actually detected by our sense of smell.

ON THE TONGUE

Taste receptors

A close look at the tongue shows that its upper surface is covered with hundreds of tiny, variously shaped bumps called papillae. The papillae grip and move food around the mouth when you chew. Many papillae have much smaller taste buds around their sides or edges. They also contain nerve endings that detect pressure, heat, cold, slipperiness, hardness, and pain. These factors combine with taste and smell in the brain to produce the overall sensation of the food being eaten.

STATS AND FACTS

NUMBER OF TASTE BUDS

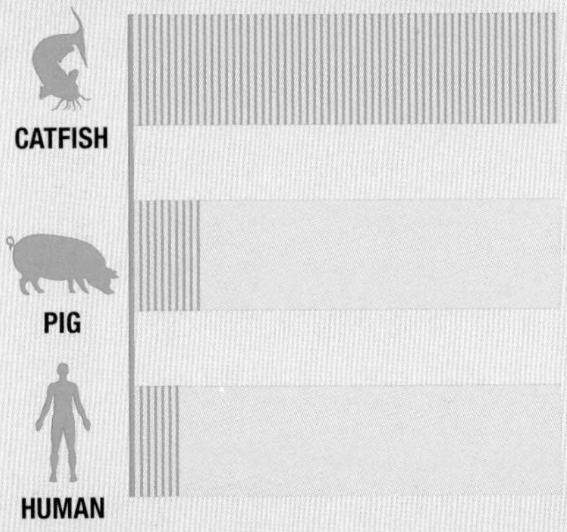

CATFISH — 100,000

PIG — 15,000

HUMAN — 10,000

NUMBER OF TASTES WE DETECT
1,000

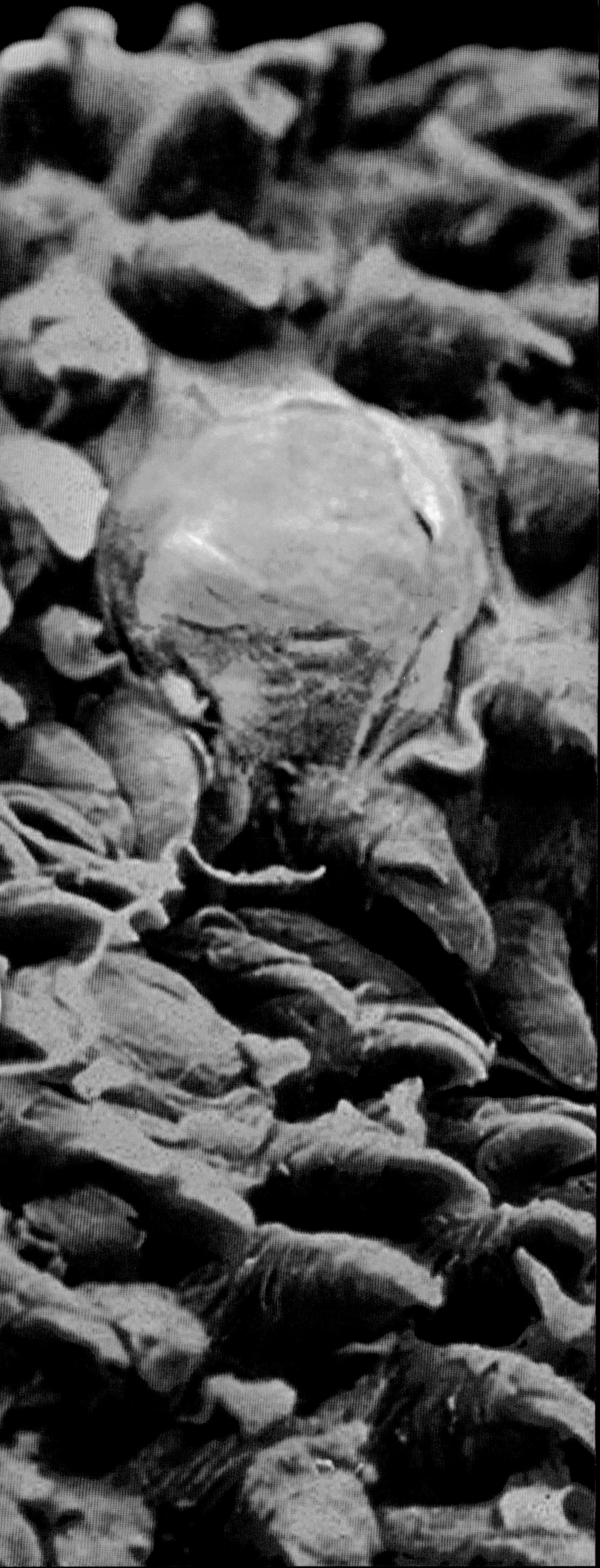

Food's-eye view

Fingerlike papillae (colored pink on this highly magnified image) are less than 1 mm long. The tongue also has about 200 mushroom-shaped papillae (in blue), each with 5–15 taste buds.

"**Taste bud cells** live for only **10–11 days** before they are replaced"

ON THE SCENT

How we smell things

Life without scents, perfumes, odors, and aromas would be very dull. Our supersense of smell can tell apart millions of different odors. It helps us sniff out harmful gases in the air or the stench of rotten food, and lets us enjoy the aromas of a delicious feast or the perfumes of flowers. The smell, or olfactory, system also has direct nerve connections into parts of the brain that deal with memories and emotions. This is why smells from our past, such as a pine forest or the seashore, can bring back strong feelings and powerful memories.

> "We have about **20 million** smell receptors **in our nose**"

FROM AIR TO BRAIN

As with taste, our sense of smell is based on chemistry. Receptor cells in the nose detect odor molecules floating in the air and send nerve messages to the brain. Unlike taste, smell is a long-distance sense—we can sniff out certain odors from hundreds of yards away.

1 Odors in air
Each of the chemicals in an odor molecule has a unique structure that binds to a particular type of receptor in the nose. Most odor molecules are small and light, and float easily in air.

Odor molecules drift in air currents

4 Bulb and brain
The receptors pass on millions of nerve messages to the olfactory bulb located just above them. The bulb sorts and coordinates these messages. It then sends them along the short, thick, nervelike olfactory tract to the brain's smell processing center.

Smell and taste center identifies the smell

Olfactory bulb processes nerve messages

Olfactory tract to brain

Brain

Nerve branches

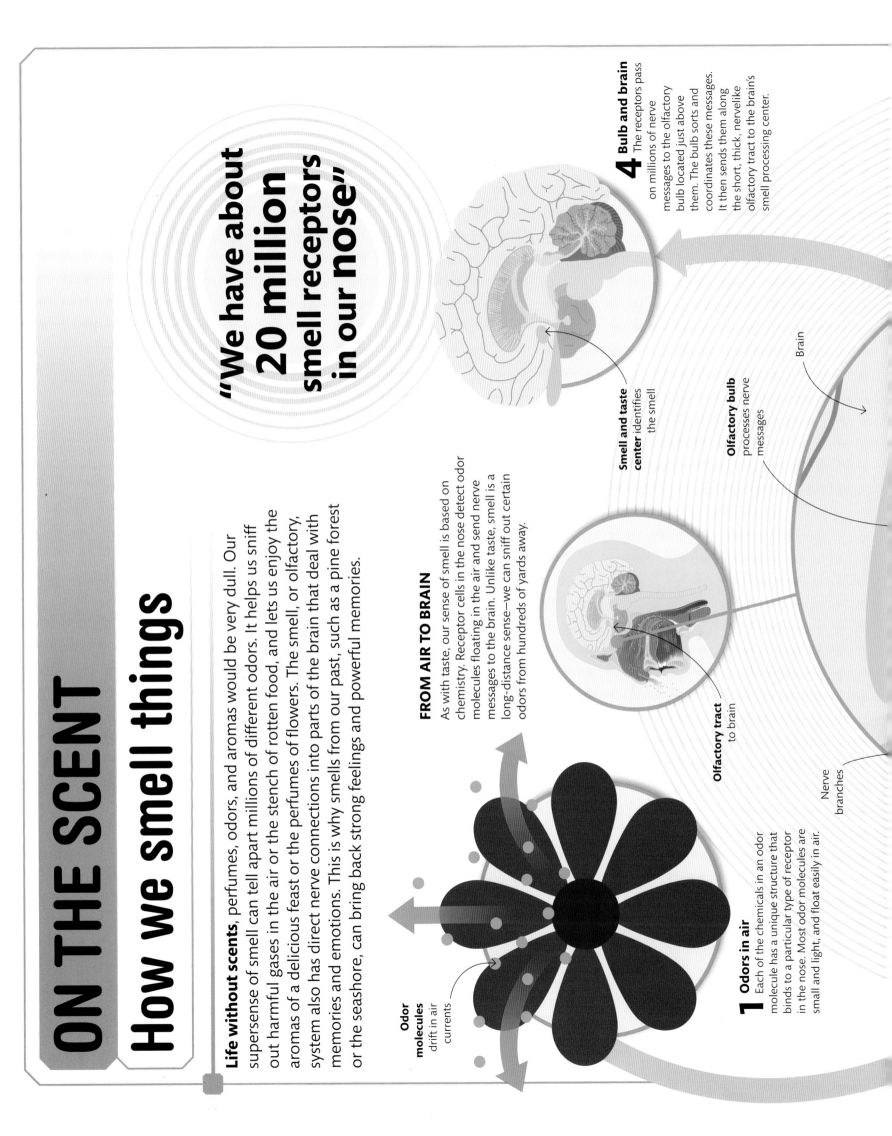

Hairlike endings detect odor molecules

SMELL RECEPTORS

Air drawn in through nostrils and into nasal chamber

2 Into the nose
When you want to smell something, you take a small sniff. This makes air, and with it the odor molecules, swirl into the nasal chamber, the space in the upper part of your nose where the receptor cells are located.

Olfactory epithelium is a layer rich in receptors

Odor molecules

Air flow

3 Smell cells
On each side of the nasal chamber is a thumbnail-sized area called the olfactory epithelium. This contains millions of smell receptors with hairlike endings. When an odor molecule lands on a suitable receptor, it sends a nerve signal to the brain.

WARNING! DANGER!
Certain smells have a fast, direct effect on the body. The foul stench of rotting food, stagnant water, and human digestive waste, or the sharp odor of strong chemicals such as acids, are all quickly identified. They warn of dangers such as germs, infection, and poisoning, and we instinctively wrinkle our nose to avoid them. This partly closes the airways, which reduces damage to the nose's delicate lining from powerful or harmful chemicals in the smell.

Nasal passage closed partially to prevent foul smell from entering

KEEPING IN TOUCH
How we feel sensations

Far more than simply sensing contact with something, touch is a super-multi-sense. It begins with a wide range of receptors, or specialized nerve endings in the skin and tissues. Various forms of contacts trigger the receptors to send patterns of messages to your brain—thousands every second. From this immense amount of information, the brain works out whether an object is hard or soft, wet or dry, smooth or rough, warm or cold, stiff or bendy, and much more.

"If the body was as tall as the Eiffel Tower, the fingertips would be able to feel ridges less than 1mm high"

TYPES OF TOUCH RECEPTORS

The skin has millions of touch receptors of various kinds. Some are near the surface; others are buried deeper. Certain types respond to several kinds of change, such as being pressed, heated, cooled, squeezed, stretched, or vibrated, while others respond to only a few types of change.

Free nerve endings are like tiny branching trees and are affected by most kinds of change in touch— they also register pain.

Merkel endings are located near the skin's surface and they are especially sensitive to medium levels of touch, pressure, and slower vibrations.

Meissner endings sit just below the epidermis and respond to very light, brief touches as well as faster vibrations.

Ruffini endings are sensitive to being stretched and squeezed; they also react to changes in temperature.

HUMAN SKIN

Pacinian endings are the deepest and largest type of touch receptor; they respond to prolonged pressure and all kinds of vibrations.

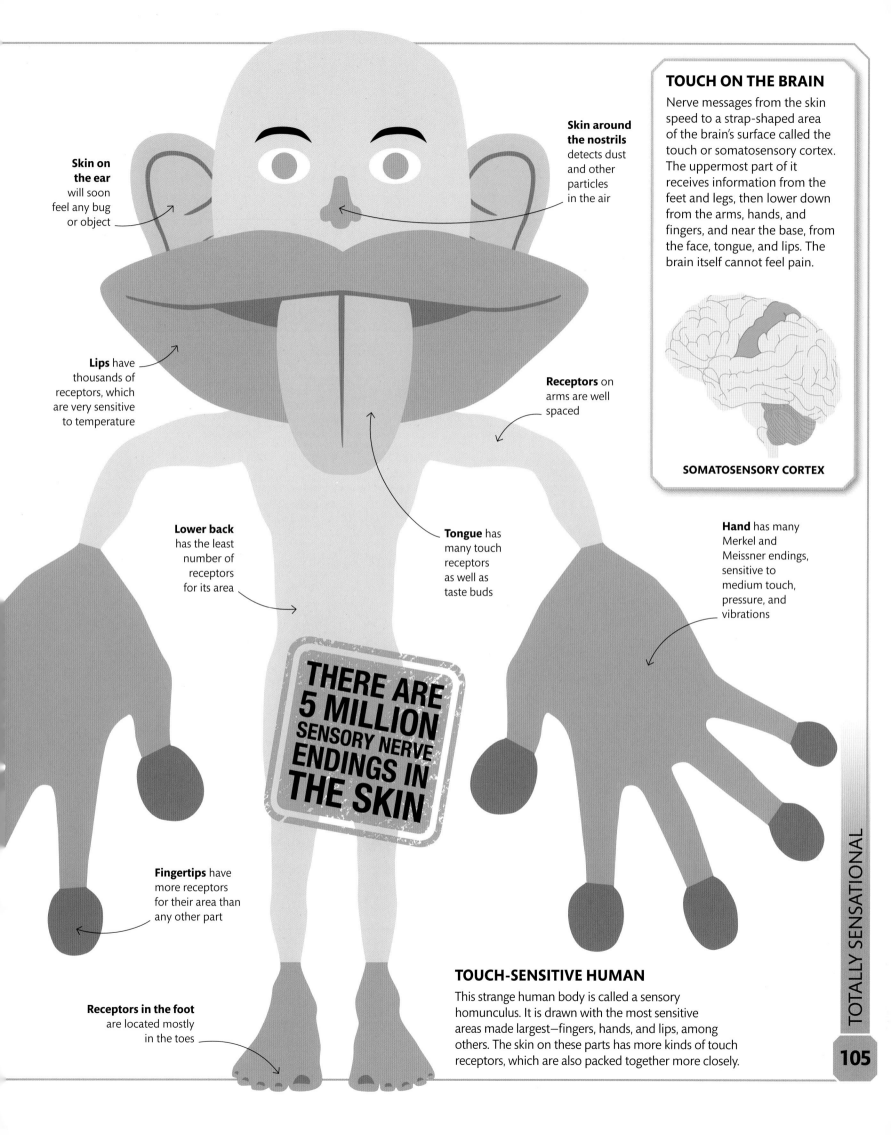

Skin on the ear will soon feel any bug or object

Skin around the nostrils detects dust and other particles in the air

TOUCH ON THE BRAIN

Nerve messages from the skin speed to a strap-shaped area of the brain's surface called the touch or somatosensory cortex. The uppermost part of it receives information from the feet and legs, then lower down from the arms, hands, and fingers, and near the base, from the face, tongue, and lips. The brain itself cannot feel pain.

SOMATOSENSORY CORTEX

Lips have thousands of receptors, which are very sensitive to temperature

Receptors on arms are well spaced

Lower back has the least number of receptors for its area

Tongue has many touch receptors as well as taste buds

Hand has many Merkel and Meissner endings, sensitive to medium touch, pressure, and vibrations

THERE ARE 5 MILLION SENSORY NERVE ENDINGS IN THE SKIN

Fingertips have more receptors for their area than any other part

TOUCH-SENSITIVE HUMAN

This strange human body is called a sensory homunculus. It is drawn with the most sensitive areas made largest—fingers, hands, and lips, among others. The skin on these parts has more kinds of touch receptors, which are also packed together more closely.

Receptors in the foot are located mostly in the toes

FEELING GROOVY

Fingertips

Faced with something new, the body's immediate instinct, if all is safe, is to feel it with the fingertips. Each finger has an estimated 15,000 touch nerve endings, packed in closest at the tip. Almost no other part of the body is as sensitive. As the fingertip moves over an object, its ridges bend and distort slightly, triggering the touch endings along their edges. The smallest thing you can feel with a single touch is 1/5000th the width of a hair.

STATS AND FACTS

FINGERPRINTING

1 in 64,000 MILLION

The chance of two fingerprints matching—more unique than even DNA

AVERAGE DIMENSIONS

↕ **0.3** mm
Height of a fingertip skin ridge

↔ **0.4** mm
Width of a fingertip skin ridge

RIDGES PER FINGERTIP

1.20–1.50

"The fingertips can feel tiny bumps that the eye cannot see"

Remarkable ridges

Up close, the skin on the fingertips looks like a chain of mountains. The ridges and grooves help grip and also sense the tiniest of variations in a surface. The round pits along the ridges are sweat pores.

THAT HURTS!

How we feel pain

Pain is certainly not welcome, but it is definitely useful. It is an early warning that some part of the body is in danger of being damaged. The natural response is to move away from the cause of the pain and rest the injured area until it heals. Most kinds of touch sensor in the skin can send pain signals to the brain. There are pain sensors inside the body as well—in joints, muscles, main blood vessels, intestines, and even bones.

Touch cortex establishes location of pain

3 Awareness of pain
The pain messages fast-track up the spinal cord to the brain's thalamus, which sends them straight into the alert mind. Messages from the skin arrive at an area called the somatosensory, or touch, cortex (see pp. 104–105).

Pain signals arrive in the brain

Frontal cortex becomes aware of pain

Parts of the limbic system are linked to emotions of pain

Thalamus relays signals to cortex

Pain signals move up the spinal cord toward the brain

PAIN PATHWAYS

The more touch sensors are squeezed, heated, or frozen, the more nerve signals—of different patterns—they send to the brain. The messages travel along nerve fibers at up to 160 ft (50 m) per second. In the brain they are routed straight to the conscious awareness, so the mind can take urgent action.

RUB IT BETTER

It can help to stroke or rub a part that hurts. Rubbing produces hundreds of signals from the other touch sensors in the area. These swamp the brain and sidetrack its attention, so that it feels the rubbing more than the pain.

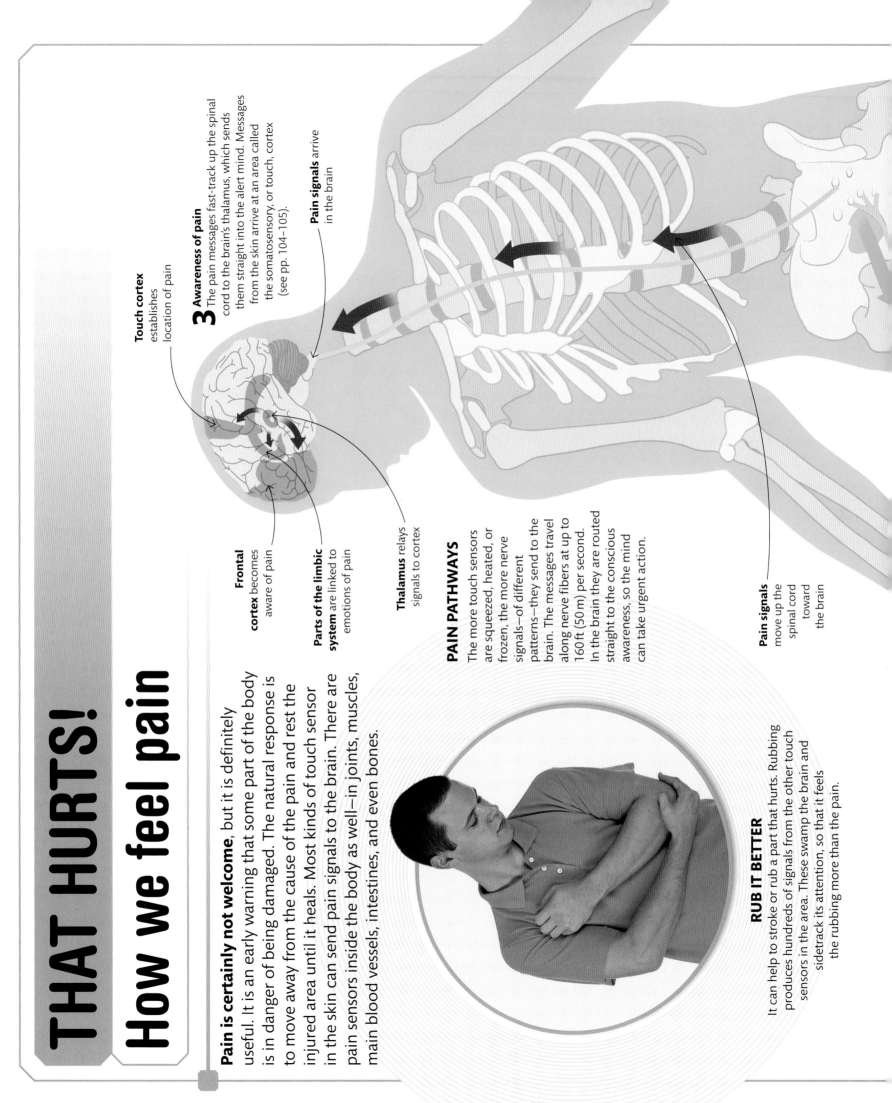

Spinal cord sends signals to leg muscles

Muscles lift leg off the pin

2 Auto-reaction
The signal reaches the spinal cord, which triggers a reflex link to the motor nerves that control the leg muscles. These contract to jerk the foot away from the site of the pain.

Messages speed along sciatic nerve to the spinal cord

Pain messages flash up tibial nerve in calf

Signals travel along plantar nerve in foot

Source of pain

1 Cause of pain
A pinprick penetrates the skin, triggering touch sensors called free nerve endings. Further damage to underlying muscles registers a split-second later.

SOME LIKE IT HOT

Spicy foods often taste hot. But they are not truly burning the mouth and tongue with heat. A substance called capsaicin in chili peppers and similar spices can trigger the nerve endings that usually detect warmth and pain. So although capsaicin is at body temperature in the mouth, the brain registers a fiery feeling.

PAIN, STRESS, AND STRAIN

Pain levels vary—even in the same person at different times. How painful an injury feels often depends on our physical and mental state when it happens. Someone who is tired usually feels pain more deeply than a person who is full of energy.

REACTION TIME TO
PAIN IS ¹⁄₁₅ OF
A SECOND

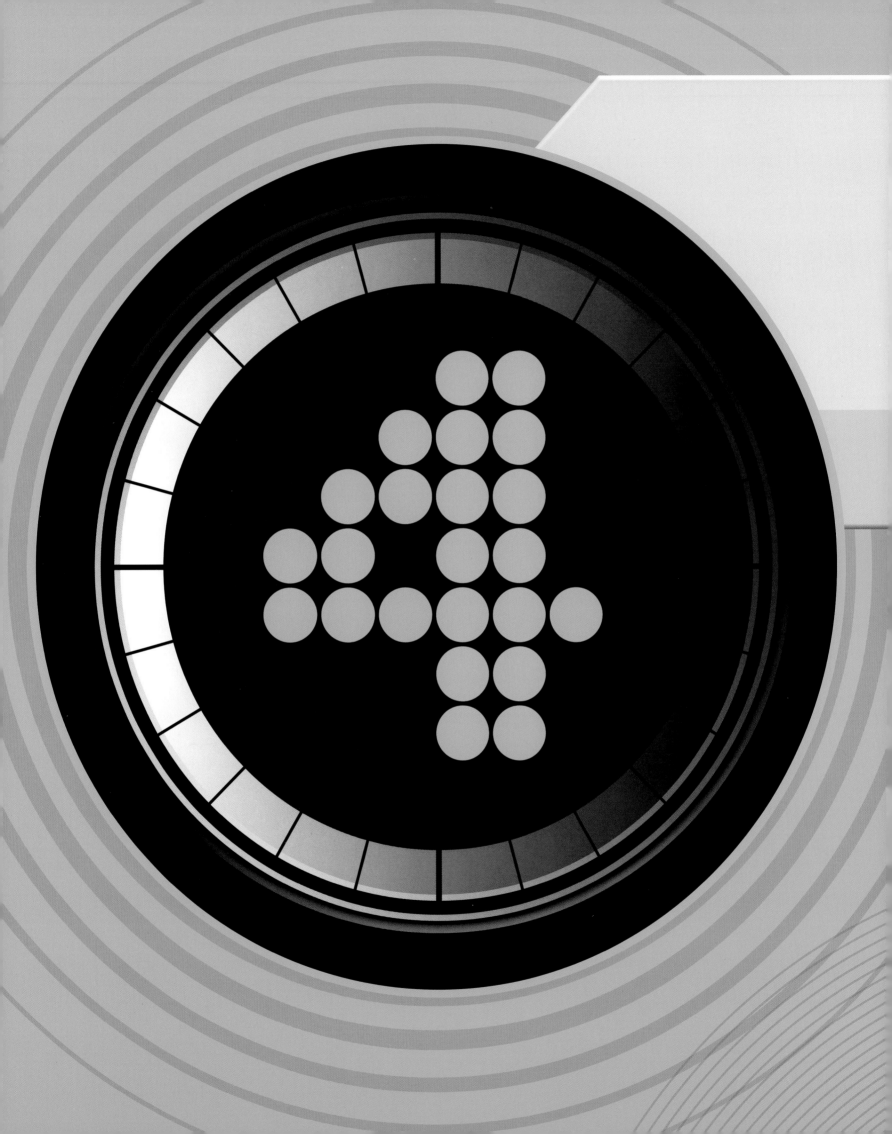

POWER SYSTEMS

Regular, reliable, and dependable, every second the lungs breathe, the heart beats, and the pulse throbs as the blood flows. The rest of the body relies on these supersystems never to pause or lose their power.

BREATHING MACHINE
Lungs and airways

The body can survive for a while without food and, for a lesser time, even without water. But the need for oxygen is constant and critical. This gas is in the air all around. Yet its need is so urgent that without it, some body parts, such as the brain, become damaged in minutes. After a few more minutes, many cells and tissues start to die. The lungs are where oxygen from the air we breathe in enters the blood. Also, waste carbon dioxide—which could poison the body if its levels rise—is removed from the blood and breathed out.

2,500 ALVEOLI WOULD FIT ON A FINGERNAIL

"The **surface area** of the **lungs** is **35 times larger** than that of the **skin**"

Cilium (plural cilia)

CLEANING YOUR AIR

The windpipe and main airway linings have millions of microhairs called cilia in a coating of sticky mucus. The mucus traps dirt and germs. The cilia bend to and fro to move these up to the throat for coughing out or swallowing.

There are 1,500 miles (2,414 km) of airways in the lungs

STATS AND FACTS

TOTAL VOLUME OF BOTH LUNGS

11–13 pints (5–6 liters)
ADULT MALE

8–11 pints (4–5 liters)
ADULT FEMALE

BREATHING CAPACITY

You take about **30,000** breaths per day, the same as blowing air into 2,000 balloons

AIR SACS IN BOTH LUNGS
600 MILLION

INSIDE THE CHEST

Fresh air travels down the windpipe, which divides into two main airways called bronchi. Each of the bronchi leads into a lung, where it branches many more times into smaller and smaller airways (bronchioles), ending in tiny air sacs called alveoli.

Larynx, or voice box, makes sounds

Trachea, or windpipe, carries air to and from the lungs

Bronchus (plural bronchi) branches from the windpipe

Bronchioles are the smaller branches from the bronchus. There are around 30,000 bronchioles in each lung

Network of capillaries encasing air sacs

ALVEOLI

Carbon dioxide is breathed out of the body

Oxygen is drawn into the capillary and is taken to the heart

Carbon dioxide moves from the blood into the alveolus

AIR SACS

Each tiny air sac, or alveolus, is surrounded by a network of the smallest blood vessels, capillaries. Oxygen in the air can easily pass through the thin alveolus and capillary walls into the blood, while waste carbon dioxide follows the opposite route—from the blood to the alveolus.

Diaphragm separates the chest cavity from the abdomen and helps inflate the lungs

POWER SYSTEMS

113

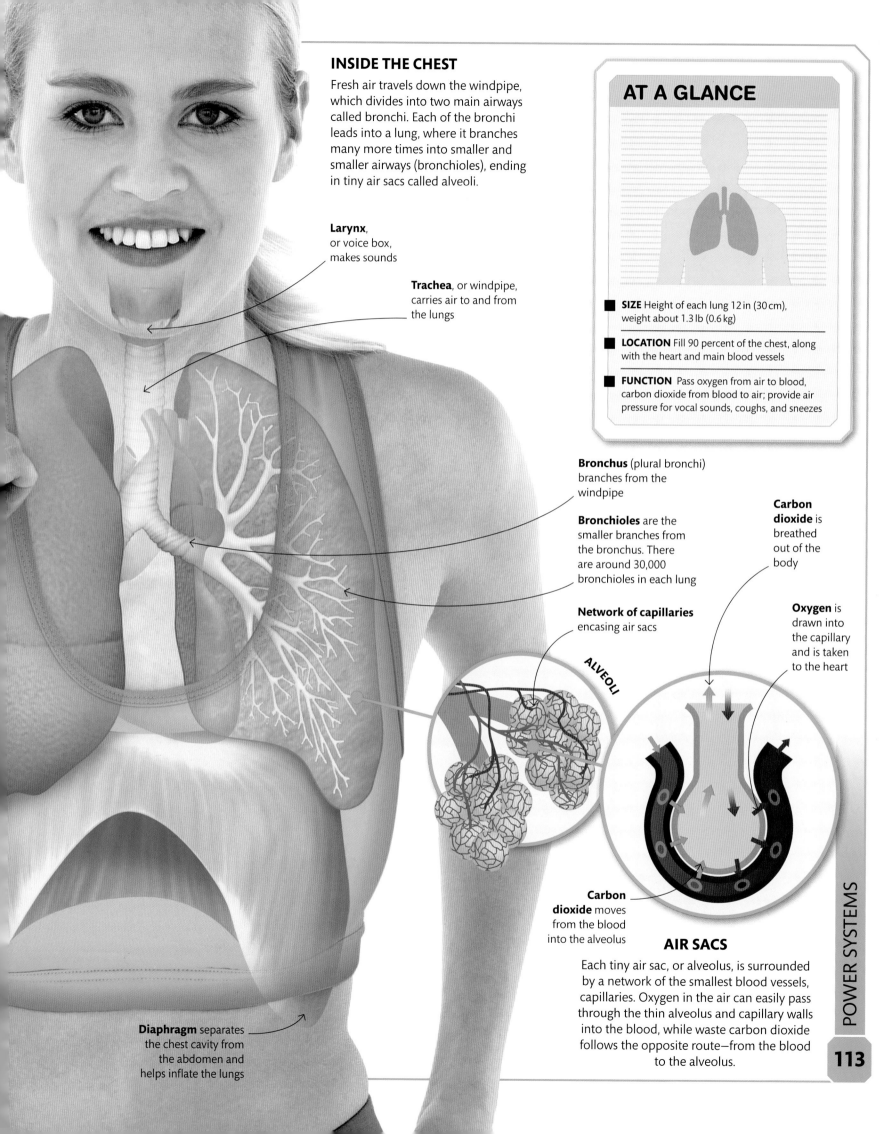

TAKE A DEEP BREATH
How the lungs work

Your lungs are never still. Every few seconds, day and night, they expand, pushing out the chest. This draws fresh, oxygen-rich air in through the mouth and nose, down the windpipe, and into the airways. Right after that, the lungs become smaller, or contract, to push out the stale air, which now contains waste carbon dioxide gas. Breathing in needs the power of the rib muscles and a sheet of muscle under the lungs, called the diaphragm to pull air in. Breathing out needs hardly any muscle effort at all.

BREATHING RATES

Busy muscles need more oxygen. The brain tells the diaphragm and rib muscles to work harder and faster, and increase the in–out air flow of 6 quarts (6 liters) per minute at rest, by up to 20 times when exercising.

RESTING
10–20
BREATHS PER MINUTE

EXERCISING
30–40
BREATHS PER MINUTE

INTENSE RUNNING
50–60
BREATHS PER MINUTE

BREATHING IN

Movement of the diaphragm and rib muscles allows the lungs to stretch out, much like a squashed sponge. This lowers the air pressure inside the lungs, so air flows in from the outside.

0.04%
Carbon dioxide

20.8%
Oxygen

COMPOSITION OF AIR

79.16%
Nitrogen

Ribs form a movable protective cage around the lungs

Lungs expand as the rib muscles tighten and the diaphragm pulls down, sucking in air

Diaphragm is a dome-shaped sheet of muscle under the lungs

Diaphragm tightens, pulling the bottom of the lungs down

You take more than 10 million breaths in a year

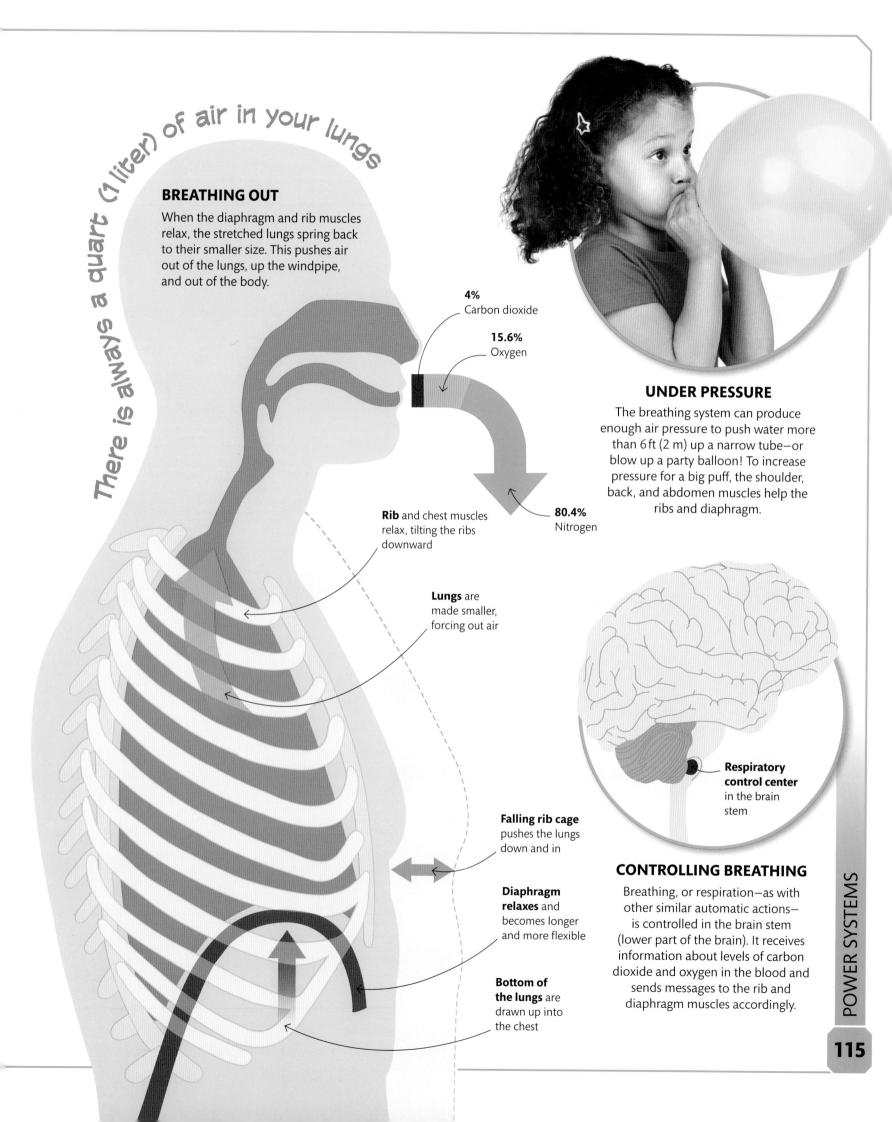

There is always a quart (1 liter) of air in your lungs

BREATHING OUT

When the diaphragm and rib muscles relax, the stretched lungs spring back to their smaller size. This pushes air out of the lungs, up the windpipe, and out of the body.

4%
Carbon dioxide

15.6%
Oxygen

80.4%
Nitrogen

Rib and chest muscles relax, tilting the ribs downward

Lungs are made smaller, forcing out air

Falling rib cage pushes the lungs down and in

Diaphragm relaxes and becomes longer and more flexible

Bottom of the lungs are drawn up into the chest

UNDER PRESSURE

The breathing system can produce enough air pressure to push water more than 6 ft (2 m) up a narrow tube—or blow up a party balloon! To increase pressure for a big puff, the shoulder, back, and abdomen muscles help the ribs and diaphragm.

Respiratory control center in the brain stem

CONTROLLING BREATHING

Breathing, or respiration—as with other similar automatic actions—is controlled in the brain stem (lower part of the brain). It receives information about levels of carbon dioxide and oxygen in the blood and sends messages to the rib and diaphragm muscles accordingly.

POWER SYSTEMS

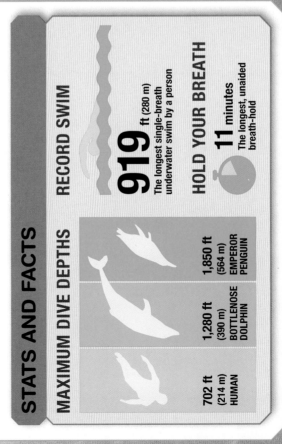

HUMAN SUB

Freediving

Deep-water divers battle against the most powerful of human instincts—to breathe. Specialized nerve endings monitor oxygen and carbon dioxide levels in the blood, especially in the arteries going to the brain. Sensors in the lower brain monitor the fluid in and around the brain. When carbon dioxide is too high, they tell the brain's breathing control center to make breathing faster and deeper to take in more oxygen. The challenge is to return to the surface before giving in to that instinct.

Plumbing the depths

Freedivers use breathing techniques that help them hold their breath longer than usual. They learn to recognize when carbon dioxide is building up, and to relax their muscles so they use less oxygen.

STATS AND FACTS

MAXIMUM DIVE DEPTHS

702 ft (214 m) HUMAN	1,280 ft (390 m) BOTTLENOSE DOLPHIN	1,850 ft (564 m) EMPEROR PENGUIN

RECORD SWIM

919 ft (280 m)
The longest single-breath underwater swim by a person

HOLD YOUR BREATH

11 minutes
The longest, unaided breath-hold

"At 33 ft (10 m) below the surface, **water pressure** collapses the **lungs** to just half their normal **volume**"

SCREAM AND SHOUT
Making sounds

The breathing, or respiratory, system does more than just take in oxygen and remove carbon dioxide. It can whisper, whistle, wail, speak, shout, scream, laugh, cry, and make many other fantastic sounds. Most come from the voice box, or larynx, in the neck. The system also makes noises when protecting itself from breathed-in dust and germs—explosive coughs and sneezes.

SNEEZE AND COUGH

A sneeze is a sudden blast of air out of the nose that blows away drops of mucus and dust at speeds of up to 100 mph (160 km/h). Coughing is used to clear the lower airways and windpipe, rattling the vocal cords as it comes out of the mouth. The air travels up to 45 mph (72 km/h) and sprays tiny drops of mucus over a distance of 10 ft (3 m)!

COMPARING LOUDNESS

Loudness, or volume, is measured in decibels (dB). The human voice can range from a whisper—just above our lower range of hearing of 0–5 dB—to a shout as loud as a chainsaw: a sound that would hurt if it was right by your ear.

> "Some **snorers** are **louder** than a low-flying jet, reaching 110 decibels"

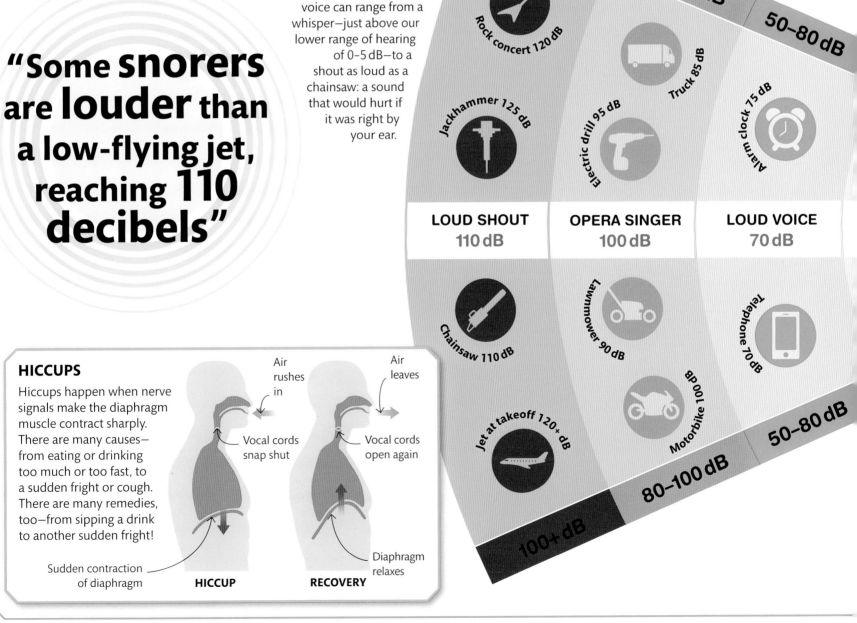

100+ dB

80–100 dB

50–80 dB

Rock concert 120 dB

Jackhammer 125 dB

Truck 85 dB

Electric drill 95 dB

Alarm clock 75 dB

LOUD SHOUT 110 dB

OPERA SINGER 100 dB

LOUD VOICE 70 dB

Chainsaw 110 dB

Lawnmower 90 dB

Telephone 70 dB

Jet at takeoff 120+ dB

Motorbike 100 dB

50–80 dB

80–100 dB

100+ dB

HICCUPS

Hiccups happen when nerve signals make the diaphragm muscle contract sharply. There are many causes— from eating or drinking too much or too fast, to a sudden fright or cough. There are many remedies, too—from sipping a drink to another sudden fright!

Air rushes in

Air leaves

Vocal cords snap shut

Vocal cords open again

Sudden contraction of diaphragm

Diaphragm relaxes

HICCUP

RECOVERY

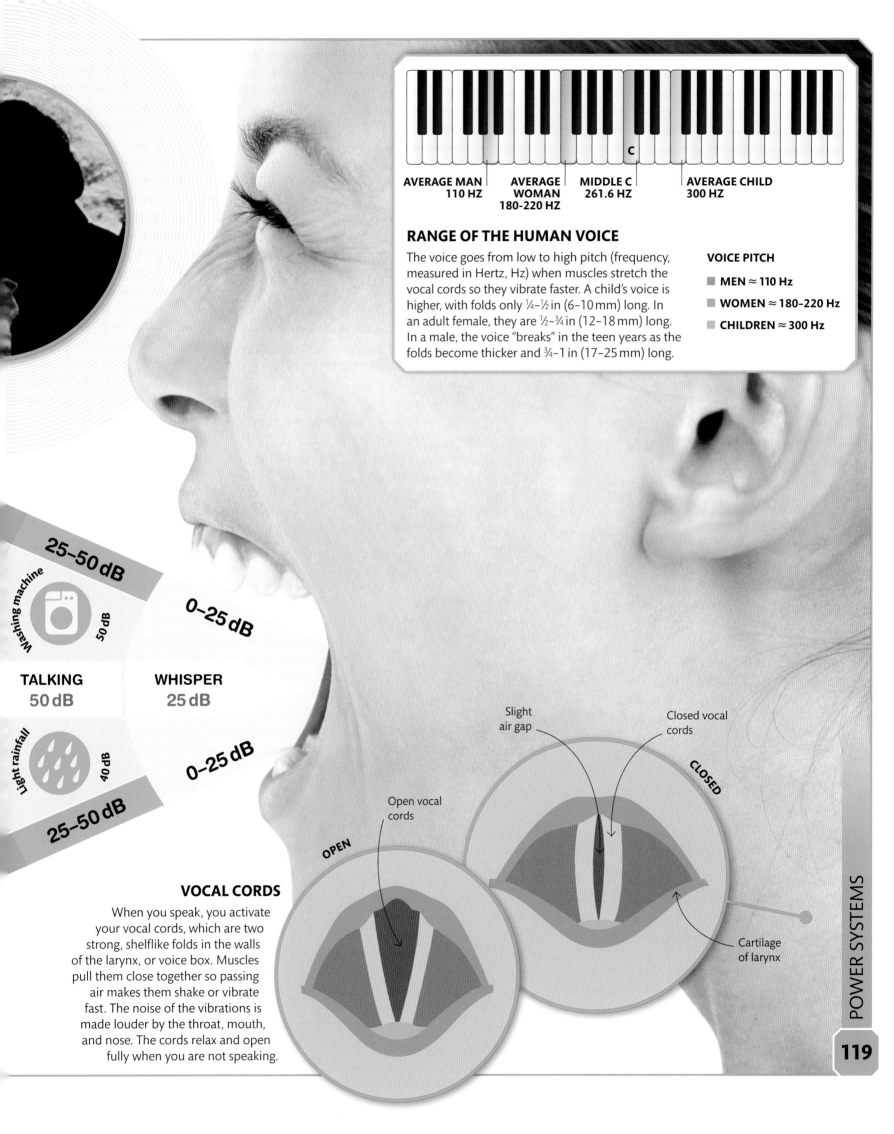

| AVERAGE MAN 110 HZ | AVERAGE WOMAN 180-220 HZ | MIDDLE C 261.6 HZ | AVERAGE CHILD 300 HZ |

RANGE OF THE HUMAN VOICE

The voice goes from low to high pitch (frequency, measured in Hertz, Hz) when muscles stretch the vocal cords so they vibrate faster. A child's voice is higher, with folds only ¼–½ in (6-10 mm) long. In an adult female, they are ½–¾ in (12-18 mm) long. In a male, the voice "breaks" in the teen years as the folds become thicker and ¾–1 in (17-25 mm) long.

VOICE PITCH

- MEN ≈ 110 Hz
- WOMEN ≈ 180-220 Hz
- CHILDREN ≈ 300 Hz

Washing machine 50 dB

25–50 dB

0–25 dB

TALKING 50 dB

WHISPER 25 dB

Light rainfall 40 dB

0–25 dB

25–50 dB

Slight air gap

Closed vocal cords

CLOSED

Open vocal cords

OPEN

Cartilage of larynx

VOCAL CORDS

When you speak, you activate your vocal cords, which are two strong, shelflike folds in the walls of the larynx, or voice box. Muscles pull them close together so passing air makes them shake or vibrate fast. The noise of the vibrations is made louder by the throat, mouth, and nose. The cords relax and open fully when you are not speaking.

POWER SYSTEMS

119

CIRCULATION CENTRAL

How blood travels

Every part of the body needs oxygen and nutrients that make energy, to stay alive. The processes of living also make wastes, which must be removed. These are the two main jobs of the circulatory system, which is made up of the beating heart, a branching network of blood vessels, and liquid blood. The system is circulatory because the same blood goes around and around. Blood also spreads heat evenly around the body from warm parts like the heart and muscles, to cooler ones such as the fingers.

BODYWIDE NETWORK

There are three main kinds of vessels. Arteries take blood away from the heart, veins carry it back, and tiny capillaries link the arteries and veins. Each artery has a name, which changes when it branches into smaller arteries. Similarly, the names of small veins change when they join into wider main veins.

BLOOD TO THE BRAIN

This medical scan shows the main artery to the brain, the internal carotid. It passes up the neck and into the skull, and then divides into smaller branches that take blood to all brain parts.

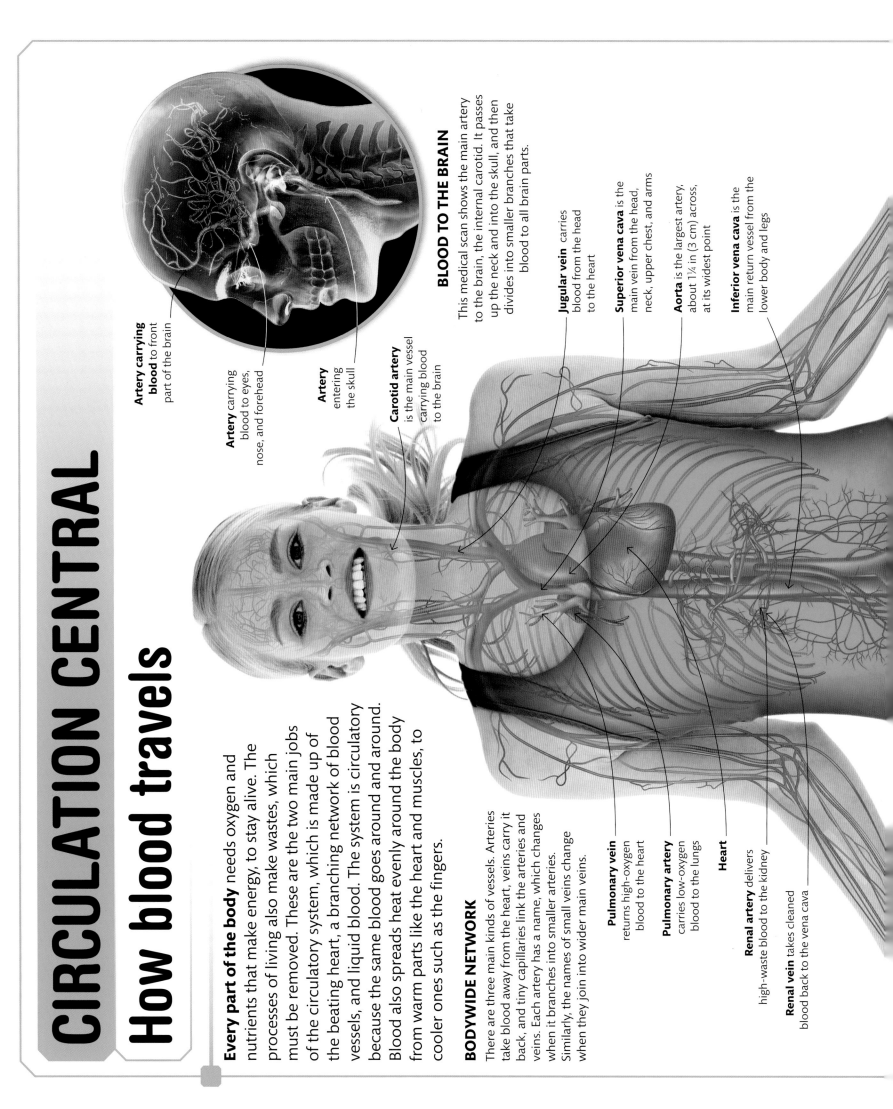

Artery carrying blood to front part of the brain

Artery carrying blood to eyes, nose, and forehead

Artery entering the skull

Carotid artery is the main vessel carrying blood to the brain

Jugular vein carries blood from the head to the heart

Superior vena cava is the main vein from the head, neck, upper chest, and arms

Aorta is the largest artery, about 1¼ in (3 cm) across, at its widest point

Inferior vena cava is the main return vessel from the lower body and legs

Pulmonary vein returns high-oxygen blood to the heart

Pulmonary artery carries low-oxygen blood to the lungs

Heart

Renal artery delivers high-waste blood to the kidney

Renal vein takes cleaned blood back to the vena cava

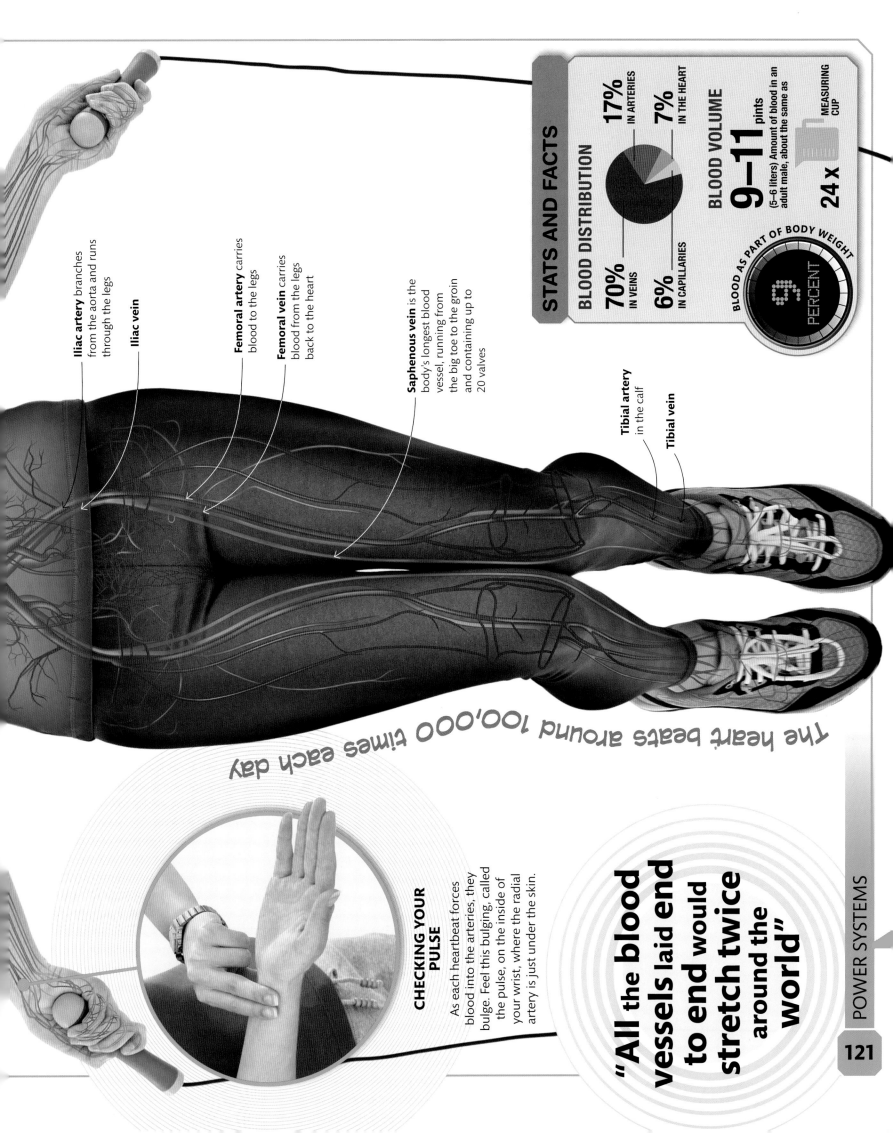

Iliac artery branches from the aorta and runs through the legs

Iliac vein

Femoral artery carries blood to the legs

Femoral vein carries blood from the legs back to the heart

Saphenous vein is the body's longest blood vessel, running from the big toe to the groin and containing up to 20 valves

Tibial artery in the calf

Tibial vein

The heart beats around 100,000 times each day

CHECKING YOUR PULSE

As each heartbeat forces blood into the arteries, they bulge. Feel this bulging, called the pulse, on the inside of your wrist, where the radial artery is just under the skin.

"All the blood vessels laid end to end would stretch twice around the **world**"

121

POWER SYSTEMS

BODY PUMP
The heart

No machine can match the heart's outstanding abilities. It works every second, day and night, for 70, 80, or even 100 years. It constantly maintains and mends itself. It responds to the body's needs by continually adjusting the amount of blood it pumps with each beat and its beating speed. This means that while the heart conserves energy during sleep, it can increase its blood output by five times during strenuous exercise.

> "Each **day** the **heart** creates **energy** that could **power** a **truck** for **20 miles** (32 km)"

PARTS OF THE HEART

The heart consists of two pumps. The left pump sends blood around the body. Blood returns to the right side, which pumps it to the lungs. Each pump has an atrium, the upper chamber, and a ventricle, the muscular lower chamber. Arteries carry blood away from the ventricles, and veins bring it back to the atria.

HOW THE HEART BEATS

The heart contracts its muscular walls to squeeze the blood inside, forcing it out into the main arteries. There are four heart valves, two in each side. These tough, flexible flaps push open easily to let blood flow the correct way, then flip shut to stop any backflow.

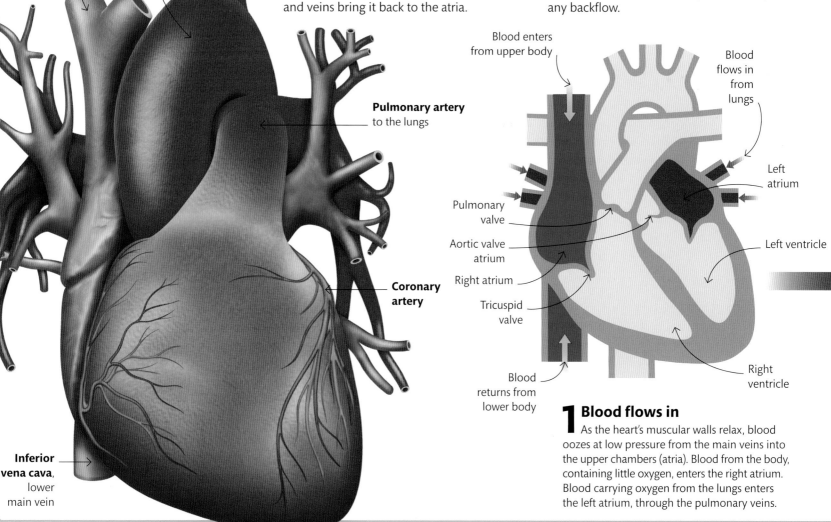

Aorta main artery, takes blood from the heart to the rest of the body

Superior vena cava, upper main vein

Pulmonary vein from the lungs

Pulmonary artery to the lungs

Coronary artery

Inferior vena cava, lower main vein

Blood enters from upper body

Blood flows in from lungs

Left atrium

Left ventricle

Pulmonary valve

Aortic valve atrium

Right atrium

Tricuspid valve

Blood returns from lower body

Right ventricle

1 Blood flows in

As the heart's muscular walls relax, blood oozes at low pressure from the main veins into the upper chambers (atria). Blood from the body, containing little oxygen, enters the right atrium. Blood carrying oxygen from the lungs enters the left atrium, through the pulmonary veins.

CORONARY SUPPLY

The heart has its own blood supply to feed it with oxygen, through the coronary arteries. They branch from the start of the aorta (the main blood vessel), loop over the heart's surface, and go down into the thick muscles of the heart walls.

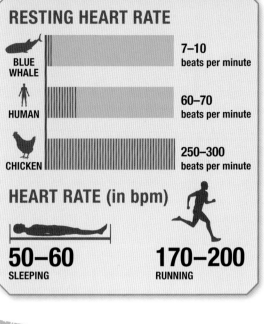

Branch of left coronary artery

Mitochondria for energy

Thick muscle fiber

HEART MUSCLE

The heart's walls are made of a special muscle called cardiac muscle, or myocardium. It contains many subunits called mitochondria, which provide a plentiful supply of energy, so the heart never tires. Mitochondria contain special DNA that regulates oxygen and energy in most body cells.

THE HEART BEATS 100,000 TIMES PER DAY

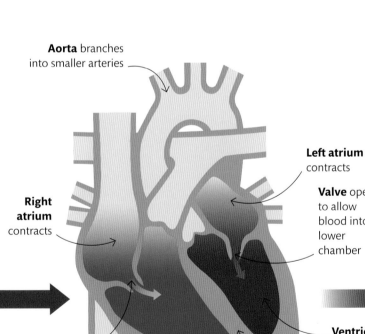

Aorta branches into smaller arteries

Right atrium contracts

Left atrium contracts

Valve opens to allow blood into lower chamber

Valve opens

Ventricle fills with blood

Septum separates the chambers

Blood flows to upper body

Aorta

Blood flows to lungs

Blood flows to lungs

Ventricles contract

Blood flows to lower body

2 Upper to lower

The walls of each upper chamber (atrium) tighten or contract to push blood through a valve into the lower chambers (ventricles). The ventricle walls are still relaxed so they stretch and bulge as the blood comes in. A wall in the middle of the heart, the septum, keeps the two sets of blood separate.

3 Blood flows out

The muscular walls of the ventricles squeeze to force blood through valves into the arteries. The aorta (main artery) takes blood rich in oxygen from the left ventricle to the body, while the pulmonary arteries from the right ventricle carry blood with low oxygen levels to the lungs.

DOORSTEP DELIVERY
Blood's network

With each thumping beat, high-pressure blood surges out of the heart into the main arteries. As these divide, each branch heads to a major organ, such as the liver, kidneys, brain, or muscles. Here the artery branch divides many more times, sending blood along its narrower, thinner branches, deep into the tissues. Finally the branches become the smallest blood vessels of all—capillaries. These have walls just one cell thick, allowing oxygen and nutrients to seep through easily to the tissues and cells around them.

THERE ARE 5 MILLION RED BLOOD CELLS IN A DROP OF BLOOD

Arteriole, a small, narrow artery

Muscles in artery wall

Thin elastic layer

Tough, protective outer layer

Endothelium, a strong blood-proof lining

ARTERY

Endothelium wall, one cell thick

Red blood cell

ARTERIES

These vessels have a strong inner lining and thick walls that contain stretchy fibers, so the artery can bulge with each pulse of high-pressure blood. The walls have muscles that contract to make the artery narrower and reduce blood flow, or relax to widen it and allow the blood to flow faster.

CAPILLARIES

These microvessels divide and join many times in just a tiny fraction of an inch, forming a web. Substances such as oxygen and sugars seep out of their thin walls into the surrounding cell as waste, such as carbon dioxide, and spent energy products seep in to be carried away.

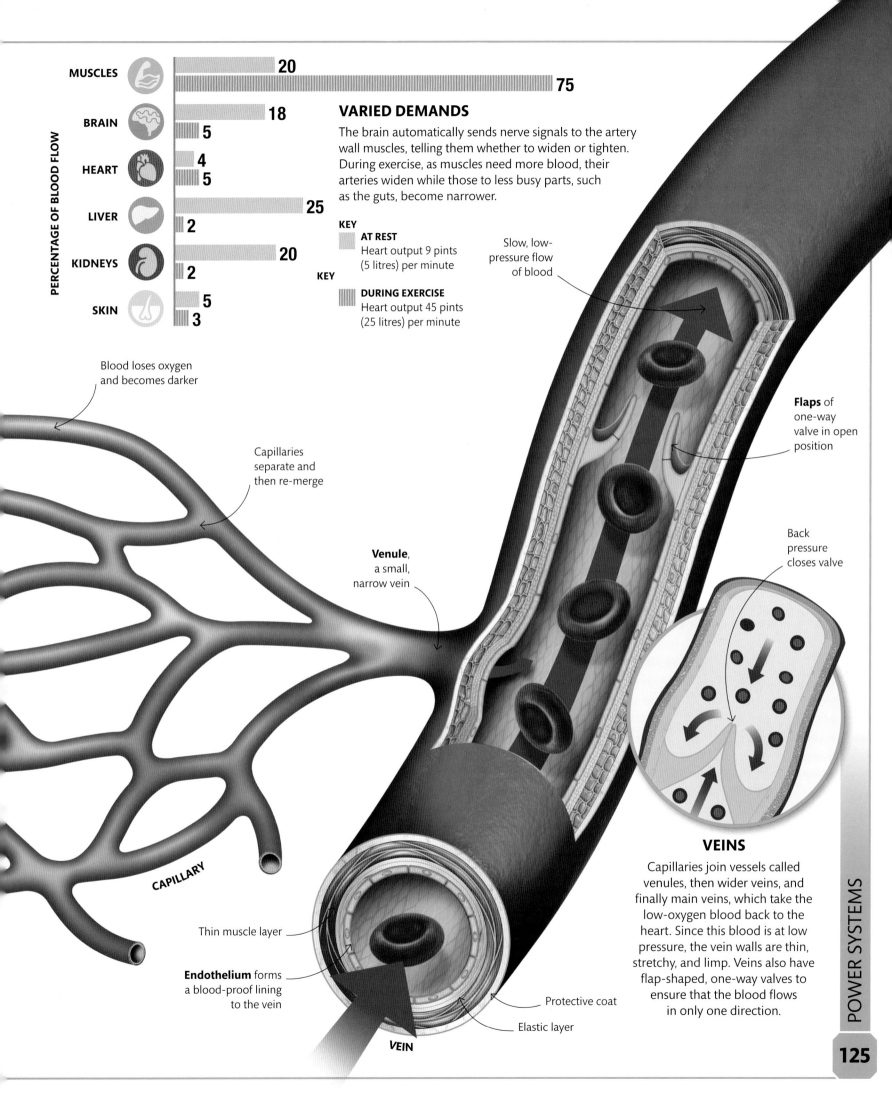

PERCENTAGE OF BLOOD FLOW

MUSCLES	20	75
BRAIN	18	5
HEART	4	5
LIVER	25	2
KIDNEYS	20	2
SKIN	5	3

VARIED DEMANDS

The brain automatically sends nerve signals to the artery wall muscles, telling them whether to widen or tighten. During exercise, as muscles need more blood, their arteries widen while those to less busy parts, such as the guts, become narrower.

KEY

AT REST
Heart output 9 pints (5 litres) per minute

KEY

DURING EXERCISE
Heart output 45 pints (25 litres) per minute

Blood loses oxygen and becomes darker

Capillaries separate and then re-merge

Slow, low-pressure flow of blood

Flaps of one-way valve in open position

Back pressure closes valve

Venule, a small, narrow vein

CAPILLARY

Thin muscle layer

Endothelium forms a blood-proof lining to the vein

Protective coat

Elastic layer

VEIN

VEINS

Capillaries join vessels called venules, then wider veins, and finally main veins, which take the low-oxygen blood back to the heart. Since this blood is at low pressure, the vein walls are thin, stretchy, and limp. Veins also have flap-shaped, one-way valves to ensure that the blood flows in only one direction.

"The body cannot feel constant speed— it only detects changes in speed"

Surviving high g-force

An F-16 jet pilot wears a g-suit with balloonlike chambers around the lower body. At high g-forces, these automatically inflate to press on the body and prevent blood from pooling in the lower legs.

FIGHTING G-FORCE

Maintaining flow

The heart and blood vessels usually adjust to cope with the effects of motion and the pull of Earth's gravity (g-force). This ensures blood reaches all parts of the body, especially the brain. But as the body speeds faster, brakes harder, or takes a sharp turn, unnaturally high forces disturb blood flow, which the heart cannot deal with. Blood then collects in the lowest parts of the body, starving the brain of oxygen and energy. This can result in a sudden loss of consciousness—a total blackout.

STATS AND FACTS

EFFECTS OF GRAVITY

Standing still, we are pulled toward Earth by the force of gravity (1 g). The faster you speed up or slow down while moving, the more g-force you feel.

3–4 g-force
ROCKET LAUNCH

4–5 g-force
ROLLER COASTER

9–12 g-force
FAST JET TURN

HUMAN g-FORCE LIMIT

g-FORCE

BLOOD VOLUME

20%

How much less blood an astronaut has in space compared with on Earth

BLOOD SUPERHIGHWAY
What's in the blood

Blood is the vital fluid that keeps the body alive. Three types of cells—red cells, white cells, and platelets—make up about half of your blood. The rest is a pale yellowish liquid called plasma. Blood performs a wide range of tasks. It carries oxygen from the lungs to all body parts, and it collects wastes, such as carbon dioxide and urea, for disposal. It contains sugar (glucose), nutrients, and chemical messengers called hormones. It even spreads out warmth from busy organs, such as the heart and muscles, to cooler parts.

"A single red blood cell can travel 300 miles (400 km) in its lifetime"

PACKED VESSELS

Inside vessels, blood flows nonstop every second of the day. In arteries it moves in short, quick bursts due to the heart's powerful beat; in veins it moves at a slower, more even speed. Within these vessels, blood is quite thin and runny, but as soon as it is exposed to air, or is cooled, it becomes thick and gooey.

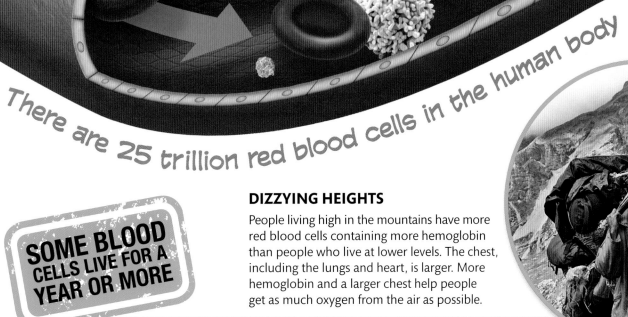

There are 25 trillion red blood cells in the human body

SOME BLOOD CELLS LIVE FOR A YEAR OR MORE

DIZZYING HEIGHTS

People living high in the mountains have more red blood cells containing more hemoglobin than people who live at lower levels. The chest, including the lungs and heart, is larger. More hemoglobin and a larger chest help people get as much oxygen from the air as possible.

Red cells
contain a substance called hemoglobin, which attaches to oxygen and carries it from the lungs to all body parts. Their average lifespan is 3–4 months.

White cells
protect against germs and help in healing. These colorless cells are flexible, like water-filled plastic bags. Their lifespans range from a day to over a year.

Plasma
is around 95 percent water. There are more than 500 substances dissolved in it, including body salts, minerals, and nutrients.

Platelets
are smaller than red or white cells. Platelets are usually rounded but become spiky when they form blood clots. Their lifespan is 5–10 days.

Platelets move to site of injury

1 Site of injury
Damaged cells and the exposed vessel wall leak substances that attract platelets. These begin a complex series of chemical changes to start clotting.

Platelet

Fibrin

Plasma

SEALING THE LEAK

When a blood vessel is cut or torn, a speedy repair process starts at once. Platelets start attaching themselves to the broken vessel wall to build up a lump called a clot, or thrombus. This keeps the blood from leaking out, and gives the vessel wall time to repair itself. The clot dissolves when the wound has healed.

2 Clotting begins
Platelets release chemicals that turn a protein called fibrinogen that is present in the plasma into sticky, threadlike fibers of another protein, fibrin. These fibers trap blood cells for clotting.

129

CLIMBING HIGH

Oxygen levels

Higher air is thinner air—and the lack of oxygen and lower air pressure can leave you gasping for breath. At 9,900 ft (3,000 m), there is just two-thirds of the oxygen at sea level, yet the respiratory system still copes. But even at this height, one person in five develops altitude sickness, and above 13,000 ft (4,000 m), one in two. It is best to climb up around 1,600 ft (500 m) a day, which allows the body to gradually increase its red cells so that it can pick up more of the scarce oxygen.

EFFECT OF ALTITUDE ON AVAILABLE OXYGEN

OXYGEN AVAILABLE COMPARED TO SEA LEVEL

6%
8%
10%
12%
14%
16%
18%
20%
22%

Sea level

Mt. Fuji, Japan
12,388 ft
(3,776 m)

Kilimanjaro, Africa
19,340 ft
(5,895 m)

Mt. Everest, Himalayas
29,028 ft
(8,848 m)

INCREASING ALTITUDE

"Your nose clogs more frequently at altitude, adding to the pressure on your lungs"

Hitting the wall

Heavy backpack adding to the body's load, the panting climber chips cautiously up an almost sheer wall of ice. Several days of getting used to the thin air has lessened the risk of feeling dizzy—or even blackout.

RED ARMY
Blood cells

The number of red blood cells in the body is astonishing—they make up about one-quarter of the total. As they journey around the body, the red pigment they contain, hemoglobin, takes up oxygen from the lungs, and then releases it when the cells reach the tissues. They also carry some waste carbon dioxide from the tissues back to the lungs, although about three-quarters of the carbon dioxide is dissolved in the liquid part of the blood, called plasma.

STATS AND FACTS

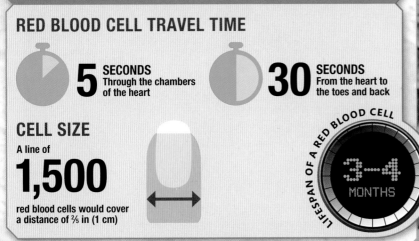

RED BLOOD CELL TRAVEL TIME

5 SECONDS
Through the chambers of the heart

30 SECONDS
From the heart to the toes and back

CELL SIZE

A line of
1,500
red blood cells would cover a distance of ⅖ in (1 cm)

LIFESPAN OF A RED BLOOD CELL
3–4
MONTHS

"We make **2.4 million** red cells **each second** of every day"

In a tangle

As red cells travel in the bloodstream, they may get stuck in threadlike clumps of the substance fibrin. This is produced after damage to the vessel wall, and will build up a sticky lump called a blood clot.

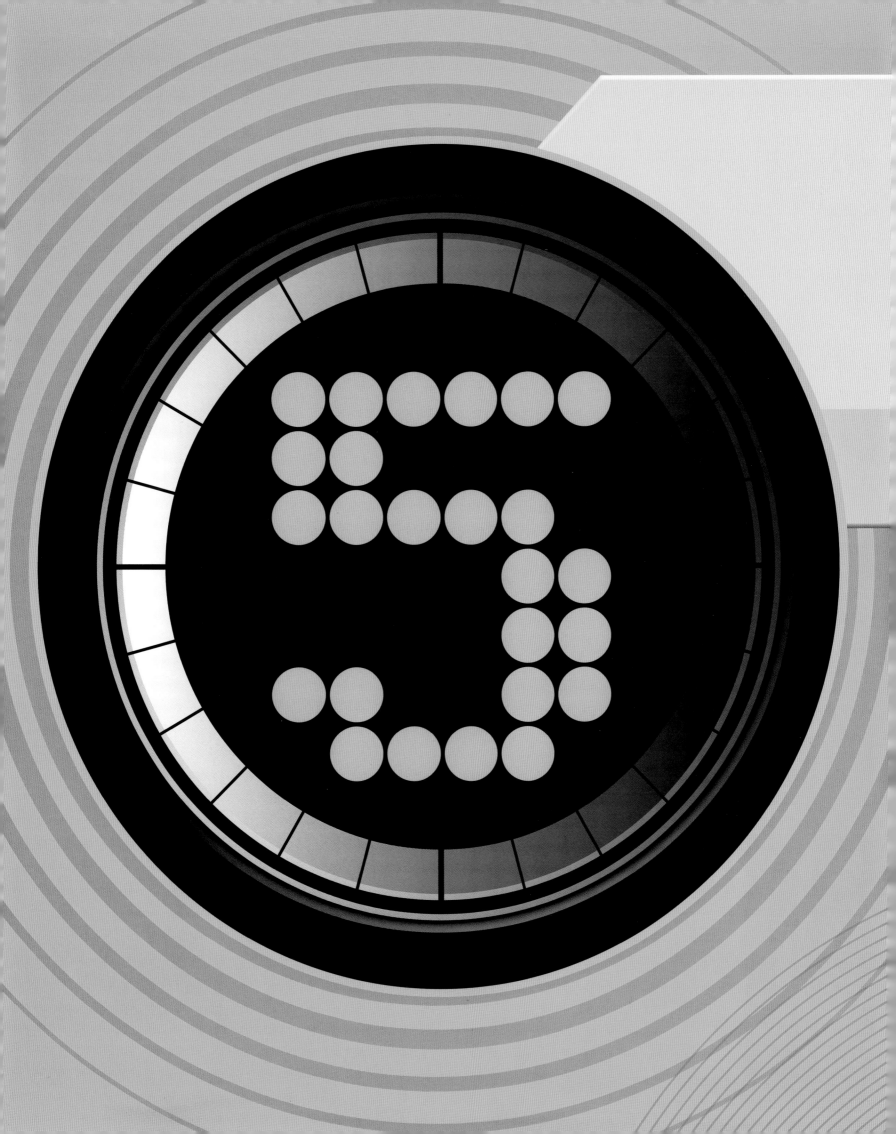

FUEL
AND WASTE

Super machines need fuel, care, adjustments, and regular removal of unwanted garbage. The digestive and excretory systems do these jobs every hour of every day, allowing the rest of the body to perform at its maximum.

FUELING THE BODY

How digestion works

As chewed food slips down the gullet toward the stomach, it begins an epic journey through the digestive tract, or passage, lasting 24 hours or more. It will be mixed with acids and other powerful digestive juices, squeezed and mashed into a lumpy soup, and have all its nutrients and goodness taken away. Then the leftovers, mixed with rubbed-off gut lining and billions of dead bacteria, will form a smelly, squishy mass that's ready for removal.

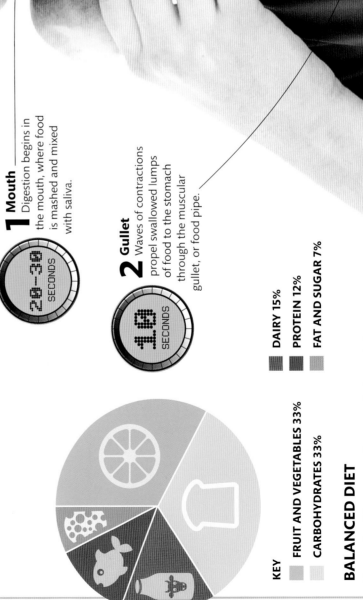

1 Mouth
Digestion begins in the mouth, where food is mashed and mixed with saliva.

20–30 SECONDS

2 Gullet
Waves of contractions propel swallowed lumps of food to the stomach through the muscular gullet, or food pipe.

15 SECONDS

KEY

- FRUIT AND VEGETABLES 33%
- CARBOHYDRATES 33%
- DAIRY 15%
- PROTEIN 12%
- FAT AND SUGAR 7%

BALANCED DIET

To stay healthy, we need to eat a balanced diet of different types of foods, ideally in the same proportions as the chart above. Too much of any single food can affect digestion and necessary supplies of energy, body-building proteins, and substances such as minerals and salts.

Liver produces bile and other digestive substances, which flow into the small intestine and break down fats

Gall bladder receives bile from the liver, stores it, and releases it into the small intestine, as and when required, to digest fatty food

Pancreas makes protein-digesting and other enzymes and releases them along a tube into the small intestine

3 Stomach
Churns to mash food further, and adds strong acids and digestive enzymes.

2 HOURS

4 Small intestine
Breaks food down into a liquid and lets nutrients pass through its lining into the blood and lymph.

6 HOURS

5 Large intestine and rectum
Absorb minerals and water from digested food, which then becomes feces.

12–19 HOURS

DIGESTION IN ACTION

The long passageway for food, from mouth to anus, is known as the gut, or digestive tract. Two organs that are not part of the tract, but make essential products for digestion, are the liver and pancreas.

YOU ARE WHAT YOU EAT

Maintaining a healthy body requires a regular input of key nutrients. Most food items contain a mix of these nutrients—for example, brown bread has carbohydrates, vitamins, minerals, and fibers.

Proteins
These are broken down into simpler units called amino acids, which are then built up into structural materials, such as bones, cartilage, muscles, and skin.

Carbohydrates
These are taken apart to make smaller subunits—sugars such as glucose—that are the main source of energy for all body cells and tissues.

Fats
Fats are essential for various parts of the body, such as cell membranes and the protective covering of nerve fibers. They also supply energy to the body.

Vitamins and minerals
More than 30 vitamins and minerals, including calcium and sodium, are vital for the smooth running of the body's chemical processes.

Fiber
Present in all fruits and vegetables, fiber provides bulk for food and helps it move along the gut. It also helps in digestion and the absorption of other nutrients.

DOWN THE HATCH
Chew and swallow

The body wastes no time when it comes to digestion—it starts at the first bite. The teeth chop and chew food to a squishy mass, while mixing it with saliva, or spit, which contains digestive substances called enzymes. The tongue keeps the food moving around until it is fully mashed. All this pulps the food into soft lumps that are easy to swallow, ready for the stomach to continue the digestion.

Sharp, straight edge for slicing

Tall and pointed

Incisors
There are two on either side of each jaw. They are chisel-shaped for cutting food.

Canines
There is one on either side of each jaw. They help tear and rip food.

Premolars
There are two of these teeth on either side of each jaw. They are wide and lumpy-topped.

CHEW ON THAT
A baby grows a set of 20 milk teeth. From the age of about six years these are replaced by 32 adult, or permanent, teeth. These have different shapes for specialized tasks, and their whitish covering—enamel—is the hardest substance in the entire human body.

Molars
There are three on either side of each jaw. They are broad for powerful crushing of food.

Nasal chamber

Hard palate, the bony shelf in the roof of the mouth

Maxilla, or upper jawbone

Upper lip

Lower lip

Tongue

Salivary ducts deliver saliva to the mouth

Sublingual gland, salivary gland under the tongue

Mandible, or lower jawbone

Submandibular gland, salivary gland under the lower jaw

THE INSIDE STORY
As three pairs of salivary glands pour out their watery saliva along tubes or ducts, the tongue shifts food to the type of teeth most suited to each stage of chewing. It also presses the chewed chunks against the hard palate, pushing the food backward down the throat.

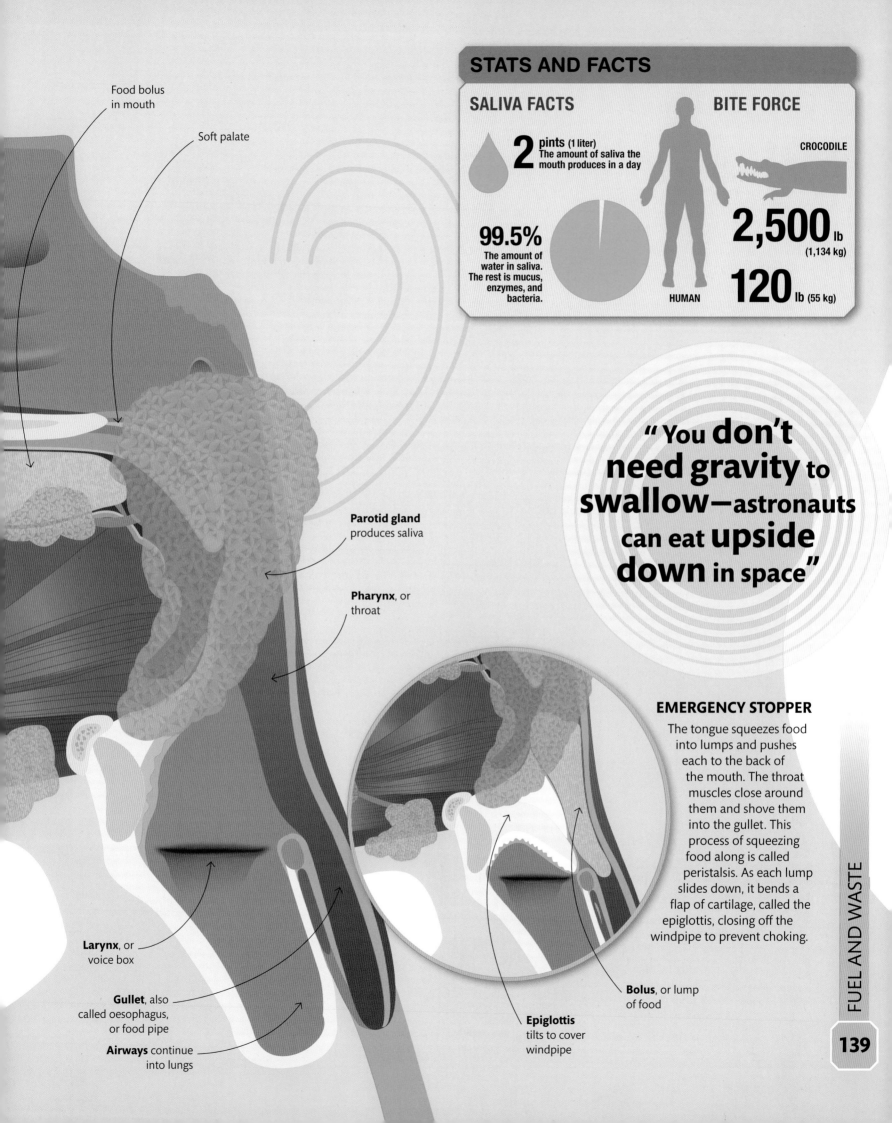

Food bolus
in mouth

Soft palate

SALIVA FACTS

BITE FORCE

2 pints (1 liter)
The amount of saliva the
mouth produces in a day

CROCODILE

99.5%
The amount of
water in saliva.
The rest is mucus,
enzymes, and
bacteria.

2,500 lb
(1,134 kg)

120 lb (55 kg)

HUMAN

Parotid gland
produces saliva

Pharynx, or
throat

" You **don't
need gravity** to
swallow—astronauts
can eat **upside
down** in space "

EMERGENCY STOPPER

The tongue squeezes food
into lumps and pushes
each to the back of
the mouth. The throat
muscles close around
them and shove them
into the gullet. This
process of squeezing
food along is called
peristalsis. As each lump
slides down, it bends a
flap of cartilage, called the
epiglottis, closing off the
windpipe to prevent choking.

Larynx, or
voice box

Gullet, also
called oesophagus,
or food pipe

Airways continue
into lungs

Epiglottis
tilts to cover
windpipe

Bolus, or lump
of food

FUEL AND WASTE

139

ACID BATH
Inside the stomach

An empty stomach is smaller than a clenched fist, folded and shriveled, while a full one—stretched tight like a balloon—can be almost soccer-ball-sized! This organ works as a store so we can eat a big meal within a few minutes, then digest it over several hours. It also continues the physical and chemical breakdown of food that began in the mouth. The stomach's powerful wall muscles churn and crush its contents, while its lining pours out powerful acids, enzymes, and other digestive juices.

STOMACH ACID IS STRONG ENOUGH TO DISSOLVE METAL

LIVING BLENDER

The thick stomach wall has three layers of muscles that lie in different directions from each other. These muscles contract in waves making the stomach long and thin, short and wide, or almost any other shape, to mix and mash the meal.

1 Chewed food enters through the valvelike esophageal sphincter into the stomach.

2 Folds in the stomach lining provide extra surface area. The lining is covered with 35,000 microscopic gastric pits that release digestive chemicals.

Gastric pits are like small pockets in the stomach lining

Hydrochloric acid and digestive enzymes pour in from the pits

Pyloric sphincter is a circular muscle that opens to let food through

Folds in stomach lining

Opening into small intestine

THE GATEKEEPERS

At both ends of the the stomach are tight rings of muscles called sphincters. These keep the food and digestive juices in the stomach while it is being churned and regulate how much food enters and leaves the stomach.

3 Gradually the digestive attack produces a sloppy soup, called chyme, ready to pass into the small intestine.

"The stomach can stretch to 20 times its size after eating"

Longitudinal muscle layer

Circular muscle layer

Diagonal muscle layer

UP IT COMES

Rotting or poisonous food irritates the stomach lining, which sends nerve signals to the brain to trigger vomiting. The stomach, the diaphragm above it, and abdomen muscles around it, all contract to push the food back into the gullet and force it out through the mouth.

Nasal passages close off

Food forced back up

Gullet, or esophagus

Muscles contract

STATS AND FACTS

DAILY PRODUCTION OF DIGESTIVE FLUIDS

Large intestine ½ pint (0.2 liters)

Small intestine 4 pints (2 liters)

Saliva 2 pints (1 liter)

Liver 2 pints (1 liter)

Pancreas 3 pints (1.5 liters)

Stomach 3 pints (1.5 liters)

95% of water in the digestive system is recycled

STOMACH VOLUME

Normal **1** pint (0.5 liter)

Maximum size **21** pints (10 liters)

ULTIMATE ACID PIT

Inside the stomach

Every time food enters our stomach, tiny gastric pits in the lining ooze out acid and enzymes to break it down. But if these digestive juices are so powerful, why does the stomach not digest itself? First, the enzymes are not active when they're made—they only become active when they mix with the acidified food. Second, the lining also produces a thick layer of mucus that stops the juices from attacking it. The mucus also makes the food more squishy and slippery so it moves through the stomach easily.

STATS AND FACTS

MEASURING ACID STRENGTH (pH)

2–3	1–2	0.8–1
Citric acid	Hydrochloric acid	Sulfuric acid
LEMON JUICE	STOMACH ACID	CAR BATTERY

WEAK   STRONG

AVERAGE THICKNESS

⅕ in (5 mm)
Whole stomach wall

1⁄16 in (1.5 mm)
Inside lining

GASTRIC PITS IN STOMACH

5,000

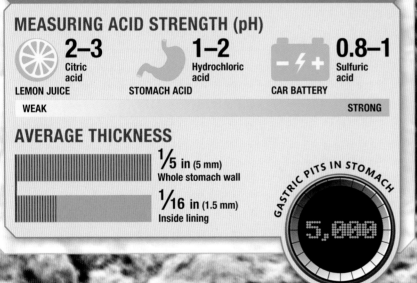

Pit profiles
In this magnified view of the stomach lining, the closely packed lumps are its mucus-making cells. Also seen are the openings to gastric pits where specialized cells produce acid while others make enzymes.

"The **medical** term for a **rumbling tummy** is **borborygmi**"

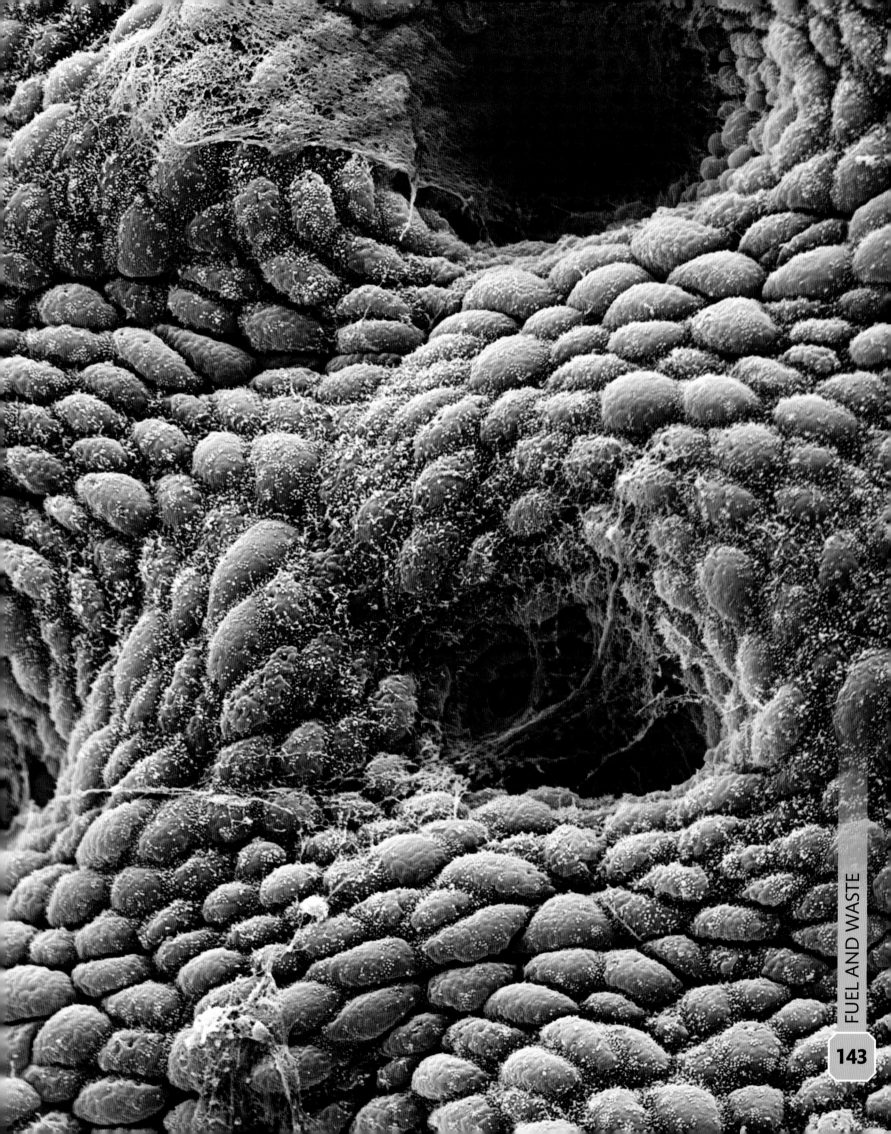

GUT REACTIONS
Inside the intestines

A few hours after a meal, globs of smelly, soupy, and partly digested food (called chyme) spurt from the stomach into the intestines every few minutes. First to deal with the chyme is the slim but very long small intestine, which breaks it down further to extract the nutrients. These pass through the lining of the intestine into the millions of blood capillaries in its wall, which carry the blood to the liver. The undigested leftovers move on to the shorter, wider large intestine, where water and a few other substances are removed before the rest travels on to leave the body.

"Your guts produce around 2 pints (1 liter) of gas every day"

TWISTS AND TURNS

The small intestine is more than 20 ft (6 m) long but only 1¼ in (3 cm) wide and has many bends, folds, and coils. It leads into the first part of the large intestine, called the cecum, which connects to the colon. The large intestine loops around the small intestine and is 5 ft (1.5 m) long (about the length of a bicycle) and 2¾ in (7 cm) wide.

1 Little squirts
As food moves out of the stomach, digestive juices from the pancreas gland and the liver are squirted into the duodenum, the first section of the small intestine. These juices help break down fats and proteins.

2 Sticky fingers
The lining of the small intestine is covered with millions of tiny, fingerlike projections called villi. The villi increase the surface area of the gut, helping nutrients to be absorbed more rapidly.

3 Soaking it up
As well as absorbing most of the water from the undigested leftovers through its lining, the large intestine absorbs body salts and minerals such as sodium.

The appendix keeps a supply of bacteria in case a digestive problem wipes them out in the main part of the gut

Rod-shaped bacteria multiply constantly

IT'S A GAS!

The large intestine is home to at least 5,000 different types of bacteria, and there are 10 times more bacterial cells there than cells in the rest of the body. They help with the last stages of digestion and with absorbing essential minerals and salts. But they also make gases such as methane, which must come out sometime.

Cells of intestinal lining

THERE ARE ABOUT 5 MILLION VILLI IN THE SMALL INTESTINE

Stomach
churns food into
a mushy soup

Pyloric sphincter
is a muscular ring
that opens to allow
food to pass into the
small intestine

Feces inside
large intestine

Wall of
large intestine

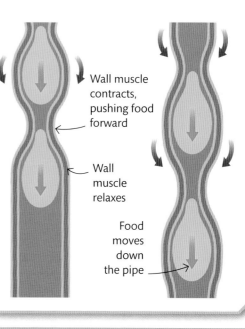

END OF THE LINE

When the food has been broken down, what
is left is a mixture of insoluble fiber and dead
bacteria. This forms pellets inside the large
intestine. Water and minerals are drawn out
of the pellets as they pass along the colon.
The pellets collect in the rectum before being
expelled through the anus.

PERISTALSIS

Food does not simply fall down the passages
of the gullet, stomach, and intestines. These
organs are packed into the body and are
under pressure from all sides. So, at every
stage their contents are pushed along by a
powerful, wavelike motion called peristalsis.
This is created by muscles in the passage
walls, which contract with a squeezing
action that pushes the food ahead.

Wall muscle
contracts,
pushing food
forward

Wall
muscle
relaxes

Food
moves
down
the pipe

Lower colon
collects feces
for removal

4 Final exit
The semi-solid leftovers,
called feces, are stored in the lower
colon and the final part of the large
intestine, the rectum. From there,
they pass out through the anus.

Rectum

The anus is a ring
of muscle that relaxes
to allow the feces out

FUEL UP!
Food as energy

You are a powerhouse of energy use. At maximum output, such as when sprinting, the body consumes more than 20 Calories (kcal) of energy per minute. Over a 12-hour day this would need the energy in 50 chocolate bars! During normal daily activities the body needs far less fuel. To stay healthy, a balance between food input and energy output is vital.

LEVELS OF ACTIVITY

All body parts use energy all the time simply to stay alive. Even during sleep the heart beats and the lungs breathe. As soon as the muscles start working, energy needs rise rapidly.

Shoulder and arm postures maintain stability

Hip, thigh, and calf muscles contract hard

Foot muscles absorb landing stress

Relaxed legs reduce energy use

LOW LEVEL
Lying flat requires the least energy because most muscles can relax, so they need energy only for their minimal life processes. Compared to lying down, standing still in a relaxed way increases energy use by two times, and slow walking by around three times.

- **SITTING** Leg and arm muscles mostly relaxed, torso and neck maintain balance

- **STANDING** Leg, torso, and neck muscles continually shift to maintain balance

- **SLOW WALKING** Leaning forward slightly gives momentum to save some energy

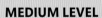

ENERGY USED PER MINUTE

2-5
CAL

MEDIUM LEVEL
As more muscles start working, they demand more oxygen and energy in the form of glucose, or sugar. This increases heartbeat and breathing rates—also muscle-powered—so push up energy needs even more. Leg muscles are the biggest and so use the most energy.

- **BICYCLING** The energy-efficient bicycle reduces energy needs greatly compared to running

- **SLOW RUNNING** Arms swing more to maintain momentum and so add to energy needs

- **JUMPING** Large, powerful leg muscles greatly increase energy costs

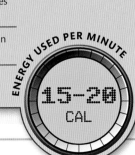

ENERGY USED PER MINUTE

15-20
CAL

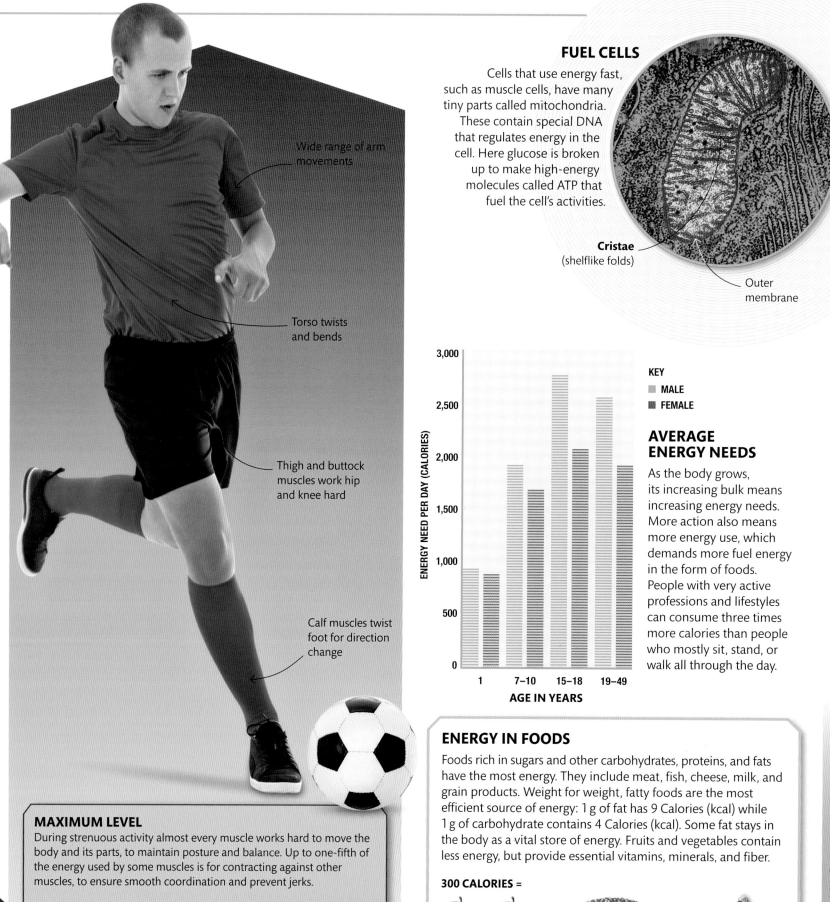

Wide range of arm movements

Torso twists and bends

Thigh and buttock muscles work hip and knee hard

Calf muscles twist foot for direction change

FUEL CELLS

Cells that use energy fast, such as muscle cells, have many tiny parts called mitochondria. These contain special DNA that regulates energy in the cell. Here glucose is broken up to make high-energy molecules called ATP that fuel the cell's activities.

Cristae
(shelflike folds)

Outer membrane

KEY
- MALE
- FEMALE

AVERAGE ENERGY NEEDS

As the body grows, its increasing bulk means increasing energy needs. More action also means more energy use, which demands more fuel energy in the form of foods. People with very active professions and lifestyles can consume three times more calories than people who mostly sit, stand, or walk all through the day.

ENERGY NEED PER DAY (CALORIES)

3,000
2,500
2,000
1,500
1,000
500
0

1   7–10   15–18   19–49

AGE IN YEARS

MAXIMUM LEVEL

During strenuous activity almost every muscle works hard to move the body and its parts, to maintain posture and balance. Up to one-fifth of the energy used by some muscles is for contracting against other muscles, to ensure smooth coordination and prevent jerks.

- **FAST RUNNING** As with walking, faster running means the arms work harder too

- **SWIMMING** Water resistance rises greatly with speed, demanding ever more muscle effort

- **SOCCER, SIMILAR SPORTS** Continual changes of speed and direction are very energy-hungry

ENERGY USED PER MINUTE

25-35
CAL

ENERGY IN FOODS

Foods rich in sugars and other carbohydrates, proteins, and fats have the most energy. They include meat, fish, cheese, milk, and grain products. Weight for weight, fatty foods are the most efficient source of energy: 1 g of fat has 9 Calories (kcal) while 1 g of carbohydrate contains 4 Calories (kcal). Some fat stays in the body as a vital store of energy. Fruits and vegetables contain less energy, but provide essential vitamins, minerals, and fiber.

300 CALORIES =

4 APPLES   =   **1 BURGER**   =   **⅙ PIZZA**

PUMPING UP THE POWER

Eating for energy

Extreme endurance is a severe test of your physical condition—including digestion, to fuel the body, and conserving water and fluids. Before endurance events, athletes "carb load", eating plenty of high-carbohydrate or starchy foods, such as pasta, bread, potatoes, and rice. These provide high-energy sugars, which are converted to glycogen (body starch) in the liver and the muscles. These energy stores can gradually be converted back to sugars during the long haul.

STATS AND FACTS

CALORIES USED

BICYCLING
24 Calories/mile
(15 kcal/km)

WALKING
80–97 Calories/mile
(50–60 kcal/km)

RUNNING
97–129 Calories/mile
(60–80 kcal/km)

SWIMMING
193–241 Calories/mile
(120–150 kcal/km)

DAILY ENERGY

MAN
2,500
Calories (kcal)

ULTRA-ATHLETE
4,700
Calories (kcal)

POLAR EXPLORER
7,000+
Calories (kcal)

"Running a **marathon** uses as much **energy** as is contained in **12 slices** of **pizza**"

Defying the dunes

Competitors in the Sahara ultra-marathon have to cover 155 miles (250 km) of desert in six days. With temperatures above 104°F (40°C), they must make sure they drink enough to replace water lost as sweat.

DETOX CENTRAL
What the liver does

Right lobe
forms four-fifths
of the liver's bulk

The liver is a true super-organ, and a list of its tasks would fill this whole book. Its many functions are mostly to do with adjusting the contents of blood, maintaining the levels of essential substances such as glucose and vitamins, and removing possibly harmful chemicals, or toxins.

SUPER STOREHOUSE

Almost one-third of the body's blood flows through the liver every minute. About one-quarter of this flow comes along two massive hepatic arteries. The rest arrives along the hepatic portal vein from the intestines. This blood is loaded with nutrients.

BREAKDOWN

The liver acts on many substances to break them into smaller, simpler pieces, in a process known as catabolism. In particular, it detoxifies the blood, which means changing possible toxins or poisons, such as the waste product ammonia, into harmless substances.

Hormones
Several hormones are taken apart, in particular insulin, which affects blood glucose levels.

Toxins
Harmful chemicals in body wastes, and those in foods and drinks, are split apart or changed to make them safe.

Blood cells
Dead or dying red blood cells are taken to pieces and their parts, especially iron, are recycled.

Germs
Specialized white cells in the liver, called phagocytes, attack and destroy germs.

Gall bladder
under right lobe stores bile, used to digest fatty foods

STORAGE

Supplies of many vital substances, such as glucose, are kept in the liver. These are released when their levels in the body fall too low. The liver stocks up on these supplies again using the digested food nutrients brought in from the intestines by the hepatic portal vein.

Glycogen
This is a form of carbohydrate made from joined-up glucose (sugar) units.

Minerals
These include iron needed for blood cells and copper for bones and connective tissues.

"The liver performs around 500 functions"

Left lobe
arches over
stomach

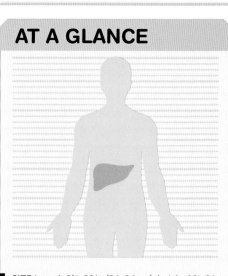
BUILDING UP

The liver is a living chemical production factory that assembles small, simple building substances into bigger ones. This process is called anabolism. Examples include the blood chemicals needed for clotting and liver hormones that affect the production of blood cells.

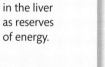

Bile

Liver makes bile, stored in the gall bladder and released into the intestines.

Fats

Some kinds of fats are held in store in the liver as reserves of energy.

Vitamins

The liver can store two years' worth of vitamin A.

Nutrients

A variety of nutrients come and go, including those for making proteins.

Heparin

This natural substance affects the clotting ability of blood and its germ-fighting abilities.

Nutrients

Building-block substances include triglycerides to make the protective membranes around cells.

Protein synthesis

Amino acids are joined in various ways to construct many kinds of proteins for cells and tissues.

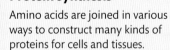

Heat

As with the heart and the kidneys, the liver is always busy and a constant source of body warmth.

BLOOD SUGAR CONTROL

Controlled by hormones such as insulin, the liver is the storehouse for blood glucose, which is needed by every cell for energy. If glucose levels fall, the liver breaks down its stores of glycogen (starch) into glucose, which dissolves into the bloodstream. If there is too much glucose, for example after too much sugary drinks or foods, the liver does the reverse and converts the extra glucose back into glycogen.

FUEL AND WASTE

151

PURIFICATION PLANT

What kidneys do

As blood flows past cells and through tissues, it collects more than 100 kinds of waste and any excess sodium, blood sugar, and water. Blood then travels to the two kidneys, taking five minutes to pass through them. Here, waste and excess substances are made into a liquid called urine.

The urine trickles along two tubes called ureters, one from each kidney, down to a storage bag— the bladder—and out of the body.

WASTE COLLECTION

Inside its tough covering, each kidney is split into three layers: the outer cortex, the inner medulla, and a space called the renal pelvis. Urine is made in the cortex and carried by tubes into the renal pelvis. From here it flows along the ureter to the bladder.

AT A GLANCE

Kidney

Bladder

Ureter

- **SIZE** Length of each kidney 4¾ in (12 cm); weight 5¼ oz (150 g); bladder 17 fl oz (500 ml) when full
- **LOCATION** Kidneys behind liver and stomach; bladder in lower front abdomen
- **FUNCTION** Kidneys filter wastes from blood, make hormones; bladder stores urine

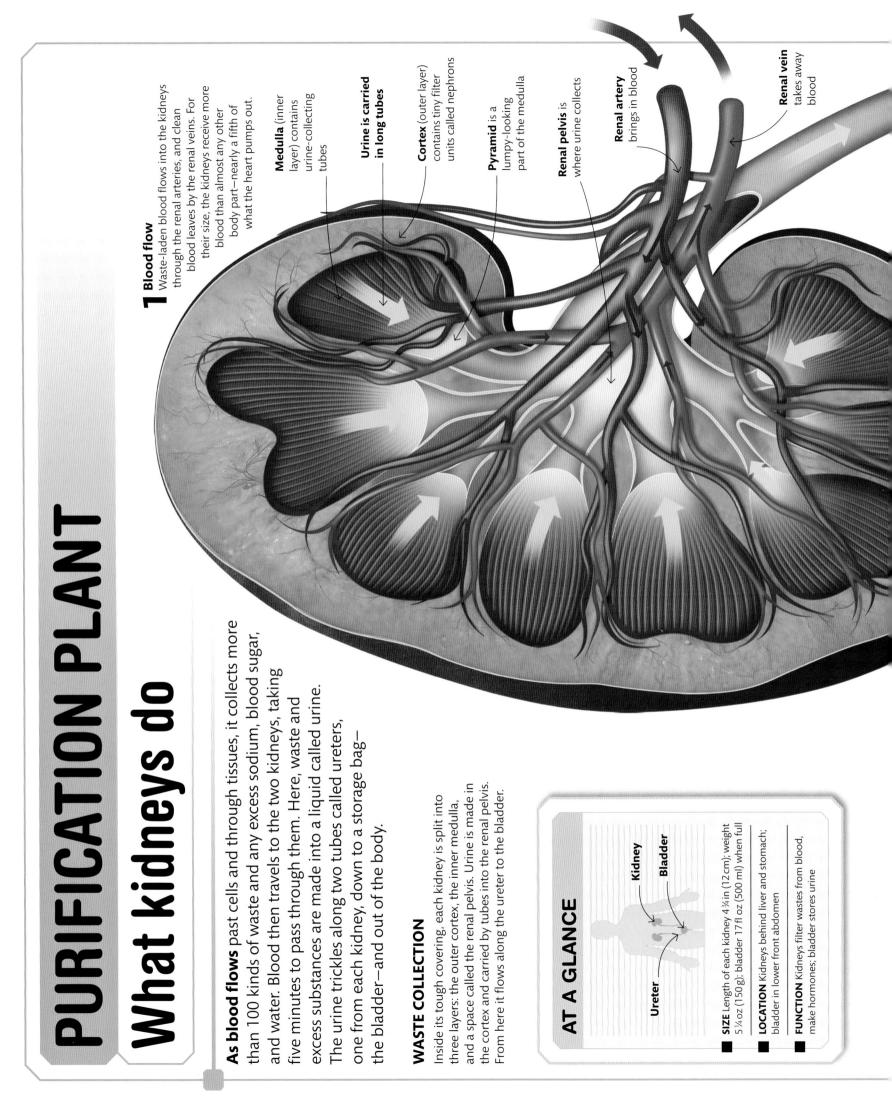

1 Blood flow
Waste-laden blood flows into the kidneys through the renal arteries, and clean blood leaves by the renal veins. For their size, the kidneys receive more blood than almost any other body part—nearly a fifth of what the heart pumps out.

Medulla (inner layer) contains urine-collecting tubes

Urine is carried in long tubes

Cortex (outer layer) contains tiny filter units called nephrons

Pyramid is a lumpy-looking part of the medulla

Renal pelvis is where urine collects

Renal artery brings in blood

Renal vein takes away blood

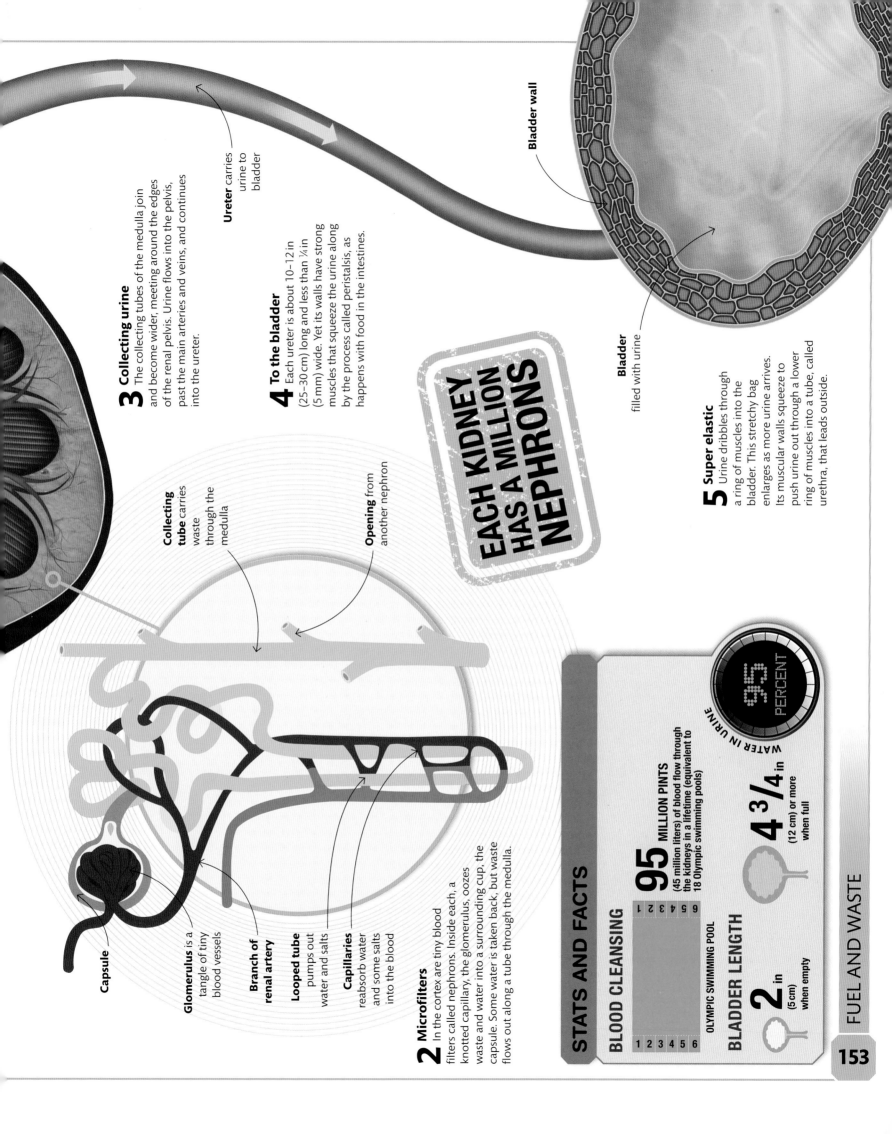

3 Collecting urine
The collecting tubes of the medulla join and become wider, meeting around the edges of the renal pelvis. Urine flows into the pelvis, past the main arteries and veins, and continues into the ureter.

Ureter carries urine to bladder

4 To the bladder
Each ureter is about 10–12 in (25–30 cm) long and less than ¼ in (5 mm) wide. Yet its walls have strong muscles that squeeze the urine along by the process called peristalsis, as happens with food in the intestines.

Bladder wall

Bladder filled with urine

5 Super elastic
Urine dribbles through a ring of muscles into the bladder. This stretchy bag enlarges as more urine arrives. Its muscular walls squeeze to push urine out through a lower ring of muscles into a tube, called urethra, that leads outside.

Collecting tube carries waste through the medulla

Opening from another nephron

EACH KIDNEY HAS A MILLION NEPHRONS

Capsule

Glomerulus is a tangle of tiny blood vessels

Branch of renal artery

Looped tube pumps out water and salts

Capillaries reabsorb water and some salts into the blood

2 Microfilters
In the cortex are tiny blood filters called nephrons. Inside each, a knotted capillary, the glomerulus, oozes waste and water into a surrounding cup, the capsule. Some water is taken back, but waste flows out along a tube through the medulla.

STATS AND FACTS

BLOOD CLEANSING

6 5 4 3 2 1

95 MILLION PINTS
(45 million liters) of blood flow through the kidneys in a lifetime (equivalent to 18 Olympic swimming pools)

OLYMPIC SWIMMING POOL

1 2 3 4 5 6

BLADDER LENGTH

2 in (5 cm) when empty

4 ¾ in (12 cm) or more when full

95 PERCENT
WATER IN URINE

FUEL AND WASTE

153

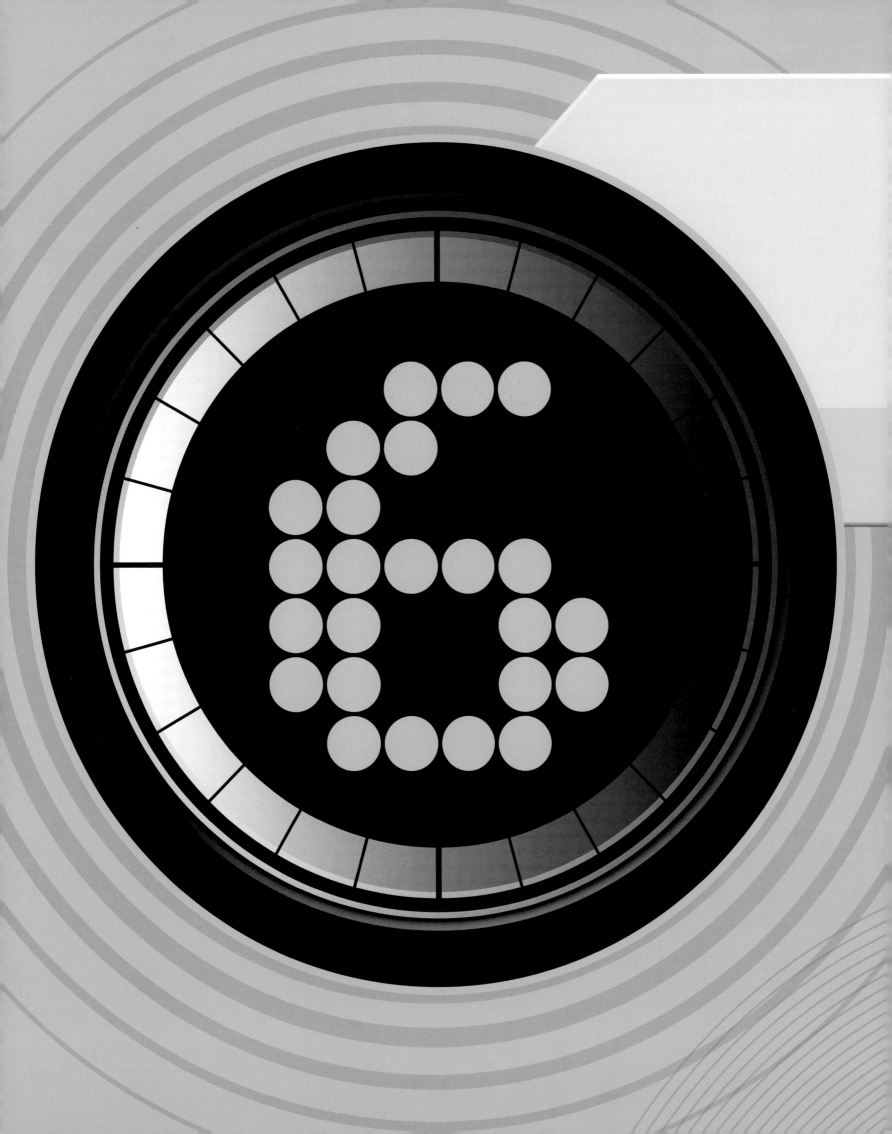

DEFENSE AND CONTROL

Our bodies are not only ideal for us—they are also an attractive home for other organisms. To keep them out, an internal army is ready around the clock to fight invaders. Meanwhile, hormones ensure the smooth operation of almost every internal process, from energy use to the thrill of fear.

SECURITY ALERT

Protecting the body

Harmful microbes we call germs are everywhere—in air, water, food, and even the human body. No wonder we need so many defenses against these tiny invaders! Every organ, from the eyes to the guts, is equipped with physical and chemical barriers to protect it from harm.

There are two systems that specialize in self-defense—the lymphatic and immune systems.

UNDERCOVER MAZE

The network of lymph vessel tubes and nodes, or glands, is like an alternative blood system. Its fluid, lymph, flows slowly because it has no pump and depends on movement to push it around the body. It supplies nutrients to tissues, removes wastes, carries germ-fighting white cells, and flows into the blood system in the chest.

SKIN AND SWEAT

The skin is a stretchy yet strong physical barrier against invaders. It also makes sweat and an oily fluid called sebum, both of which contain substances that have damaging effects on germs, such as bacteria.

WE HAVE AROUND 650 LYMPH NODES

Saliva (spit) traps and removes germs

Adenoids trap and kill eaten or inhaled germs

Nose hairs and mucus trap dust and germs

Thymus gland, where white cells mature into germ killers

Spleen stores and recycles blood cells

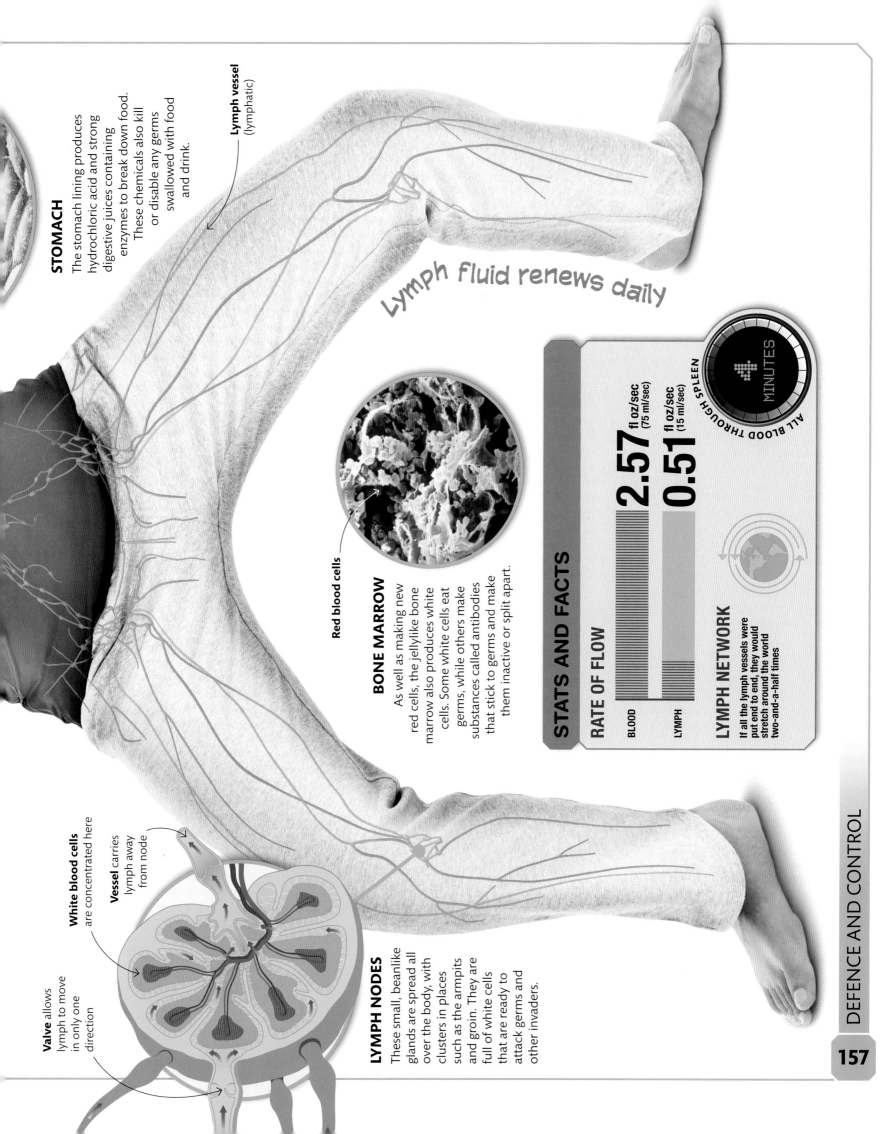

STOMACH

The stomach lining produces hydrochloric acid and strong digestive juices containing enzymes to break down food. These chemicals also kill or disable any germs swallowed with food and drink.

Lymph vessel (lymphatic)

Lymph fluid renews daily

Red blood cells

BONE MARROW

As well as making new red cells, the jellylike bone marrow also produces white cells. Some white cells eat germs, while others make substances called antibodies that stick to germs and make them inactive or split apart.

STATS AND FACTS

RATE OF FLOW

2.57 fl oz/sec (75 ml/sec)

0.51 fl oz/sec (15 ml/sec)

BLOOD

LYMPH

ALL BLOOD THROUGH SPLEEN

MINUTES

LYMPH NETWORK

If all the lymph vessels were put end to end, they would stretch around the world two-and-a-half times

White blood cells are concentrated here

Vessel carries lymph away from node

Valve allows lymph to move in only one direction

LYMPH NODES

These small, beanlike glands are spread all over the body, with clusters in places such as the armpits and groin. They are full of white cells that are ready to attack germs and other invaders.

ON THE ATTACK
Combating germs

Despite the body's super-tough defense barriers—from the skin to stomach acid—germs sometimes get inside. But the invaders are nearly always doomed because they are attacked by the armed forces of the immune system—white blood cells. There are more than 20 main types of white cells, and they work together like a crack assault team to destroy germs. One way they do this is by producing natural weapons called antibodies. Tinier than any of the invaders, billions of antibodies cause them to clump together, stop working, spill out their insides, or even explode!

GERM WARFARE

Any break in the protective outer layer of dead skin allows germs to get into tissues. Once inside, they damage cells, take nutrients from them, and multiply. If they enter the skin's blood vessels, they can spread around the body in minutes. So white cell defenses must gather fast at the war zone, ready for action.

> **"All the white blood cells together weigh twice as much as the brain"**

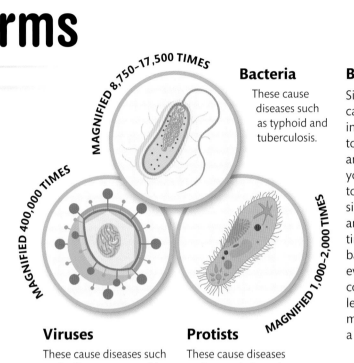

MAGNIFIED 8,750–17,500 TIMES

Bacteria
These cause diseases such as typhoid and tuberculosis.

BODY INVADERS
Single-celled germs, called protists, are similar in size and structure to body cells. Bacteria are many times smaller— you need a microscope to see them—and much simpler inside. Even tinier are viruses—around 100 times smaller than a bacteria. They have even less inside them, consisting only of short lengths of genetic material encased in a protein shell.

MAGNIFIED 400,000 TIMES

MAGNIFIED 1,000–2,000 TIMES

Viruses
These cause diseases such as the flu, common cold, measles, and mumps.

Protists
These cause diseases such as malaria and sleeping sickness.

Invading germs

Signaling substance attracts macrophages

Macrophages gather at battle site

Break in the outer layer of skin

Blood vessel

1 Raise the alarm
Damaged body cells release signaling substances that draw white cells, called macrophages, to them. These engulf some invaders, and also pick up their surface chemicals, called antigens, to pass them to other white cells.

ENGULFING GERMS

Macrophage surrounds and eats invader

ALLERGIES

The immune system is designed to defend against germs and other harmful threats. But sometimes it attacks usually harmless substances, such as those in animal fur or feathers, plant pollen, or house dust. This reaction can cause an allergy, which includes itchy watery eyes, red itching skin, or wheezy breathing. Medicines can reduce these symptoms.

STATS AND FACTS

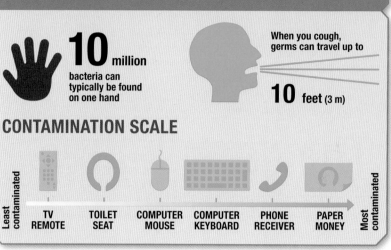

10 million bacteria can typically be found on one hand

When you cough, germs can travel up to

10 feet (3 m)

CONTAMINATION SCALE

Least contaminated						Most contaminated
TV REMOTE	TOILET SEAT	COMPUTER MOUSE	COMPUTER KEYBOARD	PHONE RECEIVER	PAPER MONEY	

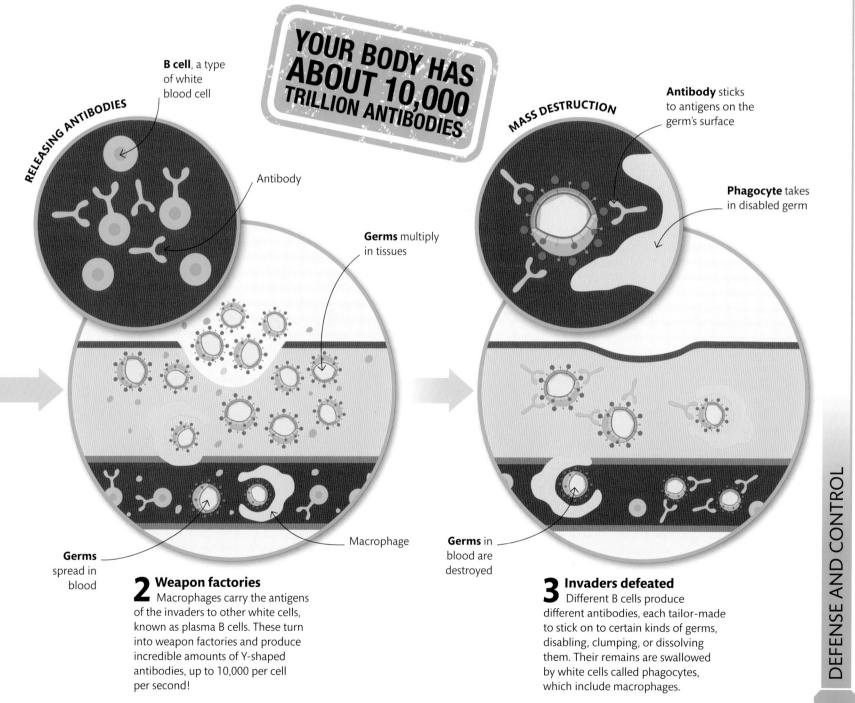

B cell, a type of white blood cell

RELEASING ANTIBODIES

Antibody

YOUR BODY HAS ABOUT 10,000 TRILLION ANTIBODIES

MASS DESTRUCTION

Antibody sticks to antigens on the germ's surface

Phagocyte takes in disabled germ

Germs multiply in tissues

Germs spread in blood

Macrophage

Germs in blood are destroyed

2 Weapon factories
Macrophages carry the antigens of the invaders to other white cells, known as plasma B cells. These turn into weapon factories and produce incredible amounts of Y-shaped antibodies, up to 10,000 per cell per second!

3 Invaders defeated
Different B cells produce different antibodies, each tailor-made to stick on to certain kinds of germs, disabling, clumping, or dissolving them. Their remains are swallowed by white cells called phagocytes, which include macrophages.

DEFENSE AND CONTROL

SEEK AND DESTROY

The germ killers

Every second, day and night, an army of white cells patrols the body. They use blood vessels as highways, then squeeze through microgaps in the blood vessel walls and pass into the fluid between tissues and cells. Their mission: to search for invaders, such as bacterial germs, the body's own damaged, dying, or dead cells, and internal parasites. Some white cells engulf and eat their victims. Others produce substances called enzymes and antibodies to break up and destroy them.

STATS AND FACTS

LIFESPAN OF MACROPHAGES

10 DAYS
Lifespan of a macrophage in an infected person

6–12 MONTHS
Lifespan of a macrophage in a healthy person

NUMBER OF MACROPHAGES

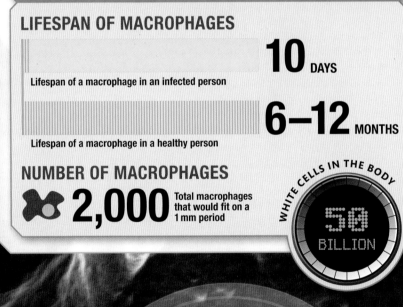

2,000 Total macrophages that would fit on a 1 mm period

WHITE CELLS IN THE BODY
50 BILLION

"A macrophage can eat **200 bacteria** before it dies"

Deadly embrace
This white cell (called a macrophage, which means "big eater") is enveloping a group of rod-shaped tuberculosis bacteria in its folds. Once inside, the bacteria will be broken down into tiny pieces.

RUNNING REPAIRS
Regeneration

Even the best machines need maintenance, repair, and the occasional replacement part. The amazing living machine that is the body is no exception. Some parts, such as skin, intestine lining, and blood cells, wear out fast and need replacing rapidly—in days, or even hours. Others, such as many of the brain's nerve cells and the heart's muscle cells, last a lifetime. On a smaller scale, the internal parts of these cells are constantly maintained and mended as some of their molecules break down and are replaced. Repairs become less efficient as we age.

"Human skin is completely regenerated every four weeks"

Fat cells are replaced every 10 years

Cartilage at end of bone protects it

POPPING OFF

Every day, more than 50 billion cells in the body die—on purpose. Each is programmed to live for only a certain amount of time. Cells die in a highly organized way: lumps called blebs form on the surface (shown above), drop off, and are cleared away by scavenging white blood cells until the entire cell is gone. This process is called apoptosis. It prevents the buildup of old, weak, damaged cells that would otherwise clog blood vessels, leak wastes, and cause other problems.

COPING WITH WEAR

Joints, such as the knee and elbow, cope with the greatest physical movement and wear. The smooth cartilage between the joints has only a limited ability to repair itself, so overuse can be harmful.

TOTAL TURNOVER

Each part of the body gets replaced at its own rate. Many of the building materials for this work come from nutrients in food, while other raw materials are recycled within the body by organs such as the liver.

Scalp hairs
last 3–6 years

Dendrites make
new links to
other neurons

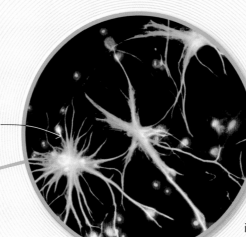

INTERNAL REWIRING

The nerve cells (neurons) in the brain
constantly change the connections
their dendrite branches make with
other nerve cells as you experience
events and form new memories.
However, it is much more difficult
to replace neurons that are damaged
by injury, although this does happen
in some parts of the brain.

Red blood cell
in open wound

Platelets
in blood
rush to the
wound

Scab forms on the
surface of the skin

SOME HEART CELLS NEVER DIE

**Fibrin
threads**
help form
a mesh

PLUGGING THE GAPS

Tiny leaks in blood vessels and
tissues are rapidly plugged by a sticky
mix of platelets, fibrin fibers, and
blood cells, in a process called blood
clotting. The clot seals any leaks and
hardens into a tough lump called a
scab. This holds the wound together
and protects it from outside infection
while the broken tissues grow back
together again. The scab
then falls off.

BRUISING

Bruises happen when
blood vessels are damaged
beneath the skin and bleed
into surrounding tissues.
The bruise slowly changes
from purple to yellow
as the clots that form
to stop the bleeding are
broken down and taken
away by white blood cells.

DEFENSE AND CONTROL

163

BODY CONTROLLERS

How hormones work

The brain and nerves, prompted by tiny electrical nerve signals, form one of the body's two control networks. The other control system uses natural chemical substances called hormones. These are made in parts of the body called hormonal, or endocrine, glands. Hormones are released into the blood, and as each one travels around the body it targets certain organs and tissues. This remarkable system uses more than 50 main hormones, made by over a dozen major hormone glands. Hormones are also produced in organs such as the heart, stomach, and liver.

HORMONE MAKERS

Endocrine glands—present in the head, chest, and abdomen—pass hormones directly into the blood supply as blood flows through the glands. Hormones influence almost every cell, organ, and function of the body.

Pineal gland
makes melatonin, which affects sleep and wakefulness

Hypothalamus
links the nervous and hormonal systems

Pituitary gland
produces hormones that control other hormone glands

Thyroid gland
controls metabolism, protein production, and body temperature

Parathyroid gland
controls calcium and phosphate mineral levels, vital for healthy bones

Thymus gland
stimulates the development of white blood cells and the growth of the body

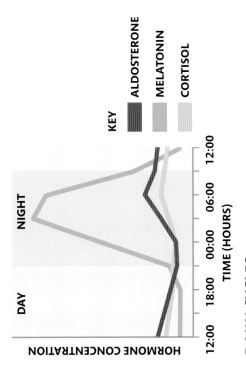

DAILY CYCLES

The level of each hormone rises and falls in a regular cycle over the course of a day. Melatonin increases in the evening to make you sleepy, then drops to wake you up; aldosterone regulates water levels; and cortisol lessens reactions to stress.

KEY

ALDOSTERONE

MELATONIN

CORTISOL

DAY   **NIGHT**

HORMONE CONCENTRATION

12:00   18:00   00:00   06:00   12:00

TIME (HOURS)

"Doctors in ancient times detected diabetes by tasting the sweetness of their patients' urine"

Adrenal gland
produces hormones that control water levels and respond to stress

Liver
influences blood vessels, fluid levels, and cell growth

Kidney
influences red blood cell production

Pancreas
produces insulin and glucagon to control blood sugar

Stomach
produces gastrin and other hormones involved in digestion

Ovary
produces female hormones, such as estrogen

MALE REPRODUCTIVE SYSTEM

Testes
release male hormones, such as testosterone

BODY REGULATORS

The thyroid gland makes two vital hormones, thyroxine (T4) and tri-iodothyronine (T3). Acting as the body's speed controllers, they increase the rate at which almost all cells and systems work, particularly:

Heart and vessels

They make the heart pump faster and more powerfully, increasing its output and the speed of blood flow.

Digestive system

The stomach produces more digestive juices and enzymes, and food moves through the gut faster.

Liver

The liver increases its processing speed of nutrients, minerals, blood cells, and other substances.

Proteins

These building blocks of cells and tissues are built up and broken down more rapidly.

Cells and tissues

More nutrients are taken in and more waste products produced. There is a general increase in energy use.

Caffeine leads to epinephrine release

DANGER, DANGER!

Stress hormones

From concerns that nag for days, to sudden shock—the body copes with stress in many ways. Hormones are the body's chemical messengers and they play an important role in keeping you calm, yet ready for action. The adrenal glands, which sit on top of the kidneys, make several stress hormones. Cortisol affects levels of blood glucose (sugar), reduces pain and swelling, increases tissue repair, and delays the body's response to injury or infection. Epinephrine also affects blood glucose levels and prepares the body to face danger—the "fight or flight" reaction.

"Epinephrine makes you perceive things you see twice as fast as normal"

STRESS AND THE BRAIN

Epinephrine's relative, norepinephrine, is also made in the adrenal glands and has similar affects. It is produced in the nervous system too, where it passes messages between nerve cells (neurons). It is particularly important for tasks that involve concentrating for long periods and focusing without distractions or daydreams, such as when you are studying for an exam.

Blood sugar
The liver releases a surge of blood glucose for use by cells, mainly the muscle cells.

Pain
Nerve signals for pain are reduced as they travel to and from the brain.

Urine
Reduced blood flow through kidneys slows down urine production (see pp. 154–55).

Breathing
Airways widen and the lungs expand faster and deeper, to get more oxygen.

Heart
The heart pumps faster and with more force, increasing blood flow and pressure, so more blood goes where it is needed.

Hearing
There is no direct effect on the ears, but the brain's hearing centers become extra-alert.

Brain
Blood flow to the brain increases so that all its parts can work at top speed.

Eyes
The pupils widen and the brain concentrates on what they see.

Mouth
Saliva production and release slow or even stop, producing a dry mouth.

Muscles
Extra blood flow, carrying oxygen and glucose, allows muscles to put in extra effort.

Sweat
The skin sweats to cool the body when muscles are active.

Digestion
Blood flow to the stomach and intestines reduces, giving the fluttery feeling of butterflies in your tummy.

"Epinephrine levels are the lowest while dreaming"

EPINEPHRINE KICK

As soon as the brain recognizes a threat—real or imaginary, planned or unexpected—it tells the adrenal glands to release epinephrine. The hormone floods through the blood network in seconds and, working with the nervous system, affects the entire body.

AT A GLANCE

- **LOCATION** Adrenal glands sit on top of kidneys
- **SIZE** Height ¾ in (2 cm); length 3 in (8 cm); weight ³⁄₁₆ oz (5 g)
- **FUNCTION** The adrenal glands produce hormones, including the stress hormones, cortisol, epinephrine, and norepinephrine, as well as those affecting urine production.

DEFENSE AND CONTROL

167

THRILLS AND SPILLS

Adrenaline rush

There's nothing quite like the rush of excitement you get when taking part in something that involves speed or taking risks, such as skiing, snowboarding, mountain-biking, or skydiving. This thrilling feeling is a result of the hormone adrenaline, released when the body is facing possible danger. High-energy sugar floods into the blood and enters cells, speeding up their processes and, in turn, the heart, putting both body and mind on edge.

STATS AND FACTS

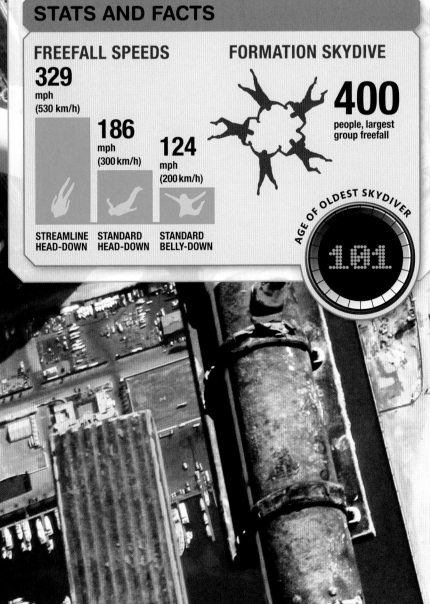

FREEFALL SPEEDS

329 mph (530 km/h)

186 mph (300 km/h)

124 mph (200 km/h)

STREAMLINE HEAD-DOWN

STANDARD HEAD-DOWN

STANDARD BELLY-DOWN

FORMATION SKYDIVE

400 people, largest group freefall

AGE OF OLDEST SKYDIVER

101

A skydiver leaps from a plane with only a parachute to save him. He freefalls for around a minute, supported only by the air pushing upward, before opening his parachute to glide safely back to Earth.

"The **highest ever freefall** was from **24 miles** (39 km) above the ground"

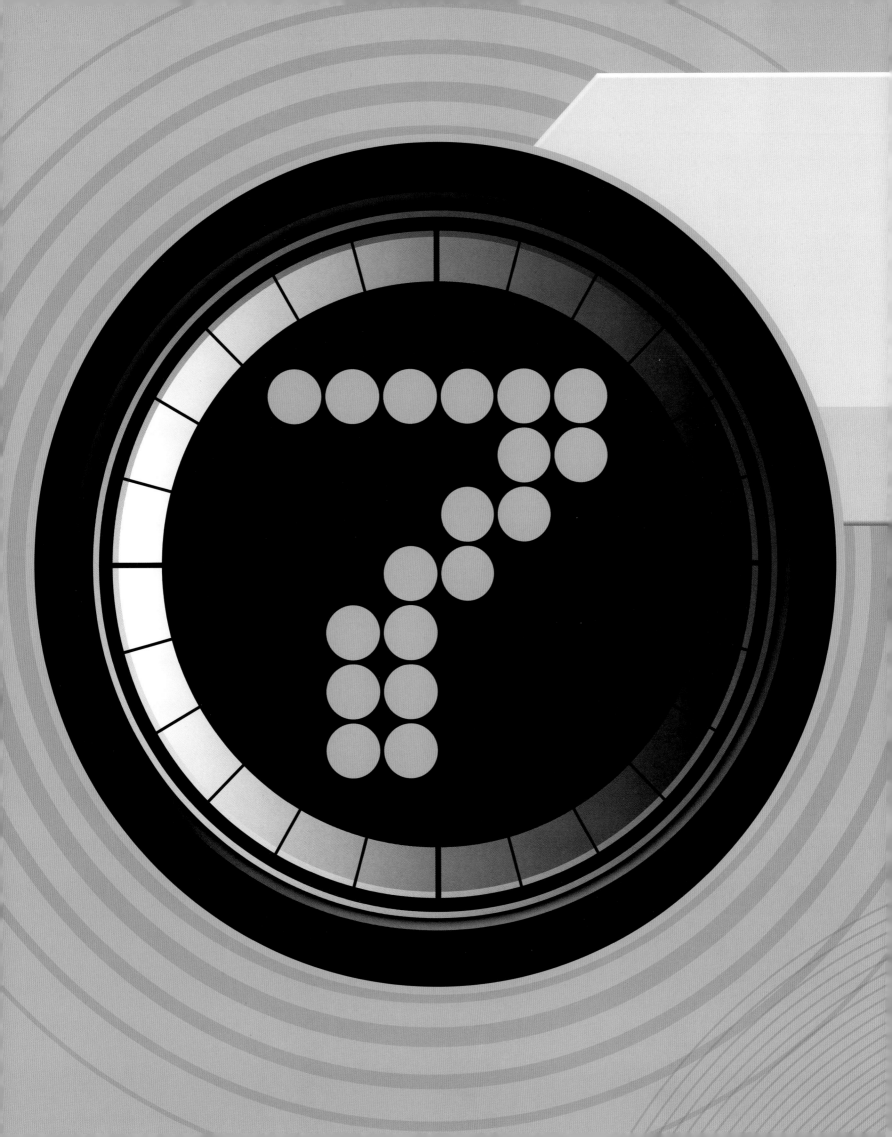

NEW LIFE AND GROWTH

Incredibly, every human starts life as just one cell. To turn into an adult with trillions of cells involves an amazing process of growth and development. Learning how to use and coordinate all the body's systems takes years of practice. Becoming a superhuman is not an easy process!

MAKING A SUPERHUMAN
The first week

Every amazing human body, with its billions of cells, begins as a single cell—a tiny speck smaller than this period. The speck is an egg cell from the mother, which has been fertilized by a sperm cell from the father. After a few hours, the fertilized egg begins to divide into two cells, then four cells, then eight, and so on. Several days later it becomes a hollow ball of cells, called a blastocyst. It is still about the same size as the original egg but it now consists of more than 300 cells.

SPERM MEETS EGG

Of the millions of sperm, swimming by lashing their tails, only a few hundred make it to the relatively huge egg. Only one sperm manages to get through the egg's tough outer layer to the inside, where its genetic material joins with the genetic material of the egg.

Zona pellucida is a tough protective layer

1 Sperm reaches egg A sperm cell touches the outer layer of an egg cell.

Male pronucleus, the male genetic material

2 Sperm enters egg The sperm cell dissolves and burrows through the outer layer. Only a single sperm will penetrate the egg.

3 Sperm head The sperm head leaves its outer covering behind and moves toward the pronucleus of the egg.

AT A GLANCE

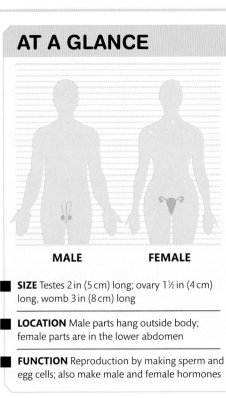

MALE **FEMALE**

- **SIZE** Testes 2 in (5 cm) long; ovary 1½ in (4 cm) long, womb 3 in (8 cm) long

- **LOCATION** Male parts hang outside body; female parts are in the lower abdomen

- **FUNCTION** Reproduction by making sperm and egg cells; also make male and female hormones

Fluid-filled chamber inside the blastocyst

Inner cells form the baby

Blood-rich lining of the womb, also called the uterus

Fallopian tube

Outer cells form the placenta, which attaches to the womb lining

Ovary

Inner chamber of womb

THE WOMB

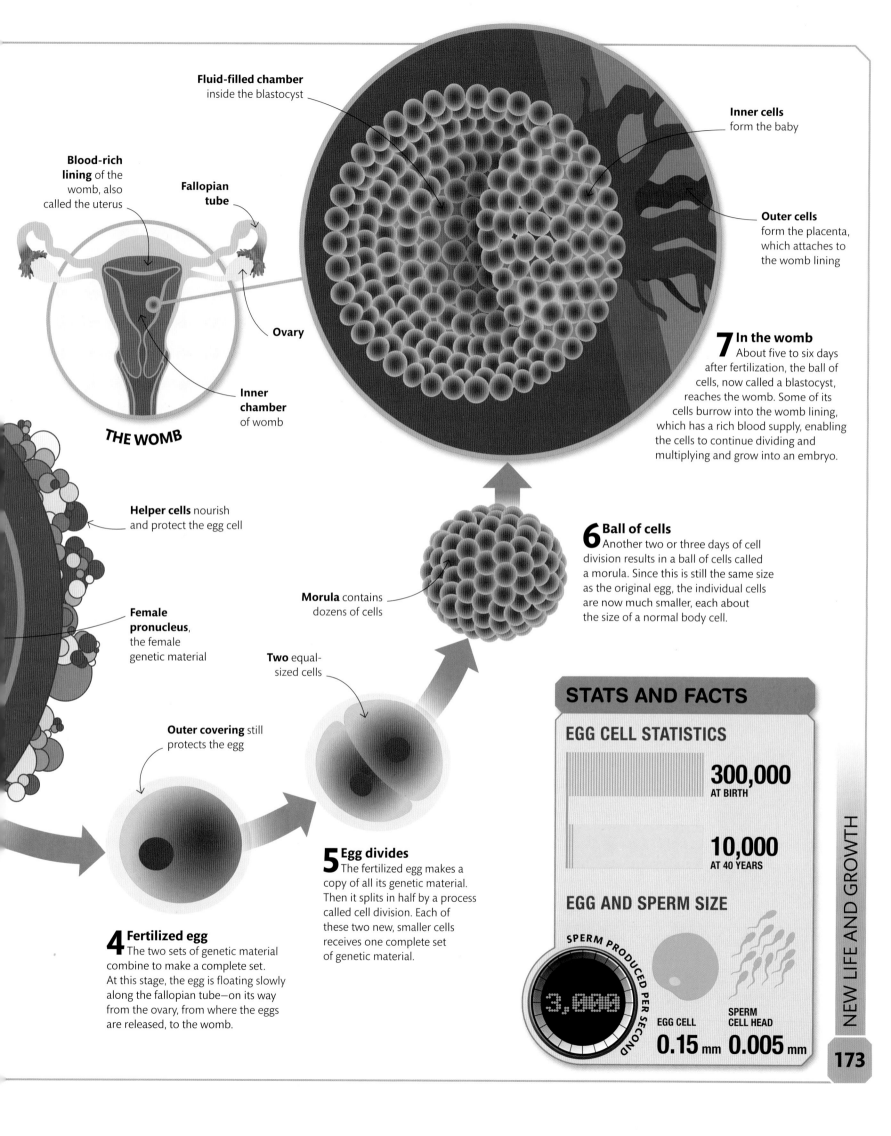

7 In the womb
About five to six days after fertilization, the ball of cells, now called a blastocyst, reaches the womb. Some of its cells burrow into the womb lining, which has a rich blood supply, enabling the cells to continue dividing and multiplying and grow into an embryo.

Helper cells nourish and protect the egg cell

6 Ball of cells
Another two or three days of cell division results in a ball of cells called a morula. Since this is still the same size as the original egg, the individual cells are now much smaller, each about the size of a normal body cell.

Morula contains dozens of cells

Female pronucleus, the female genetic material

Two equal-sized cells

Outer covering still protects the egg

5 Egg divides
The fertilized egg makes a copy of all its genetic material. Then it splits in half by a process called cell division. Each of these two new, smaller cells receives one complete set of genetic material.

4 Fertilized egg
The two sets of genetic material combine to make a complete set. At this stage, the egg is floating slowly along the fallopian tube—on its way from the ovary, from where the eggs are released, to the womb.

STATS AND FACTS

EGG CELL STATISTICS

300,000
AT BIRTH

10,000
AT 40 YEARS

EGG AND SPERM SIZE

SPERM PRODUCED PER SECOND

3,000

EGG CELL
0.15 mm

SPERM CELL HEAD
0.005 mm

IN THE WOMB

Life before birth

After just one week, the tiny human embryo—as small as the dot on this i—settles into the womb lining. Here it begins to grow and develop at an astonishing rate. Parts start forming—first the brain and the head, then the main body, followed by the arms and legs. By two months, all the main organs, including the eyes, beating heart, silent lungs, and twitching muscles, have formed—even though the embryo is smaller than a thumb.

SQUEEZED FOR SPACE

From two months until birth at around nine months, the developing baby is called a fetus. This is mainly a time of growth, the greatest of our whole life. Also, small details, such as toenails, fingernails, eyebrows, and eyelashes, are added to the body. The immense increase in size—more than 3,000 times heavier between two months and birth—means the baby becomes a tighter fit inside the womb.

8 months

Sucking reflex strengthens, the heart beats at a of rate 140 per minute, and lungs and stomach are ready to work. Height is 18 in (46 cm), weight is 85 oz (2,400 g).

7 months

Scalp hair, eyebrows, and eyelashes lengthen, and a protective greasy layer, called vernix, forms on the skin. Height is 16 in (40 cm), weight is 46 oz (1,300 g).

6 months

The baby responds to noises, kicks and thumps, its body develops brown baby fat, and there is still enough room to move in the womb. Height is 14 in (35 cm), weight is 23 oz (650 g).

Placenta embedded in the womb wall

Mother's blood vessels in placenta

LIFE SUPPORT SYSTEM

The baby cannot breathe or eat in the womb. Oxygen and nutrients from the mother's blood pass through thin membranes, inside the disk-shaped placenta, to the baby's blood.

Low-oxygen blood from baby

Umbilical cord to baby

High-oxygen blood to baby

8 MONTHS

7 MONTHS

6 MONTHS

BABY SCAN

A machine called an ultrasound scanner beams high-pitched, harmless sound waves into the womb. It then detects the bounced-back echoes and forms an image. These scans are used during pregnancy to check that the baby is developing normally.

4 months
Facial features are recognizable, eyes blink, fingers and toes are distinct, and fingerprints are formed. Length is 4½ in (11 cm), and weight is 4 oz (100 g).

STATS AND FACTS

TIMELINE OF DEVELOPING UNBORN CHILD

👁 EYES	**20** days
🔔 HEART	**22** days
🦵 LEGS	**28** days
👃 NOSE	**35** days

21 weeks
The time the fetus takes to grow to the size and weight of a banana

5,000
CELLS PER SEC
ADDED AT MOST RAPID GROWTH

5 MONTHS

4 MONTHS

3 MONTHS

5 months
Mother feels the baby's movements. The baby makes faces, yawns, and sucks its thumb. Length is 6 in (16 cm), weight is 11 oz (300 g).

Umbilical cord
connects the baby to the mother's placenta

3 months
The heart is beating, the muscles make early movements, and even the kidneys are working. Length of the fetus is 2½ in (6 cm), and weight is 0.5 oz (15 g).

Amniotic fluid around baby helps keep the baby warm and lets it move about easily

Womb's
muscular wall

175

NEW LIFE AND GROWTH

NEW KIDS ON THE BLOCK

Multiple births

Multiple births are two or more babies born from the same pregnancy. For identical twins, one fertilized egg divides into two cells, and then each develops into a baby. For identical triplets, one of these divided cells splits again and each develops into a baby, and so on. These babies have the same genes and so are either all girls or all boys. Nonidentical twins happen when two separate fertilized eggs develop into babies. For nonidentical triplets, there are three fertilized eggs, and so on.

STATS AND FACTS

CHANCES OF MULTIPLE BIRTHS

1 birth in 300,000 is quadruplets

1 birth in 4,500 is triplets

1 birth in 70 is twins

Single birth

PREGNANCY PERIOD

40 WEEKS
NORMAL BIRTH

36 WEEKS
TWIN BIRTH

MULTIPLE BIRTHS IN HUMANS

1.5 PERCENT

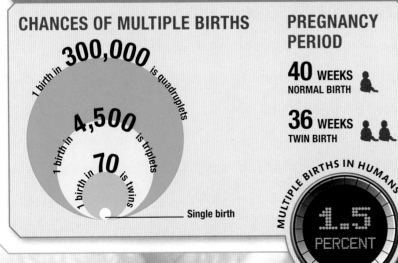

"The **largest** ever multiple birth to **survive** were **octuplets**, born in 2009 in the US"

GROWING UP
The early years

Can you remember being a new baby? You did little more than sleep, feed, and of course cry when hungry, uncomfortable, or frightened. But you could also look, listen, smell, and feel—and during those early years, you learned faster than at almost any other time. Starting to walk seemed so difficult and you probably fell over dozens of times. This was partly because you were "top heavy"—your head was very large compared with your body. After that there was no stopping you from growing and learning new skills at an incredible rate every day.

"From 18 months a child understands 10 or more new words every day"

THE FIRST TEN YEARS

Each baby is an individual and develops at her or his own rate in size, physical skills, learning, and other abilities. Many youngsters may be slightly ahead or behind the average ages shown here, but nearly all catch up eventually.

Holding toy in a pincerlike grip

Scribbling with crayons

Stacking and balancing building blocks

0-1 YEARS
When babies first arrive they have little control over anything their body does. Within months they have learned to reach for objects, move about, and communicate basic needs.

- **PHYSICAL SKILLS** Sits up, rolls over, crawls, stands, holds out arms

- **MANUAL SKILLS** Grasps objects, plays with feet and hands

- **MENTAL AND SOCIAL SKILLS** Responds with smiles and squeals, makes babbling sounds

1-2 YEARS
This is the main period for learning to talk and walk. The hand and fingers gradually come under more accurate control to produce a variety of different grasps and grips.

- **PHYSICAL SKILLS** Walks, jogs, runs, kicks ball, throws ball

- **MANUAL SKILLS** Scribbles, picks up small objects, drinks from a cup

- **MENTAL AND SOCIAL SKILLS** Learns single words, understands short sentences

2-3 YEARS
Better hand-eye coordination makes catching and throwing easier. Words are made into simple sentences—toddlers can now take part in conversations and understand instructions.

- **PHYSICAL SKILLS** Balances on one foot, twirls around, pedals a tricycle

- **MANUAL SKILLS** Draws straight lines, places shaped objects correctly, builds brick towers

- **MENTAL AND SOCIAL SKILLS** Knows names; talks in simple sentences, understands more

BRAIN BOOST

One of the most rapid spurts of growth occurs in the brain. At birth it is only 30 percent of adult size, but has all the neurons it needs. It shoots up in size to 80 percent by age three, and almost adult size at 12 years. Much of this increase is due to the nerve cells making millions of new connections every day as the child learns new skills.

25–30% adult size

95–98% adult size

AT BIRTH

AT 12 YEARS

Bouncing a ball off one knee shows leg-eye coordination

Dressing and undressing self without help

A CHILD'S BRAIN MAKES 700 NEW NERVE LINKS A SECOND

Children need 10–12 hours of sleep to grow

3–6 YEARS

"Self-centered" problems, such as temper tantrums, come under control as children start mixing with others at playgroup and school. Also, they make progress in writing and drawing.

- **PHYSICAL SKILLS** Catches ball, skips, hops on a leg

- **MANUAL SKILLS** Draws people, animals, and objects; copies shapes and matches colours; writes names, dresses without help

- **MENTAL AND SOCIAL SKILLS** Understands sharing, relates to helping others

6–10 YEARS

At this age, physical development and skill levels improve rapidly with practice. A growing self-awareness makes youngsters realize they are individuals as well as part of various social groups.

- **PHYSICAL SKILLS** Plays sports, develops fine motor skills

- **MENTAL SKILLS** Develops self-control, thinks independently, begins to question others

- **SOCIAL SKILLS** Develops close friendships, seeks privacy, appreciates need to control strong feelings

NEW LIFE AND GROWTH

179

TEEN TIME

Reaching puberty

The teenage years, ages 13 to 19—and just before them—are times of enormous change. Under the control of hormones, a child's body grows into that of an adult. It goes through a big growth spurt, changing shape and proportions. Younger girls and boys have much the same overall body outlines, but these change as outward features develop differently for women and men. Hormones also bring transformations within the body, as the reproductive parts begin to work. This time is called puberty.

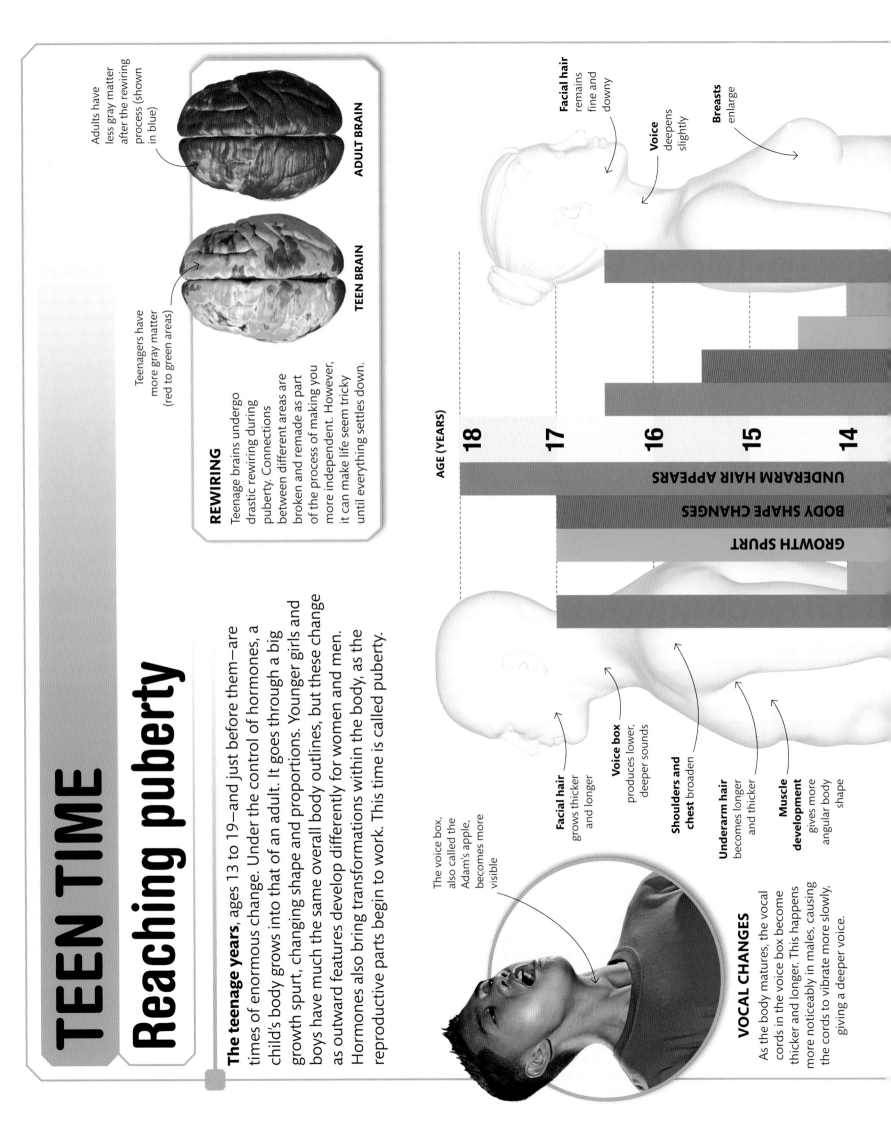

Adults have less gray matter after the rewiring process (shown in blue)

ADULT BRAIN

Teenagers have more gray matter (red to green areas)

TEEN BRAIN

REWIRING

Teenage brains undergo drastic rewiring during puberty. Connections between different areas are broken and remade as part of the process of making you more independent. However, it can make life seem tricky until everything settles down.

Facial hair remains fine and downy

Voice deepens slightly

Breasts enlarge

AGE (YEARS)

18

17

16

15

14

REWIRING

UNDERARM HAIR APPEARS

BODY SHAPE CHANGES

GROWTH SPURT

Facial hair grows thicker and longer

Voice box produces lower, deeper sounds

Shoulders and chest broaden

Underarm hair becomes longer and thicker

Muscle development gives more angular body shape

The voice box, also called the Adam's apple, becomes more visible

VOCAL CHANGES

As the body matures, the vocal cords in the voice box become thicker and longer. This happens more noticeably in males, causing the cords to vibrate more slowly, giving a deeper voice.

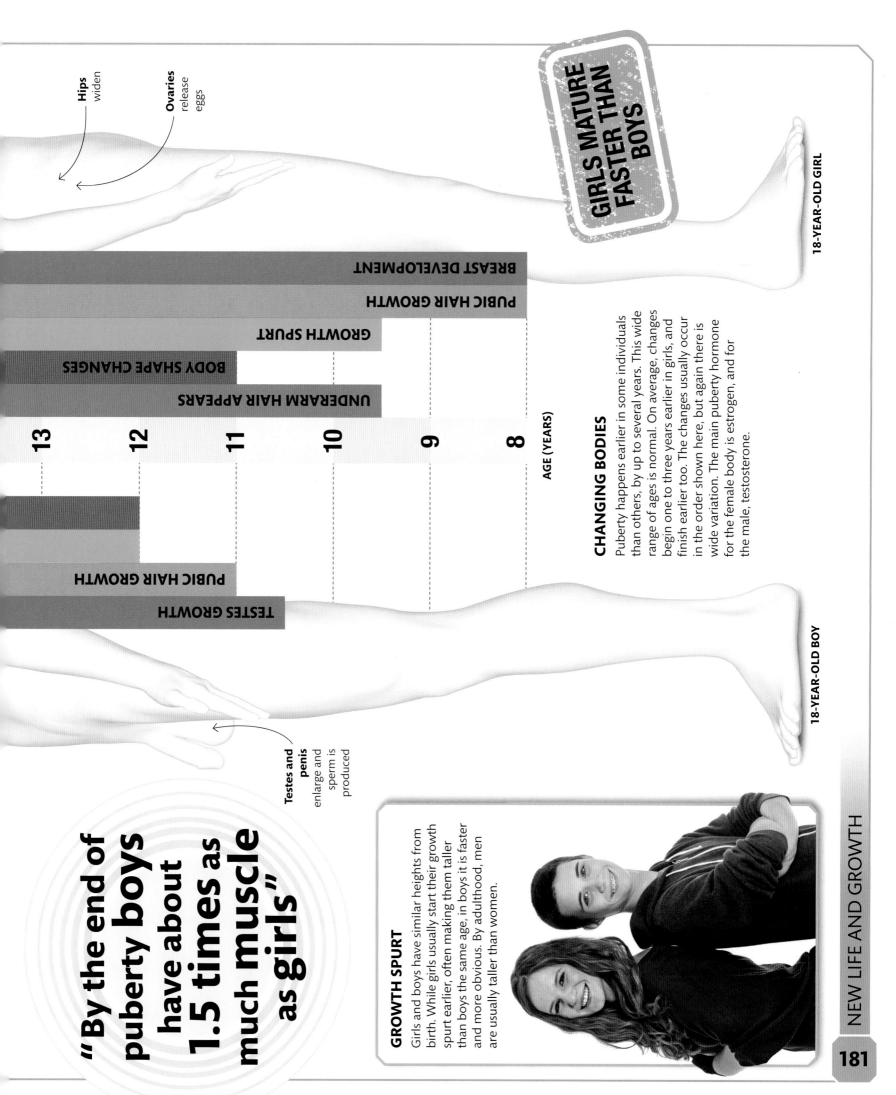

Hips **widen**

Ovaries **release eggs**

GIRLS MATURE FASTER THAN BOYS

18-YEAR-OLD GIRL

BREAST DEVELOPMENT

PUBIC HAIR GROWTH

GROWTH SPURT

BODY SHAPE CHANGES

UNDERARM HAIR APPEARS

PUBIC HAIR GROWTH

TESTES GROWTH

13 · 12 · 11 · 10 · 9 · 8

AGE (YEARS)

CHANGING BODIES

Puberty happens earlier in some individuals than others, by up to several years. This wide range of ages is normal. On average, changes begin one to three years earlier in girls, and finish earlier too. The changes usually occur in the order shown here, but again there is wide variation. The main puberty hormone for the female body is estrogen, and for the male, testosterone.

18-YEAR-OLD BOY

Testes and penis enlarge and sperm is produced

"By the end of puberty boys have about 1.5 times as much muscle as girls"

GROWTH SPURT

Girls and boys have similar heights from birth. While girls usually start their growth spurt earlier, often making them taller than boys the same age, in boys it is faster and more obvious. By adulthood, men are usually taller than women.

PHYSICAL PROGRESS
Growth and change

All living things, including humans, pass through a series of life changes. The body reaches maximum size, strength, and coordination at around 20–30 years of age. These features begin to fade from about 40–45 years of age, very slowly at first. But the brain continues to gather experience with memories and knowledge that can help wise thinking and decision-making.

BONE GROWTH

When the baby is still in the womb, bones first form as structures of cartilage. These harden into true bone tissue over the years. Height mainly increases by the leg bones lengthening at sites called growth plates.

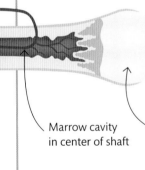

Early bone

In a newborn baby, the shaft of the bone has hardened into bony tissue while other parts are still mostly cartilage.

Marrow cavity in center of shaft

End of bone, composed of cartilage

Growing bone

In childhood, bones lengthen as cartilage from the growth plate and secondary growth site hardens into bone.

Growth plate

Secondary growth site

Spongy bone

Former growth plate

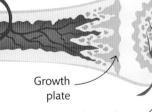

Compact bone

Mature bone

Lengthening of the bone slows and stops by the late teens. Almost all cartilage has hardened into continuous bone.

GETTING OLDER

The skeleton reaches its full size around the age of 20–23 years. Muscles continue to become bulkier for a few more years, and detailed coordination also improves with practice.

Head is still relatively large

Arms begin to lengthen

Heart and lungs grow fast

Slim body with little fat

Long bones of leg begin main growth

Shoulder and arm muscles gain power

Chest and abdomen muscles strengthen

Limb muscles start to get bulky

10 years

Rate of height increase peaks for girls, and a year or two later for boys. This is due mainly to growth of the long bones in the legs—the femur in the thigh, and the tibia and fibula in the lower leg.

17 years

Most girls reach their full height and changes of puberty are almost complete. About half of boys are still finishing their growing spurt. Muscle development is 80 percent complete.

ALL MUSCLE FIBERS ARE PRESENT FROM BIRTH

KEEP ON RUNNING

As with the entire life cycle, the rate of aging is different in different people. Keeping the body and mind active, helped by the right long-living genes, some people—such as Briton Fauja Singh—can run a marathon race when over 100 years young.

Hair begins to thin, sooner for men than women

Eyesight and hearing begin to decline

Hair loses color and turns gray

Abdomen muscles are flat and tense

Skin becomes wrinkly

Back and other muscles weaken

Bones are thinner and more brittle

Joints reach best condition

Weight-bearing joints start to wear out

Joints continue to wear

25 years
The average body is at its greatest height and maximum upright posture. Muscles are ready for their fullest development, although this depends largely on the amount of physical exercise and training.

60 years
Some joints begin to stiffen, skin loses its stretchiness, and there is a slight height loss. With reduced activity, fat gathers more easily. Senses gradually become less sharp and reactions slower.

80 years
Muscles gradually lose their power. The backbones and the cartilage disks between them slowly shrink, so the body may stoop forward. Senses diminish, and brain power and memories lessen.

NEW LIFE AND GROWTH

183

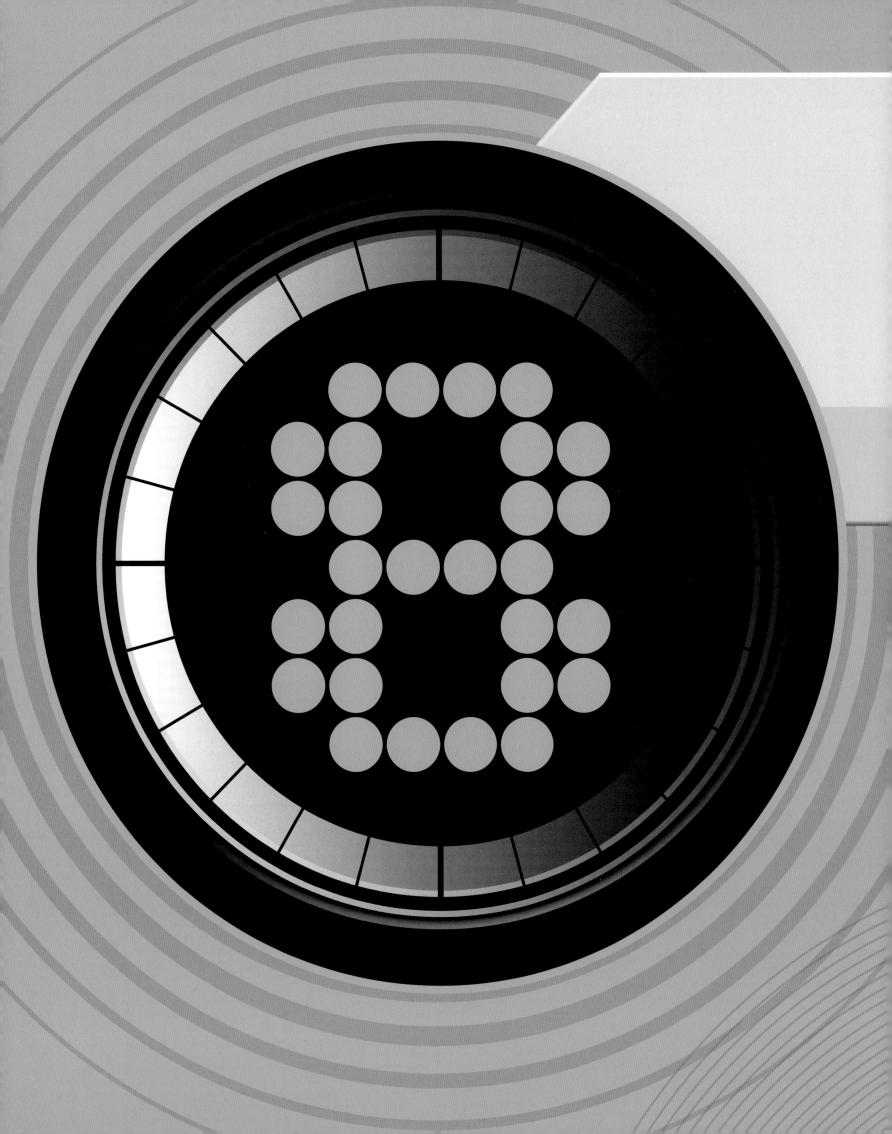

FUTURE HUMANS

Humans could change far more in the next 100 years than they have in the last 200,000 years. Computer technology, robotics, genetic engineering, and biotechnology are the forces driving a very different kind of human "evolution"—and powering us into the future.

STAYING ALIVE

Increasing longevity

Do you ever imagine what it will be like to be old? In the future, the difference between old and young could disappear. Scientists are slowly starting to discover what causes living things to age and die. They can already make worms, flies, and mice live longer, so what about humans? One day it might be possible to halt aging, but for now growing old is not something we can opt out of. Even so, there are many things we can do to stay healthy for longer, such as keeping fit and eating a good diet.

"The oldest person on record, Jeanne Calment, reached the **age of 122"**

Brain cells
These can rewire, making new connections, but very few are renewed.

Eyelashes
These fall out regularly and are replaced every 2 months.

Lens cells
These cells in the eye last well into old age.

Taste bud cells
These wear out quickly—most last no more than 10 days.

Red blood cells
These cannot divide to form new cells so they die and are replaced by the bone marrow every 120 days.

Heart muscle cells
These are rarely replaced—less than 1 percent a year.

Wrinkles appear when skin loses its elasticity

SHRINKING THE FUTURE

Why do our bodies grow older and die? Telomeres (the protective ends of chromosomes, shown in red) seem to play a part. As cells divide, the telomeres shrink, making the cells more vulnerable. Scientists think exercise might slow down aging by producing a chemical that helps telomeres last longer.

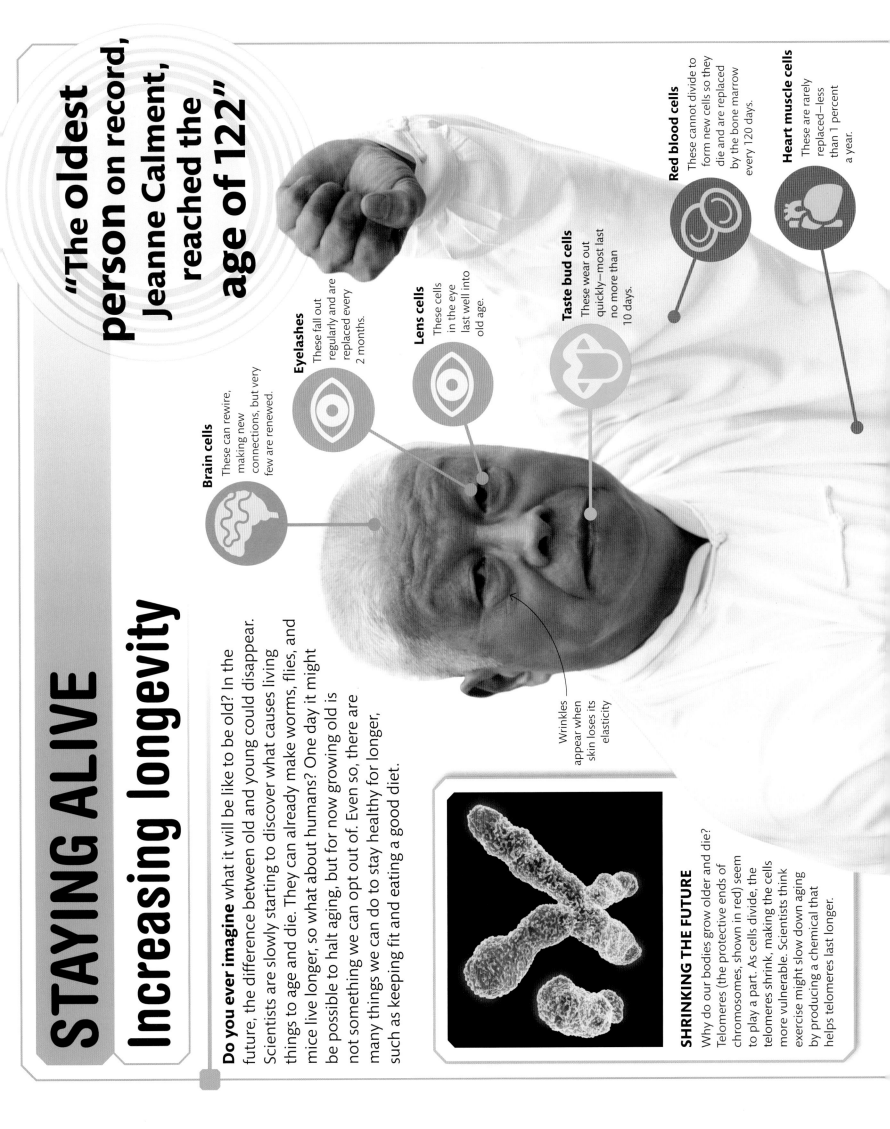

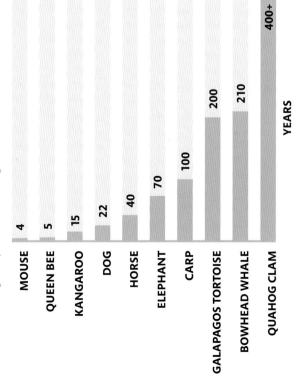

Skeletal muscle cells
These last 15 years—much longer than smooth muscle cells, found in the blood vessels and bladder, which last only a few days.

Intestinal cells
Renew the entire gut several times throughout life.

Intestine lining
These cells are rubbed off by the passage of food and last only five days.

Skin cells
These are shed every day and renewed from below the surface every four weeks.

Bone cells
The entire skeleton is replaced every 10 years.

Joints suffer the most wear and tear, but can now be replaced

YOUNG AT HEART
On average, people in developed countries now live 5–10 years longer than they did in the 1970s. That means there are many more older people in the world than there used to be. By 2020, there will be over a billion people aged over 60, and 70 percent more elderly people in the world than there were in 2000.

Regular exercise can improve mobility and help fight off disease

HOW WE COMPARE WITH OTHERS
Flies can die within a week, while oak trees might live 1,000 years. Bigger organisms generally live longer than smaller ones. No one knows exactly why, but bigger animals and plants have fewer predators, can store more food, and reproduce when they are older. These things help them live longer.

Animal	Years
MOUSE	4
QUEEN BEE	5
KANGAROO	15
DOG	22
HORSE	40
ELEPHANT	70
CARP	100
GALAPAGOS TORTOISE	200
BOWHEAD WHALE	210
QUAHOG CLAM	400+

YEARS

TO BOLDLY GO

Life in space

After millions of years of evolution, humans are perfectly at home on Earth. We are well adapted to living in our water-covered world that spins around the Sun. But what if life on Earth becomes impossible in the future? If a terrible disease threatens humanity, or climate change scorches our planet into a baking desert, the entire human race might have to pack its bags and head for the stars. Could we start afresh in the dark depths of space?

Human body
frozen for thawing later

FEWER THAN 550 PEOPLE HAVE GONE TO SPACE

Eggs frozen in liquid nitrogen for storage

LIFE IN SPACE

In space, everyday chores are way out of this world. Even simple shopping trips could mean dodging dust-storms, bursts of sun radiation, and winds colder than Earth's South Pole! What would you drive? Maybe this electric, voice-steered Eurobot—its two arms are great for everything from exploring rough terrain to packing your shopping.

SEED SHIPS

Should Earth become unlivable and we had no place else to go, in an attempt to ensure the continuity of our species we could send seed ships into space. These uncrewed spacecraft carrying human cells or embryos could artificially restart our civilization.

SPACE COLONIES

Water, sunlight, food, and gravity are essential things humans would need in order to survive in space. If we were unable to find another livable planet, we could build a space station. Spinning slowly, like a giant mouse wheel, it would make its own gravity. Vast mirrors could catch sunlight to grow plants for food.

"437 days is the longest time a person has spent in space at a stretch"

Freeze pod is vacuum sealed

SUSPENDED ANIMATION

It could take hundreds of years to reach a livable planet, but no one can survive that long. We could freeze people to stop them from aging and thaw them back to life on arrival. But while scientists can freeze sperm for 40 years, they do not know how to freeze and revive humans yet. A method of instantly freezing all the cells in the body is needed, or else it could rot!

Gloves zip onto suit

Biosuit is fitted, light, and flexible

Helmet with built-in communication devices

SPACE WARDROBE

Today's spacesuits have about 14 layers, including thermal underwear, breathing apparatus, and a toughened outer shell. To live in space forever, we will need simpler space fashions that are much more comfortable.

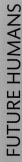

SPARES AND REPAIRS
Mini machines

When sickness wages war inside your body, you need help to get well again. Today, we swallow medicines—chemicals that drift through our blood, fighting disease. Tomorrow, our bodies may fight back with help from nanobots—mini surgical robots about the same size as body cells. Engineers can already build micromachines from atoms and molecules. In the future, technological advances may allow them to make robots with microscopic sensors that can pinpoint rogue cells or bacteria and destroy them.

Body building

Nanobots could be preprogrammed to find damaged or diseased parts of your body and repair them. Racing round the motorways of your bloodstream, they might use onboard cameras to identify rogue cells. Some may use miniature robot arms to dismantle germs, atom by atom, while others could pump medicines into diseased cells.

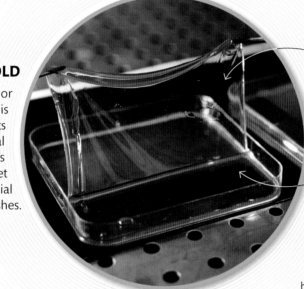

NEW SKIN FOR OLD

Skin usually heals after a cut or burn, but not if the damage is serious. Fortunately, scientists have now developed artificial skin. It takes just three weeks to grow 11 square feet (1 sq m) in these special culture dishes.

Artificially grown human skin being removed from a culture dish

Red blood cell in the bloodstream

Gel contains nutrients needed by skin cells to grow

Nanobot in blood vessel could detect and remove blockages or cancerous cells, and fight illnesses

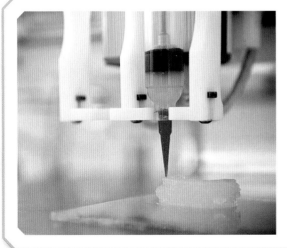

3D PRINTING

Inkjet computer printers draw pictures on paper by squirting ink. In a similar way, 3D printers make objects by squirting plastic. They use nozzles that slide back and forth, building up an object in thin layers. Doctors are now using 3D printers to make instant plastic replacements for body parts, such as fingers and ears. In the future, printers could use cells to print organs made of living tissue.

Nanobot rushes to the site of damage to help our natural defences repair it

"Nanobots would be about one-tenth the width of a human hair"

Damaged area of blood vessel

REPLACEMENT ORGANS

If one of your body organs is damaged, you might need to replace it. Organs are donated by people who have died or from friends or family. In future, specially bred animals could donate whole organs or cells. This idea is called xenotransplantation. Another possibility would be to use a person's own stem cells to grow replacement tissues. This would get around the problem of the patient having to take drugs to prevent his or her body from attacking the donated organ.

Pancreas cells
These help us make insulin and digest food. Replacements from animals could help cure diabetes.

Red blood cells
These cells could be used to make artificial blood, reducing the need for blood transfusions.

Eye tissues
Instead of transplants, people with damaged corneas, or eye tissues, could have specially grown replacements.

BIONIC BODIES

Rebuilding the body

Would you like zoom lenses for eyes, arms that can lift cars, or legs that could speed you down a track faster than a cheetah? All these things could become quite common within the next 100 years, helping you stay fit and active. Although our bodies constantly rebuild themselves, they wear out eventually. But as we slowly swap aging flesh and broken bone for more and more bionic—mechanical and electronic—replacements, a whole world of possibilities opens up for enhancing our bodies beyond their current physical capabilities.

Battery pack powers exoskeleton

EXOSKELETONS

Invented in 1846, artificial legs are a big help for people who have lost limbs. For paralyzed people, exoskeletons are better. Bionic walking assistance systems are designed to help such people walk again using electronic chest-mounted sensors. As you rock from side to side, electric motors, powered by a battery backpack, move your legs using sturdy braces.

Braces fitted onto legs enable forward motion

"Exoskeletons can make people 25 times stronger"

Plug-in memory chip could cure memory loss or give instant information

Visual processing chip automatically identifies objects and sends information to the brain

How the retina works
A bionic retina works like a digital camera plugged into the eye. A sensor chip picks up light from objects and converts it into electric signals. A processor chip fires the signals into the brain area that recognizes objects. This fools the brain into thinking it is looking through a camera.

Pacemaker with built-in battery corrects irregular heartbeats or heart failures

Bionic retina uses a sensor chip to convert viewed images into electrical signals

Artificial nose uses bionic sensors to detect and identify chemicals

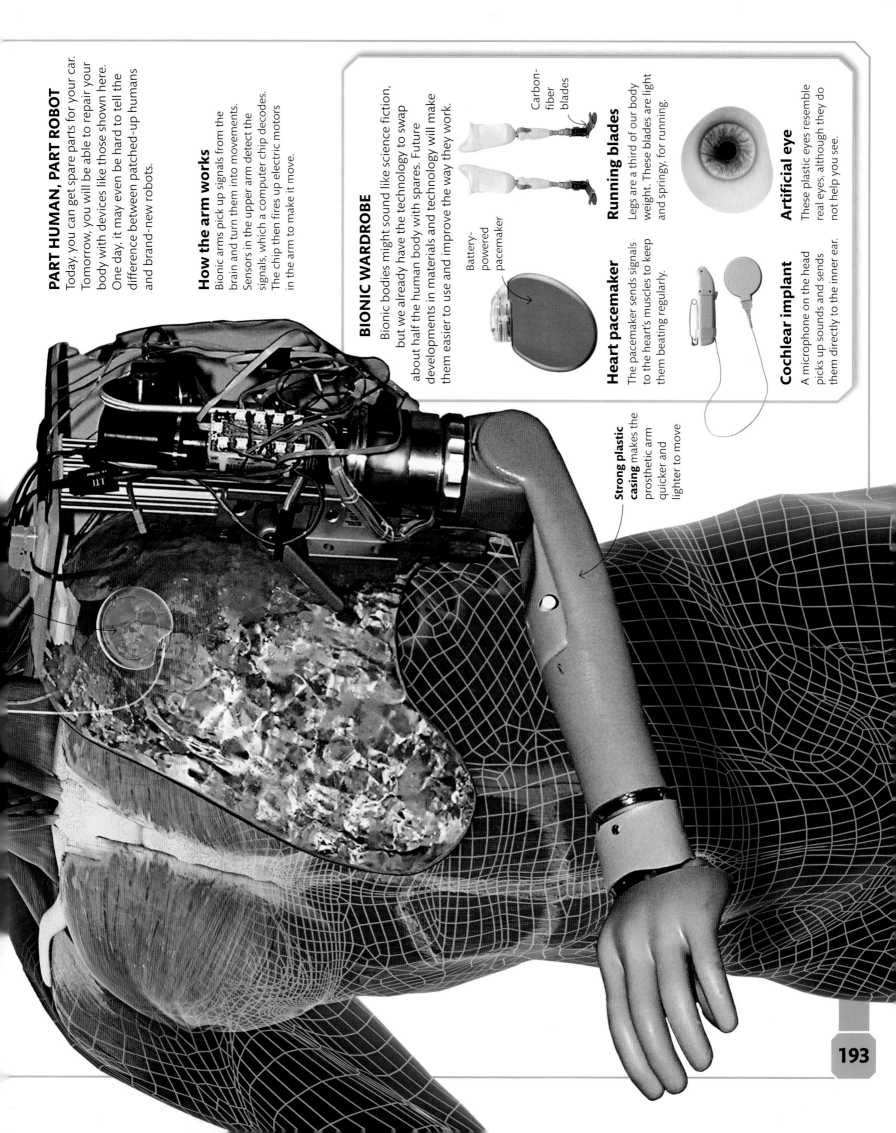

PART HUMAN, PART ROBOT

Today, you can get spare parts for your car. Tomorrow, you will be able to repair your body with devices like those shown here. One day, it may even be hard to tell the difference between patched-up humans and brand-new robots.

How the arm works

Bionic arms pick up signals from the brain and turn them into movements. Sensors in the upper arm detect the signals, which a computer chip decodes. The chip then fires up electric motors in the arm to make it move.

BIONIC WARDROBE

Bionic bodies might sound like science fiction, but we already have the technology to swap about half the human body with spares. Future developments in materials and technology will make them easier to use and improve the way they work.

Carbon-fiber blades

Running blades

Legs are a third of our body weight. These blades are light and springy, for running.

Artificial eye

These plastic eyes resemble real eyes, although they do not help you see.

Battery-powered pacemaker

Heart pacemaker

The pacemaker sends signals to the heart's muscles to keep them beating regularly.

Cochlear implant

A microphone on the head picks up sounds and sends them directly to the inner ear.

Strong plastic casing makes the prosthetic arm quicker and lighter to move

193

ALL IN THE GENES
Genetic engineering

Babies aren't crystal balls: you can't look in their eyes and see their future. How we turn out is a mixture of nature (determined by genes) and nurture (received from the world around us). Scientists now know far more about genes and how they control development. That could make it easier to engineer superhumans who will never suffer terrible diseases. But could it open the door to a scary future where perfect "designer" children are churned out like plastic dolls from a factory?

ANIMAL CLONING HAS A 95–99% FAILURE RATE

DESIGNER BABIES

Should parents be able to choose their baby's sex before it's born? What about other features? Once scientists fully understand the human genome (our complete genetic information), they might engineer any aspect of a newborn child as easily as choosing options on a new car. Should humans dare to design life better than nature?

GENE THERAPY

Engineering our genes could bring huge benefits to humanity, such as curing types of cancer. Some illnesses happen when genes in our cells mutate (go wrong and develop harmfully). In gene therapy, cells containing faulty genes are removed from a person's body, the genes are replaced with working ones, and then the cells are injected back again, curing the disease.

"You share 50 percent of your DNA with a banana"

CLONING

Extract the genetic information from your body and grow it into another person, and you'll get a clone (an identical copy of yourself). In 1996, scientists cloned a sheep called Dolly. In future, cloning could make identical babies or mass-produce farm animals for food. Or it could make stem cells, general-purpose body-repair cells that could help cure illnesses such as heart disease, Parkinson's, and diabetes.

CHOOSING CHARACTERISTICS

As a future parent, you might design your baby from a menu, a bit like ordering a takeout meal. Doctors could give you a list of options from which you pick the ones you prefer. Many would think this unethical, but who knows how far we would go down the route of picking our "perfect child."

EYES
You could choose your baby's eye color. Cloning could also help avoid genetic eye disorders and some kinds of blindness.

HAIR
Babies could be designed with a certain hair color, with straight or curly hair, and natural resistance to baldness in later life.

INTELLIGENCE
It might not be possible to clone smarter children. Scientists believe how we are raised is just as important as genetic factors.

HEIGHT
Plants have long been selectively bred to make them taller or shorter. Future babies might be engineered the same way.

SEX
In some countries, male babies are still valued more. If too many parents choose boys, what will happen to the human race?

ABILITIES
A strong child could grow into an Olympic champion, but most human abilities do not depend on our bodies in such a simple way.

BRAIN GAINS
The future brain

Everything you've ever learned, everything that's ever happened to you, and everything you know about everyone you've ever met is packed into a lump of mush the size of a pudding bowl balanced on top of your head—your brain. Humans have managed perfectly well with the way our brains work for several million years, but the development of powerful computers, over the last 50 years or so, has given us amazing new opportunities. Could we blend computer technology with our brains to make ourselves much smarter?

AUGMENTED REALITY

Augmented reality is a way of adding handy information from the Internet to things you can see in front of you. These electronic glasses can draw maps, look up facts, and project useful information about your surroundings before your eyes. They can also display emails, pinpoint friends who happen to be nearby, and allow you to listen to sound files.

Wearable computers will be able to display information about the objects around you.

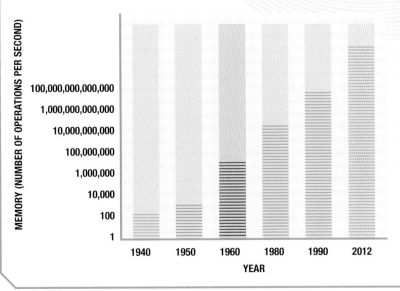

SUPERCOMPUTER POWER

Could the human brain become redundant in the future? Computer processing power has rocketed by a factor of 100 thousand trillion over the last 75 years, but it still pales by comparison with the human brain. Where we win over machines is in our ability to store memories. This allows us to solve problems in a shorter number of steps than any computer running today can achieve.

MEMORY (NUMBER OF OPERATIONS PER SECOND)

100,000,000,000,000
1,000,000,000,000
10,000,000,000
100,000,000
1,000,000
10,000
100
1

1940 1950 1960 1980 1990 2012

YEAR

Electrodes in the skull cap pick up electrical activity in the brain and send signals to a computer

MIND OVER MATTER

What if we could plug human brains into computers? We could look up interesting facts just by thinking about them or download new languages straight to our memories. It would be good news for paralyzed people. They could control wheelchairs, televisions, or household appliances by thought alone.

Neuron passes signals to other neurons

MERGING WITH MACHINES

Brains are made of neurons (nerve cells), while computers have electronic versions called transistors. If we want to merge brains and computers, we'll need to make neurons talk to transistors. In this experimental computer, a neuron (orange) has been grown on a transistor (green) that can switch it on and off.

Transistor can switch neurons on and off

HUMAN COMPUTER

Human brains have taken millions of years to evolve. The modern human brain is about 30–35 percent bigger than that of our ancestor, *Homo erectus*, who lived hundreds of thousands of years ago. Computer brains have evolved faster. Today's supercomputers are much more powerful than they were 50 years ago. Linking computers to our brains could make us smarter much faster than evolution alone.

"The most powerful computers are only half as powerful as a mouse's brain"

THE NEXT GENERATION
Future humans

What does the future hold for us? If computers and robots can do jobs better than humans, what will be left for us to do? Perhaps there will not be any "ordinary humans" in the future. Earth might be filled with genetic clones or metal cyborgs with human brains at the controls. Perhaps our planet will be a barren wasteland and we will all be living up in space. There is no doubt about one thing: future humans will certainly be "super"; the only question is, just how human will they be?

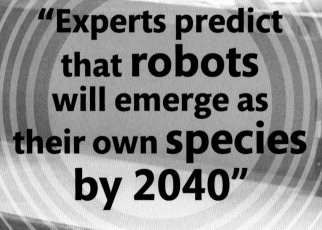

"Experts predict that robots will emerge as their own species by 2040"

メニュー
三種盛丼 ¥900
マグロ ウニ イクラ ¥1200
まぐろ丼 ¥700
具大 ¥1500
うに丼 ¥2000
ねぎとろ丼 ¥700
ねぎいくら丼 ¥800
ねぎとろ丼 ¥900
スペシャル
ねぎとろサーモン ¥900
まぐろいくら ¥800

ねぎとろ
いくら丼
¥800

まぐろ
づけ丼
¥8

ねぎとろ
スペシャル
¥900

まぐろ

本日のコレ

季節の海鮮丼
¥1500

Fiction or future?

If today's technological advancements are anything to go by, a future well beyond fiction awaits us. So, don't be surprised if tomorrow your coworker, neighbor, or even best friend is a robot.

199

FUTURE HUMAN

GLOSSARY

ABDOMEN
The lower part of the main body (the trunk), below your chest.

ABSORPTION
The process by which nutrients from digested food are taken in through the wall of your small intestine and passed into your blood.

ALLERGY
An illness caused by overreaction of the body's *immune system* to a normally harmless substance.

ANTIBODY
A substance made by the body that sticks to germs and marks them for destruction by white blood cells.

ANTIGEN
A foreign substance, usually found on the surface of germs such as bacteria, which triggers the immune system to respond.

ARTERY
A blood vessel that carries blood away from your heart to your body's tissues and organs.

AUTONOMIC NERVOUS SYSTEM (ANS)
The part of the nervous system that controls unconscious functions such as heart rate and the size of the pupils in your eyes.

AXON
A long fiber that extends from a *nerve cell (neuron)*. It carries electrical signals away from the cell.

BACTERIUM (PLURAL BACTERIA)
A small type of microorganism. Bacteria live everywhere. Some types cause disease in humans, but some are beneficial and help keep your body functioning properly.

BLOOD
A liquid tissue containing several types of cell. Blood carries oxygen, salts, nutrients, minerals, and hormones around your body. It also collects waste for disposal, such as carbon dioxide that is breathed out by your lungs.

BLOOD VESSEL
Any tube that carries blood through your body.

BONE
A strong, hard body part made chiefly of calcium minerals. There are 206 bones in an adult skeleton.

BRAIN STEM
The part of the base of your brain that connects to your *spinal cord*. This controls functions such as breathing and heart rate.

CALCIUM
A mineral used by your body to build bones and teeth. Calcium also helps muscles move.

CAPILLARY
The smallest type of blood vessel. Your body contains thousands of miles of capillaries.

CARBOHYDRATE
A food group that includes sugars and starches that provide your body's main energy supply.

CARTILAGE
A tough, flexible type of connective tissue that helps support your body and covers the ends of bones in joints.

CELL
The smallest living unit of your body.

CENTRAL NERVOUS SYSTEM
Your brain and spinal cord together make up your central nervous system. One of the two main parts of the nervous system.

CEREBELLUM
A small, cauliflower-shaped structure at the base of the back of your brain that helps coordinate body movements and balance.

CEREBRAL CORTEX
The deeply folded, outer layer of your brain. It is used for thinking, memory, movement, language, attention, and processing sensory information.

CEREBRAL HEMISPHERE
One of the two symmetrical halves into which the main part of your brain (the *cerebrum*) is split.

CEREBRUM
The largest part of the brain, which is involved in conscious thought, feelings, and movement.

CHROMOSOME
One of 46 threadlike packages of deoxyribonucleic acid (DNA) found in the nucleus of body cells.

CONCEPTION
The time between fertilization of an egg cell by a sperm and settling of an embryo in the lining of the womb.

DENDRITE
A short fiber that extends from a *nerve cell (neuron)*. It carries incoming electrical signals from other nerve cells.

DNA
A long molecule found inside the nucleus of body cells. DNA contains coded instructions that control how cells work and how your body grows and develops.

DIGESTION
The process that breaks down food into tiny particles that your body can absorb and use.

DIGESTIVE ENZYME
A substance that speeds up the breakdown of food molecules.

ENDOCRINE GLAND
A type of gland, such as the pituitary gland, that releases *hormones* into your bloodstream.

ENZYME
A substance that speeds up a particular chemical reaction in the body.

EPIGLOTTIS
A flap of tissue that closes your windpipe when you swallow food to stop the food entering your windpipe.

EPINEPHRINE (ADRENALINE)
A hormone that prepares your body for sudden action in times of danger or excitement. Epinephrine is produced by glands on top of the kidneys.

FAT
A substance found in many foods that provides energy and important ingredients for cells. The layer of cells just under the skin is full of fat.

FECES
Solid waste that is made up of undigested food, dead cells, and bacteria that are left after digestion and eliminated from your anus.

FERTILIZATION
The joining of a female egg (ovum) and male sperm to make a new individual.

GENES
Instructions that control the way your body develops and works. Genes are passed on from parents to their children.

GENOME
The deoxyribonucleic acid (DNA) contained in a set of *chromosomes*. In humans there are 46 chromosomes.

GERM
A tiny living thing that can get into your body and make you ill. Bacteria and viruses are types of germ.

GLAND
A group of specialized cells that make and release a particular substance, such as an enzyme or a hormone.

GLUCOSE
A simple type of sugar that circulates in the bloodstream and is the main energy source for the body's cells.

GRAY MATTER
Brain tissue that consists

largely of the cell bodies of neurons. The outer layer of the brain is gray matter.

HEMOGLOBIN
A substance in red blood cells that carries oxygen around the body.

HERTZ
A unit used to measure the frequency of sound waves. The higher the frequency, the higher the pitch of the sound.

HIPPOCAMPUS
A part of the brain that helps us lay down long-term memories.

HORMONE
A chemical produced by *glands* in order to change the way a different part of the body works. Hormones are carried by the blood.

HYPOTHALAMUS
A small structure in the base of your brain that controls many body activities, including temperature and thirst.

IMMUNE SYSTEM
A collection of cells and tissues that protect the body from disease by searching out and destroying germs and cancer cells.

INFECTION
If germs invade your body and begin to multiply, they cause an infection. Some diseases are caused by infections.

JOINT
A connection between two bones. The knee is the biggest joint in the human body. The bones are usually connected by ligaments.

KERATIN
A tough, waterproof protein found in hair, nails, and the upper layer of your skin.

KILOHERTZ
See hertz.

LIGAMENT
A tough band of tissue that connects bones where they meet at joints.

LIMBIC SYSTEM
A cluster of structures found inside the brain and vital in creating emotions, memory, and the sense of smell.

LYMPHATIC SYSTEM
A network of vessels that collect fluid from body tissues and filter it for germs, before returning the fluid to the bloodstream.

LYMPHOCYTE
A white blood cell specialized to attack a specific kind of germ. Some lymphocytes make antibodies.

MACROPHAGE
A white blood cell that swallows and destroys germs such as bacteria, cancer cells, or debris in damaged tissue.

MELANIN
A brown-black pigment that is found in your skin, hair, and eyes and gives them their color.

METABOLISM
A term used to describe all the chemical reactions going on inside your body, especially within cells.

MINERAL
A naturally occurring solid chemical, such as salt, calcium, or iron, that you need to eat to stay healthy.

MITOCHONDRION (PLURAL MITOCHONDRIA)
A tiny structure found inside cells that releases energy from sugar.

MOLECULE
A single particle of a particular chemical compound. A molecule is a cluster of atoms—the smallest particles of an element—bonded together permanently.

MOTOR NEURON
A type of nerve cell that carries nerve impulses from your central nervous system to your muscles.

MUCUS
Slippery liquid found on the inside of your nose, throat, and intestines.

MUSCLE
A body part that contracts (gets shorter) to move your bones or internal organs.

MUSCLE FIBER
A muscle cell.

NERVE CELL
See neuron.

NERVE IMPULSE
A tiny electrical signal that is transmitted along a nerve cell (*neuron*) at high speed.

NEURON
A term for a nerve cell. Neurons carry information around your body as electrical signals.

NUCLEUS
The control center of a cell. It contains DNA-carrying chromosomes.

NUTRIENTS
The basic chemicals that make up food. Your body uses nutrients for fuel, growth, and repair.

ORGAN
A group of tissues that form a body part designed for a specific job. Your heart is an organ.

OSTEON
Tubular structures that make up compact bone. Also known as Haversian system.

OVUM
Also called an egg, this is the female sex cell, which is produced by, and released from, a woman's ovary.

OXYGEN
A gas, found in air, that is vital for life. Oxygen is breathed in, absorbed by the blood, and used by cells to release energy from glucose (a simple sugar).

PERISTALSIS
The wave of muscular squeezes (contractions) in the wall of a hollow organ that, for example, pushes food down the esophagus during swallowing.

PROTEINS
Vital nutrients that help your body build new cells. Food such as meat, eggs, fish, and cheese are rich in proteins.

PROTIST
A single cell organism—some cause diseases in humans.

ABBREVIATIONS USED IN THIS BOOK

°C	degrees Celsius
Cal	Calories—equal to 1 kcal
cm	centimeter
dB	decibel
°F	degrees Fahrenheit
fl oz	fluid ounce
ft	foot
g	gram or gravity
Hz	hertz—see glossary for definition
in	inch
kg	kilogram
kHz	kilohertz—equal to 1,000 Hz
km	kilometer
km/h	kilometers per hour
lb	pound
m	meter
min	minute
ml	milliliter
mm	millimeter
mph	miles per hour
oz	ounce
s or sec	second
sq	square

RED BLOOD CELL
A disc-shaped cell that contains haemoglobin (a protein that carries oxygen and makes your blood red).

REFLEX
A rapid, automatic reaction that is out of your control, such as blinking when something moves toward your eyes.

RETINA
A layer of light-sensitive neurons lining the back of each eye. The retina captures images and relays them to the brain as electrical signals.

ROD CELL
A light sensitive cell in the back of the eye. They work in dim light but do not detect color (see also *cones*).

SALIVA
The liquid in your mouth. Saliva helps you taste, swallow, and digest food.

SEBUM
An oily liquid that keeps your hair and skin soft, flexible, and waterproof.

SENSORY NEURON
A type of nerve cell (neuron) that carries impulses from your sense organs to the central nervous system.

SENSORY RECEPTOR
A specialized nerve cell or the end of a sensory neuron that detects a stimulus, such as light, scent, touch, or sound.

SPERM
The male sex cells, which are made in, and released from, a man's testes.

SPHINCTER
A ring of muscle around a passageway or opening that opens and closes to control the flow of material, such as urine or food, through it.

SPINAL CORD
A column of nerve cells (neurons) that runs down your backbone and connects your brain to the rest of your body.

SPINAL NERVE
One of the 31 pairs of nerves that branch out from your spinal cord.

SWEAT
A watery liquid produced by glands in the skin. Sweat cools the body as it evaporates.

SYNAPSE
The junction where two nerve cells (neurons) meet but do not touch.

SYSTEM
A group of organs that work together. Your mouth, stomach, and intestines make up your digestive system.

TENDON
A cord of tough connective tissue that links muscle to bone.

TISSUE
A group of cells that look and act the same. Muscle is a type of tissue.

TOXIN
A poisonous substance released into the body by a disease-causing bacterium.

ULTRASOUND
An imaging technique that uses inaudible, high-frequency sound waves to produce pictures of a developing baby in the womb or of body tissues.

VEIN
A blood vessel that carries blood toward your heart.

VELLUS HAIR
One of the millions of fine, soft hairs that grow all over your body.

VENULE
A small blood vessel (smaller than a vein) that returns blood to the heart.

VIRUS
A kind of germ that invades cells and multiplies inside them. Diseases caused by viruses include the common cold, measles, and influenza.

VITAMINS
One of a number of substances, including vitamins A and C, needed in small amounts in your diet to keep your body healthy.

VOCAL CORDS
The small folds of tissue in your voice box that vibrate to create the sounds of speech.

VOICE BOX (LARYNX)
A structure at the top of the windpipe that generates sound as you speak. The sound is created by folds of tissue that vibrate as you breathe out.

WHITE BLOOD CELL
Any of the colorless blood cells that play various roles in your immune system.

WHITE MATTER
Brain tissue made up mainly of the axons (long fibers) of nerve cells. The inner part of the brain consists largely of white matter.

WINDPIPE (TRACHEA)
The main airway leading from the back of your throat to your lungs, where it branches into bronchi.

INDEX

ACKNOWLEDGMENTS

Dorling Kindersley would like to thank Jane Parker for the index; Katie John and Steve Setford for proofreading; Samina Ali and Ethen Carlin for design assistance; Natasha Rees for additional design; Adam Brackenbury for creative retouching; Gill Pitts and Kaiya Shang for editorial assistance; Chris Rao, John Spiliotis, and Alexandra Ashcroft for additional consultancy; Annabel Hobbs for hair and makeup, and for modelling: Grace Derome, Kate Byrne, Laura Cathryn, Thomas Snee, and Dhillon Boateng.

DK India would like to thank Divya P R, Vaibhav Rastogi, and Riti Sodhi for design assistance; Kanika Mittal, Heena Sharma, Vikas Chauhan, and Arun Pottirayil for assistance with artworks; Dharini Ganesh, Himani Khatreja, and Sonia Yooshing for editorial assistance.

Picture Credits
The publisher would like to thank the following for their kind permission to reproduce their photographs:

(Key: a-above; b-below/bottom; c-centre; f-far; l-left; r-right; t-top)

1 Fotolia: He2 (c). **2-3 Corbis:** TempSport / Dimitri Iundt (b). **3 Fotolia:** He2 (c). **4 Corbis:** Demotix / Pau Barrena (tr). **6 Photoshot:** PYMCA (tr). **Science Photo Library:** Eye Of Science (bl). **7 Dreamstime.com:** Yuri_arcurs (bl). **Science Photo Library:** Carl Goodman (tr). **8 Getty Images:** Gallo Images / Danita Delimont (cl). **NASA:** (bc). **9 Dreamstime.com:** Anatoliy Samara (cra); Seqoya (crb). **Getty Images:** Aurora / David McLain (tc). **10 Getty Images:** E+ / azgAr Donmaz (bl). **10-11 Corbis:** Blend Images / John Lund (c). **11 Corbis:** (tc). **12-13 Science Photo Library:** Pasieka (c). **15 Science Photo Library:** Simon Fraser (t). **16 Science Photo Library:** Dr. Torsten Wittmann (bc). **17 Science Photo Library:** Steve Gschmeissner (crb). **18 Dreamstime.com:** Ron Chapple (bc). **18-19 Dorling Kindersley:** Zygote Media Group (c). **19 Dreamstime.com:** Ruslan Nassyrov (crb). **Science Photo Library:** Power And Syred (tc). **23 Dreamstime.com:** Jun Mu (tc/Red Fingerprint); Vince Mo (tc/Blue Fingerprint). **Science Photo Library:** Power And Syred (crb). **24 Alamy Images:** imageBROKER (c).

Science Photo Library: Tony Mcconnell (cra). **25 Dreamstime.com:** Alxyago (c); Tyler Olson (cr). **26-27 Getty Images:** Stone / David Trood. **29 Dreamstime.com:** Drx. **30-31 Getty Images:** AFP. **32 Photoshot:** Picture Alliance / Rolf Vennenbernd (crb). **33 NASA:** (crb). **34-35 Getty Images:** AFP. **36 Science Photo Library:** Steve Gschmeissner (crb). **38-39 Corbis:** BJI / Blue Jean Images (t). **39 Dreamstime.com:** Brenda Carson (bl). **40-41 Corbis:** TempSport / Dimitri Iundt. **42-43 Science Photo Library:** Steve Gschmeissner. **44 Science Photo Library:** Martin Oeggerli (cl). **46-47 Corbis:** Pete Saloutos. **48 Fotolia:** Gelpi (crb). **49 Dreamstime.com:** Alexsutula (tr). **50-51 Corbis:** Gerlach Delissen. **56-57 Corbis:** Paul Souders. **58 Science Photo Library:** Nancy Kedersha (cra). **60-61 Science Photo Library:** Thomas Deerinck, NCMIR. **63 Science Photo Library:** Tom Barrick, Chris Clark, SGHMS (bl). **64-65 Corbis:** Demotix / Pau Barrena. **66 Getty Images:** Cultura / Hybrid Images (cra). **67 Science Photo Library:** Don Fawcett (crb). **68-69 Getty Images:** Moment Select / Fredrik Lonnqvist. **70 Dreamstime.com:** Lenanet (clb). **71 Pearson Asset Library:** Trevor Clifford / Pearson Education Ltd (tc). **72 Dreamstime.com:** Monkey Business Images Ltd (crb). **73 Corbis:** Allana Wesley White (cr). **Dreamstime.com:** Ljupco Smokovski (crb). **74-75 Getty Images:** Topic Photo Agency (cb). **75 Getty Images:** Photographer's Choice / Bob Elsdale (cr). **79 123RF.com:** martinak (tc). **80-81 Corbis:** Simon Marcus. **83 Dreamstime.com:** Eveleen007 (tl). **84-85 Science Photo Library:** Omikron. **86-87 Dorling Kindersley:** Duncan Turner (c). **87 Alamy Images:** Objowl (br). **88-89 Getty Images:** Aflo / Enrico Calderoni. **92-93 Science Photo Library:** Steve Gschmeissner. **95 Dreamstime.com:** Grigor Atanasov (cra). **96-97 tim-mckenna.com. 98 Corbis:** Holger Scheibe (l). **99 123RF.com:** tang90246 (tr). **100-101 Science Photo Library. 103 Dreamstime.com:** Atholpady (crb). **Science Photo Library:** Steve Gschmeissner (tl). **106-107 Science Photo Library:** Martin Dohrn. **109 Corbis:** Tim Clayton / TIM CLAYTON (cb). **112-113 Getty Images:** Stone / Michele Westmorland. **114 Getty Images:** Visuals

Unlimited / Dr. David Phillips (cra). **118-119 Science Photo Library:** Dr. Gary Settle (t). **119 Dreamstime.com:** Martinmark. **120 Science Photo Library:** Zephyr (tl). **123 Science Photo Library:** (tl, ca). **124 Getty Images:** Visuals Unlimited, Inc. / Thomas Deerinck (bc). **126-127 Getty Images:** Iconica / Tyler Stableford. **128 Dreamstime.com:** Zzvet (br). **130-131 Giri Giri Boys/Yusuke Sato. 132-133 Science Photo Library:** CDC / Science Source. **140 Science Photo Library:** Dr. K.F.R. Schiller (clb). **142-143 Science Photo Library:** Eye Of Science. **144 Science Photo Library:** University "La Sapienza", Rome / Professors P. Motta & F. Carpino (bl). **145 Science Photo Library:** (tr). **147 Dreamstime.com:** Diana Valujeva (l). **Science Photo Library:** Bill Longcore (tr). **148-149 Dreamstime.com:** Klemen Misic. **156 Science Photo Library:** Custom Medical Stock Photo / Richard Wehr (crb); Professors P.M. Motta, K.R. Porter & P.M. Andrews (tr). **157 Science Photo Library:** Prof. P. Motta / Dept. Of Anatomy / University "La Sapienza", Rome (c). **160-161 Science Photo Library. 162 Science Photo Library:** Steve Gschmeissner (clb). **162-163 Getty Images:** The Image Bank / PM Images (c). **163 Dreamstime.com:** Bidouze Stéphane (bl). **Science Photo Library:** UCLA / Nancy Kedersha (tc). **166-167 Photoshot:** PYMCA (t). **166 Corbis:** Eleanor Bentall (b). **168-169 Corbis:** dpa / Daniel Ramsbott. **175 Dreamstime.com:** Giovanni Gagliardi (cla). **176-177 Alamy Images:** Inspirestock Inc.. **178 Alamy Images:** Tetra Images (crb). **Getty Images:** Asia Images / Yukmin (clb). **179 Camera Press:** Ian Boddy (cl). **Dreamstime.com:** Yuri_arcurs (r). **180 Corbis:** Hiya Images (bc). **PNAS:** 101(21):8174-8179, May 25 2004, Nitin Gogtay et al, Dynamic mapping of human cortical development during childhood through early adulthood © 2004 National Academy of Sciences, USA (tl). **181 Dreamstime.com:** Christine Langer-püschel (br). **182-183 Science Photo Library:** David Gifford (Seven Ages of Man). **183 Corbis:** Reuters / Andy Clark (tc). **186-187 Corbis:** Imaginechina (c). **186 Science Photo Library:** Pasieka (bc). **188-189 Science Photo Library:** Christian Darkin (t). **188 ESA:** ÖWF / P. Santek (cr). **Science Photo Library:** (bc).

189 NASA: Rick Guidice (bl). **Science Photo Library:** Volker Steger (bc). **190 Corbis:** Cornell / Lindsay France (bl). **Science Photo Library:** Klaus Guldbrandsen (c). **192 Getty Images:** (cla). **192-193 Dorling Kindersley:** Medimation (b). **194 Corbis:** Waltraud Grubitzsch / epa (clb). **194-195 Science Photo Library:** Hannah Gal (c). **195 Science Photo Library:** Bluestone (tc). **196 Corbis:** Blend Images / Colin Anderson. **197 Science Photo Library:** Mpi Biochemistry / Volker Steger (c); Philippe Psaila (tc). **198-199 Getty Images:** The Image Bank / SM / AIUEO

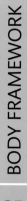

"Champion long jumpers can leap 5 times their body length"

Fast flight

As this long jumper hits the takeoff board, her power leg straightens the hip, knee, ankle, and toe joints in turn. All her leg bones together convey the forward and upward forces to the rest of the body.

BARE BONES
Inside bone

Bones are far from solid—otherwise your skeleton would be five times heavier! Each bone has an outer shell of a very strong, dense substance called compact bone. Inside it is a more spongelike layer, which has struts and rods of bone with spaces between for fluids and other tissues. This clever design makes bones light but strong, like honeycomb. In the middle of most bones is jellylike bone marrow.

"Bones can support more weight than concrete"

Periosteum, outer "skin" of the bone

Shell-like layer of compact bone

Blood vessels supply nutrients, minerals, and energy

Osteocyte cell body inside chamber

"Tentacles" reach into surrounding bone tissue

TRAPPED IN

Compact bone is full of tiny chambers that contain cells called osteocytes. Each cell lives for tens of years trapped inside its chamber, where it helps maintain the surrounding bone and keep it healthy.

REPAIRING BONE

A broken or cracked bone starts to repair itself almost right away. Blood clots in the break to stop further leaks. White blood cells gather to fight infection and clear away dead cells and tissues. Other cells make fibers that grow between the broken ends. Cells called osteoblasts then produce spongy bone that, in the outer layer, hardens into compact bone.

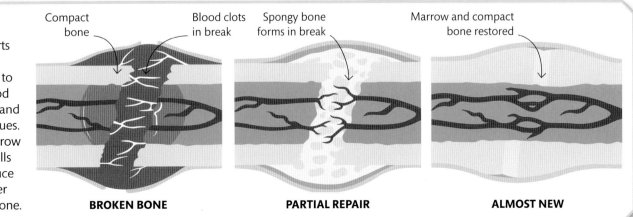

Compact bone

Blood clots in break

Spongy bone forms in break

Marrow and compact bone restored

BROKEN BONE

PARTIAL REPAIR

ALMOST NEW

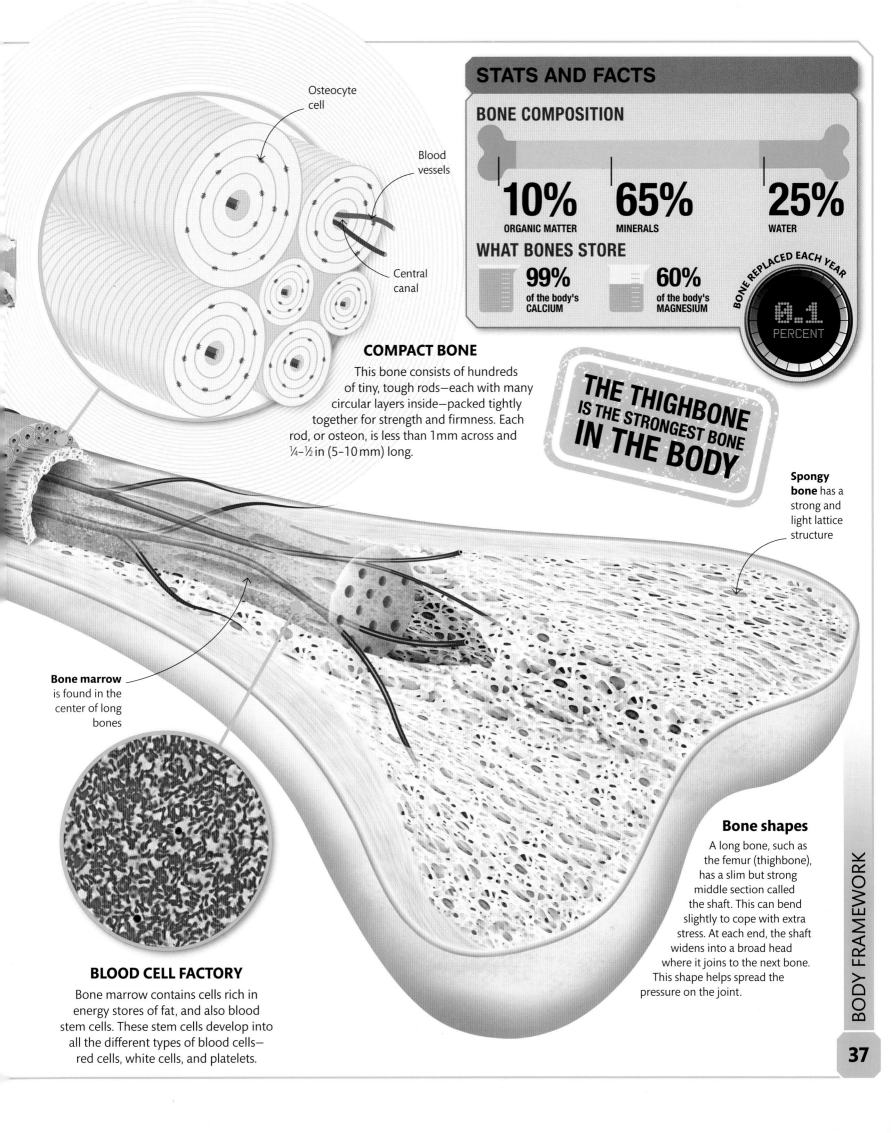

Osteocyte
cell

Blood
vessels

Central
canal

COMPACT BONE

This bone consists of hundreds
of tiny, tough rods—each with many
circular layers inside—packed tightly
together for strength and firmness. Each
rod, or osteon, is less than 1mm across and
¼–½ in (5–10 mm) long.

THE THIGHBONE IS THE STRONGEST BONE IN THE BODY

Spongy bone has a strong and light lattice structure

Bone marrow is found in the center of long bones

BLOOD CELL FACTORY

Bone marrow contains cells rich in
energy stores of fat, and also blood
stem cells. These stem cells develop into
all the different types of blood cells—
red cells, white cells, and platelets.

Bone shapes

A long bone, such as
the femur (thighbone),
has a slim but strong
middle section called
the shaft. This can bend
slightly to cope with extra
stress. At each end, the shaft
widens into a broad head
where it joins to the next bone.
This shape helps spread the
pressure on the joint.

BODY FRAMEWORK

37

BEND AND SWIVEL

How joints work

From the smallest finger knuckle to the big, sturdy knee, the body has more than 400 joints. Here bones come together and are linked to each other. Most familiar are the movable joints, which occur from the jaw down to the toes. Each movable joint has its own design that combines flexible freedom of movement with enough strength and stability to ensure that the bone ends do not come apart. But there are also fixed joints—in the skull, lower backbone, and hipbones—where the bones are stuck together with a kind of living glue.

PIVOT

The joint between the the base of the skull and the uppermost bone of the spine is like a dome that fits into a socket. This joint allows the head to move from side to side.

JOINT DESIGNS

Different kinds of joints are named after the shapes of the bones they consist of or the type of movement they allow. Usually, the lesser the range of movement, the stronger and more stable the joint.

ELLIPSOIDAL

Some of the eight wrist bones have oval-shaped surfaces that fit together like an egg in an eggcup. The bones tilt as they roll against one another.

SADDLE

The bones of the joint at the base of the thumb have a double-curved shape, like a horse's saddle. They can tilt in any direction but cannot twist.

BALL AND SOCKET

The ball-shaped top of the femur (thighbone) slots into a bowl-like socket in the pelvis (hipbone) to give a wide range of motions—to and fro, sideways, and twisting.

SHOCK ABSORBERS

In most joints, the areas where the bones meet are covered with cartilage, which is smooth and slightly squashy to absorb pressure. A thin layer of slippery fluid reduces friction even more. The knee has two extra cartilage cushions, each called a meniscus, between the bones for extra steadiness.

Femur (thighbone)

Meniscus acts as a shock absorber

Tibia

Ligaments hold bones together

Smooth cartilage keeps the bones from rubbing

KNEE JOINT

HINGE

Hinge joints in the knees and the finger and toe knuckles, let these bones move backward and forward, but they cannot move sideways or twist.

GLIDING

The seven angular, box-shaped ankle bones have little tilting motion. They can slide to and fro as well as sideways against each other.

DOUBLE JOINTED

People whose joints can bend much more than normal are sometimes called double jointed. While there is only one joint, the straplike ligaments that hold the bones together, and the muscles that pull them, are super stretchy and allow extra movement.

Fingers moving beyond range of normal joint

"There are 150 joints that cannot move"

Limbering up
Gymnasts increase the range of movement in their joints by carefully exercising the muscles, tendons, and ligaments around them. They learn how to relax the muscles fully so that they can be stretched further.

FLIPPING OUT
Flexibility

There are several reasons for hypermobility—the ability of some joints to bend and twist more than usual. The bone ends might be a slightly different shape, such as flatter rather than bowl-like. Some people naturally produce more collagen—the part of ligaments that holds bones together—than others, which makes their ligaments stretchier. Variations in hormone levels, especially that of the female hormone estrogen, can also affect ligament strength.

STATS AND FACTS

BACKBONE JOINTS

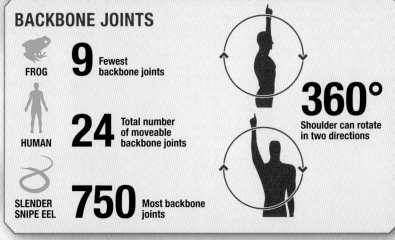

FROG	**9**	Fewest backbone joints
HUMAN	**24**	Total number of moveable backbone joints
SLENDER SNIPE EEL	**750**	Most backbone joints

360°
Shoulder can rotate in two directions

"**One** person in **30** has **extra-flexible** joints"

"Your **skeleton** starts out as cartilage, then gradually hardens into **bone**"

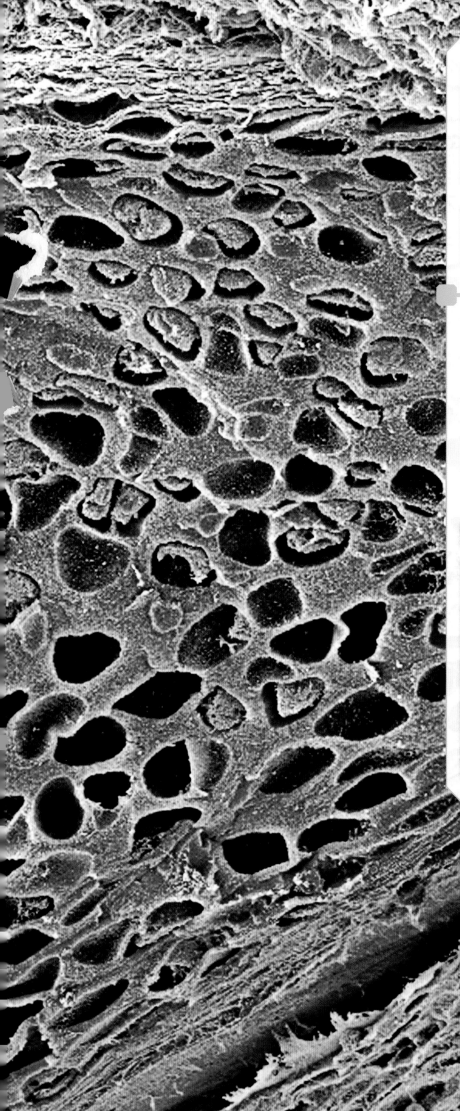

TOTALLY SMOOTH
Cartilage

Cartilage is one of the body's simplest tissues, but it plays a vital role—it keeps the ends of your bones from wearing away where they meet at the joints. It has only one type of cell, the chondrocyte. These cells surround themselves with a substance called the cartilage matrix, which contains no nerves, blood vessels, or other tissues. Cartilage is smooth and hard-wearing, yet a bit squashy and slippery. It also forms various stiff-yet-flexible body parts, such as the nose and ear flaps.

STATS AND FACTS

QUALITY
Cartilage is
5–10 TIMES
more slippery than ice

COMPOSITION
Cartilage is up to
80%
water

BODY PERCENTAGES
Cartilage forms
1–2%
of the whole human body

Cartilage makes up
100%
of a shark's skeleton

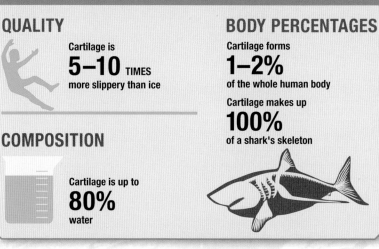

Living in the matrix
Mature chondrocytes (brown) spend their lives in tiny pockets in the cartilage matrix. This matrix is made up of collagen —a component of skin and bone—squishy chondroitin, and stretchy elastin, also found in skin.

FLEX IT!
Muscle power

Muscles account for every movement of the body, from an eye blink to a speeding sprint to a massive power-lift. Each of the hundreds of muscles is precisely controlled by nerve signals from the brain. With practice, common movements such as walking, running, eating, and writing are automatically organized by the relevant parts of the brain. We only realize how complex this control is when we learn a new skill, from threading a needle to snowboarding.

Biceps bends elbow

Latissimus dorsi, the broadest muscle of back, pulls extended arms back to the side of the body

Gluteus maximus, a large muscle that extends the bent thigh

BUILT FOR SPEED

The biggest muscles are in the legs, and they hurl the body forward in a burst of speed. But other muscles are working in coordination, too—in the body and arms to keep the balance, in the chest to breathe, and in the head and eyes to aim at the finish.

Hamstring muscles join rear thigh muscles to upper shin

Calf muscle bends knee and straightens ankle

Sartorius bends hip and knee and twists thigh. It is used when you sit in cross-legged position

MUSCLE FIBERS

A muscle contains bundles of two kinds of fibers, each less than 1 mm wide and ¼–2 in (5–40 mm) long. Fast-twitch fibers shorten rapidly with great force but tire quickly. Slow twitch-fibers contract gradually but keep going for longer.

Muscles on the front of the leg bend ankle upward

MUSCLES MAKE UP 40% OF YOUR BODY WEIGHT

Deltoid lifts and swings arm

Neck muscles move the head or keep it steady

Superior rectus muscle rotates the eye upward

Medial rectus muscle rotates the eye inward

SWING AND SWIVEL

Each eye is moved by six very thin, ribbonlike muscles—the most precise and fastest-acting. One swivels the eye up, another down, the third to the left, the fourth to the right. The other two muscles make fine adjustments, especially when the head moves one way and the eyes swing the other way, to keep the gaze on one object.

Flexor muscles in arm bend wrist, fingers, and thumb

Quadriceps (thigh muscles) bend hip and straighten knee

"650 skeletal muscles help to shape your body"

Tapering end of muscle

Tendon, with strong, rope-like fibers

TENDONS

Achilles tendon joins calf muscle to ankle bone

Fibers anchored into bone

LIGAMENTS

HOLDING IT TOGETHER

In most muscles, each end becomes narrower and attaches to a tendon, the other end of which fixes firmly into a bone and passes on the muscle's pulling force. Bones are held together at joints by ligaments. Many joints have several ligaments to stop the bones from moving too far or coming apart.

Ligaments, strong, stretchy elastic straps anchored into bones

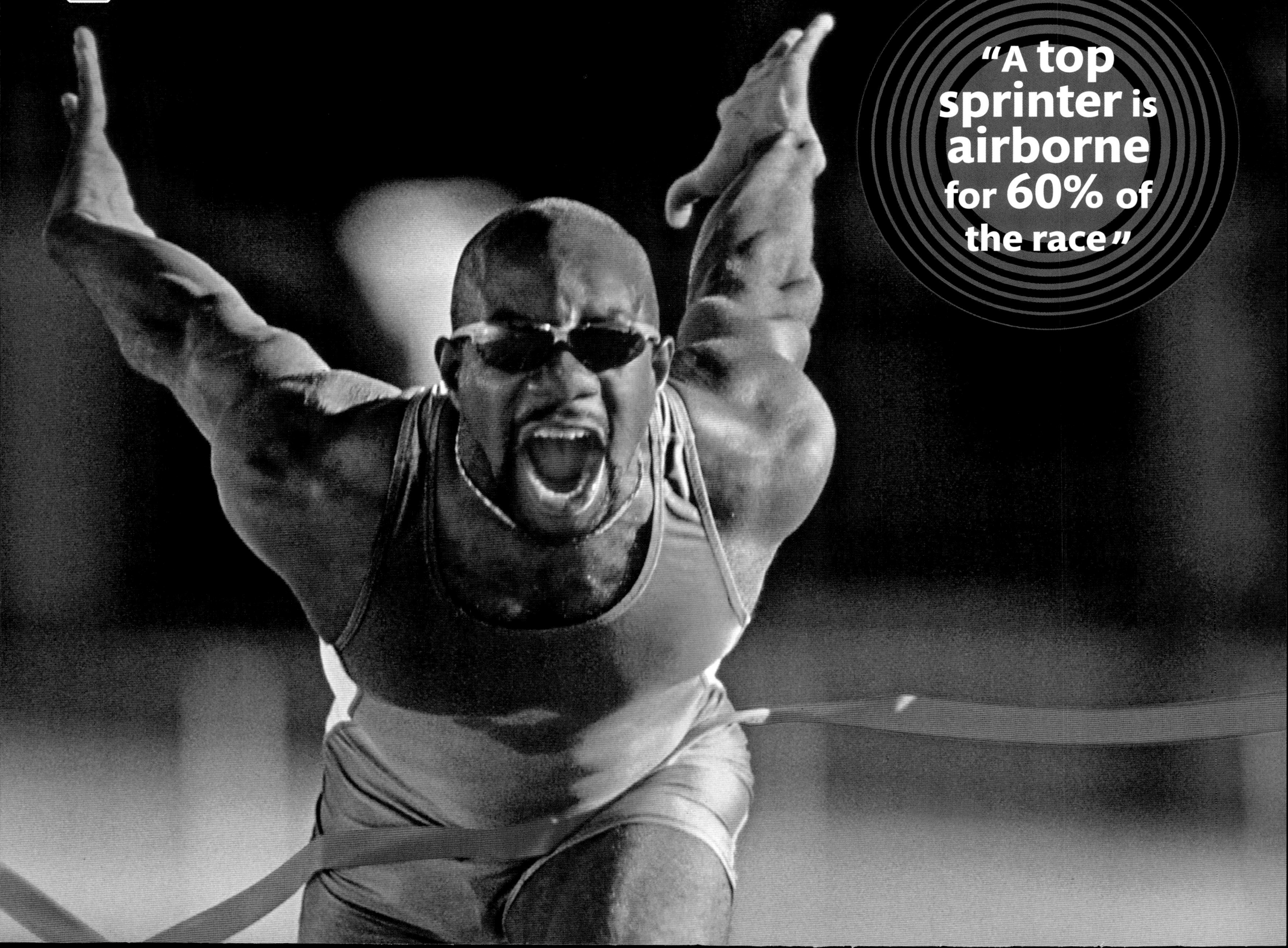

"A top sprinter is airborne for 60% of the race"

SUPER SPRINTER

Muscles at max

As the hypertuned sprint body blasts into action, more than 600 muscles—in top condition and with precise coordination—work together to propel the body along the track. The gluteus, biceps femoris, and other upper thigh muscles provide most of the forward power, while the deltoids, biceps, triceps, and others pump the arms for added momentum. All the while, the lungs take in more air for extra oxygen. Every detail counts—success is measured in thousandths of a second.

STATS AND FACTS

ACCELERATION POWER

Accelerative power is measured in watts per kilogram (power to weight ratio)

HUMAN	25
GREYHOUND	60
CHEETAH	120
CAR	140

WATTS PER KILOGRAM (2.2 LB)

SPRINTING SPEEDS

TOP SPRINTERS MAKE 4.5 STRIDES PER SECOND

FASTEST 110 yd SPRINT

09.58 SECONDS

Dipping to the finish

This sprinter sweeps his arms back to reduce air resistance and leans his body forward to cross the line at the earliest possible instant. Every stage of a sprinter's race has its detailed muscle action plan.

TEAMWORK
Muscle groups

Muscles rarely work alone. Almost every movement has several muscles, even dozens, acting as a team. A single muscle can only pull or contract—it cannot forcefully push. So muscles are arranged in groups, for example, around a bone. One group pulls the bone one way; another muscle team pulls the bone another way, another twists it, and so on. So even a seemingly simple movement is an amazing feat of multicoordination.

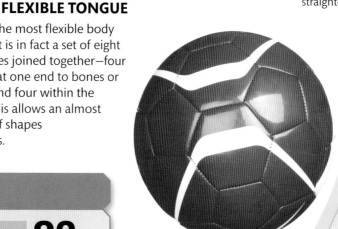

Crosswise muscles poke tongue out

Superior, or surface muscles curl up tongue

FLEXIBLE TONGUE

The most flexible body part is in fact a set of eight muscles joined together—four attached at one end to bones or other tissues, and four within the tongue itself. This allows an almost endless range of shapes and movements.

EXERCISE MAKES MUSCLES THICKER

Four muscles at front of thigh, together called the quadriceps, pull thigh forward and straighten knee

Extended leg with knee straightened

2 Front hip and thigh muscles—the quadriceps—unbend the knee and make the foot swing at great speed

STATS AND FACTS

Arm		**23**
Leg		**35**

NUMBER OF MUSCLES IN EACH LIMB

MUSCLE COORDINATION

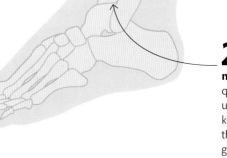

You use **8 muscles** (4 pairs) to chew food

You use **35 muscles** to hold a pen

The hamstrings, which consist of three muscles, contract to swing thigh back and bend knee

FACIAL EXPRESSIONS

The face has more than 50 muscles, some as slim as elastic bands. Several do not join to bones, but to each other, as tendons merge at connecting sites. This happens at each corner of the mouth, where seven muscles merge. Tiny movements greatly alter our facial expressions. As the frontalis muscles in the forehead contract they raise the eyebrows from a quizzical look, to surprise, to astonishment!

SURPRISE

Flexed leg bent at the knee, ready to swing for the kick

Hamstrings at rest

Quadriceps stretched by the shortening of the hamstrings

1 Rear hip and thigh muscles (hamstrings) contract to bring the leg back and bend the knee

Standing leg at rest

MUSCLES IN ACTION

The hip and thigh have the bulkiest, strongest muscles to move the leg to and fro. For a kick, muscles at the front pull fast and hard to swing the thigh forward at the hip and straighten the knee for a double-action power-hit.

"Muscle cells produce enough heat every day to boil almost 2 pints (1 liter) of water for an hour"

BODY FRAMEWORK

49

SUPER STRENGTH

Holding power

You don't need to move your muscles to make them work hard—simply tightening them can produce a huge amount of force. Holding a position requires raw strength. But attention to balance and posture is also important, because it prevents individual muscles from wasting energy by working against other muscles that are pulling the body out of alignment. With just a slight change in the position of his legs, this gymnast can reduce the power needed by his arm muscles by almost one-seventh.

STATS AND FACTS

WEIGHT DISTRIBUTION

- 7% HEAD
- 10% ARMS
- 50% TRUNK
- 20% THIGHS
- 12% LOWER LEGS

LIFTING CAPACITY

ANT
50
times own
body weight

3
times own
body weight
WEIGHTLIFTER

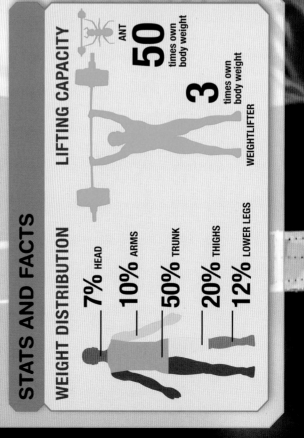

"All the body's muscles pulling in **one direction** would produce a force of **22 tons**"

Hanging around

Gymnastic rings are an ultimate test of upper body strength—about a quarter of muscle bulk is in the shoulders, arms, and hands. To hold a position, some muscle groups contract while others relax, then swap over.

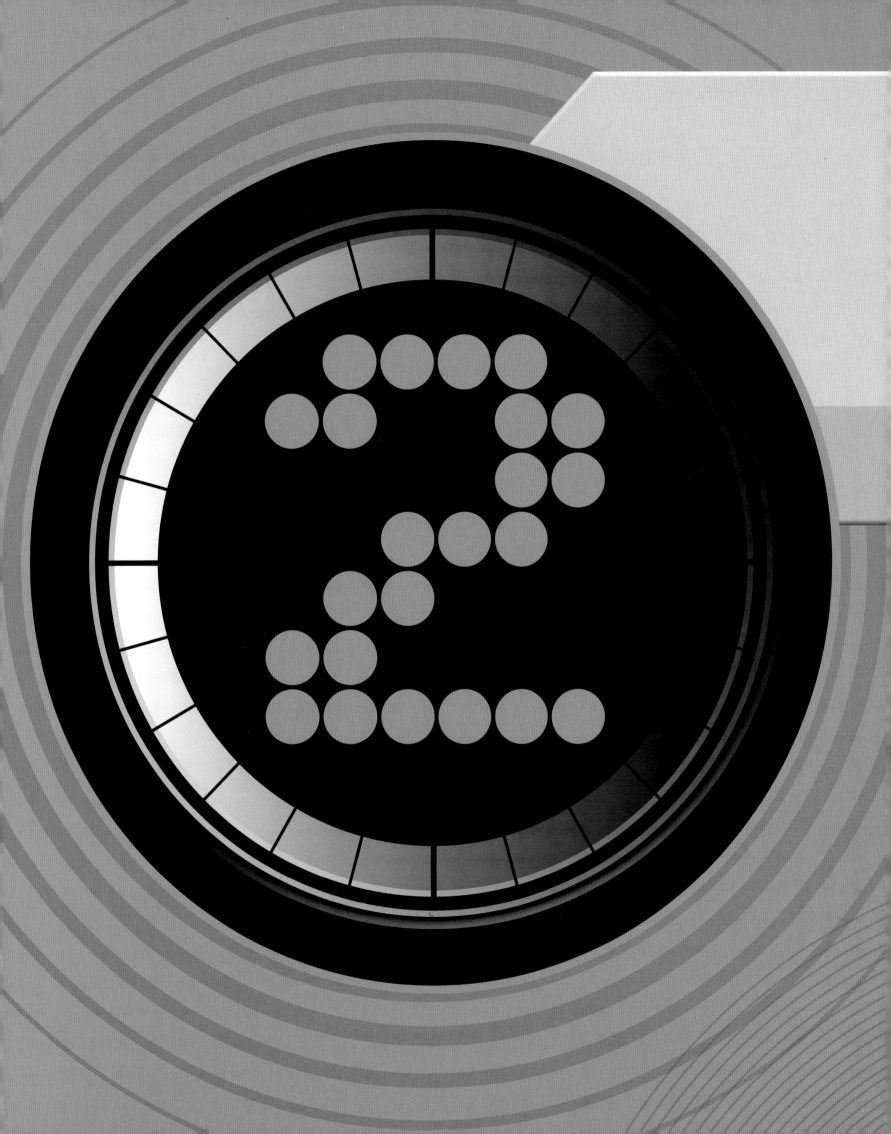

MISSION CONTROL

From its prime position at the top of the body, the all-knowing superbrain is aware of what happens outside the body—and inside, too. Every second, millions of messages carry never-ending thoughts, feelings, memories, and emotions.

TOTAL INTRANET

Nerve network

With spidery branches extending into almost every tiny corner of the body, the nervous system is an immense communications network—your own internal internet. It carries billions of nerve signals every second as micropulses of electricity. The signals are flashed to and from the brain and also directly between body parts. The brain and spinal cord form the central nervous system, while the bodywide branching nerves form the peripheral nervous system.

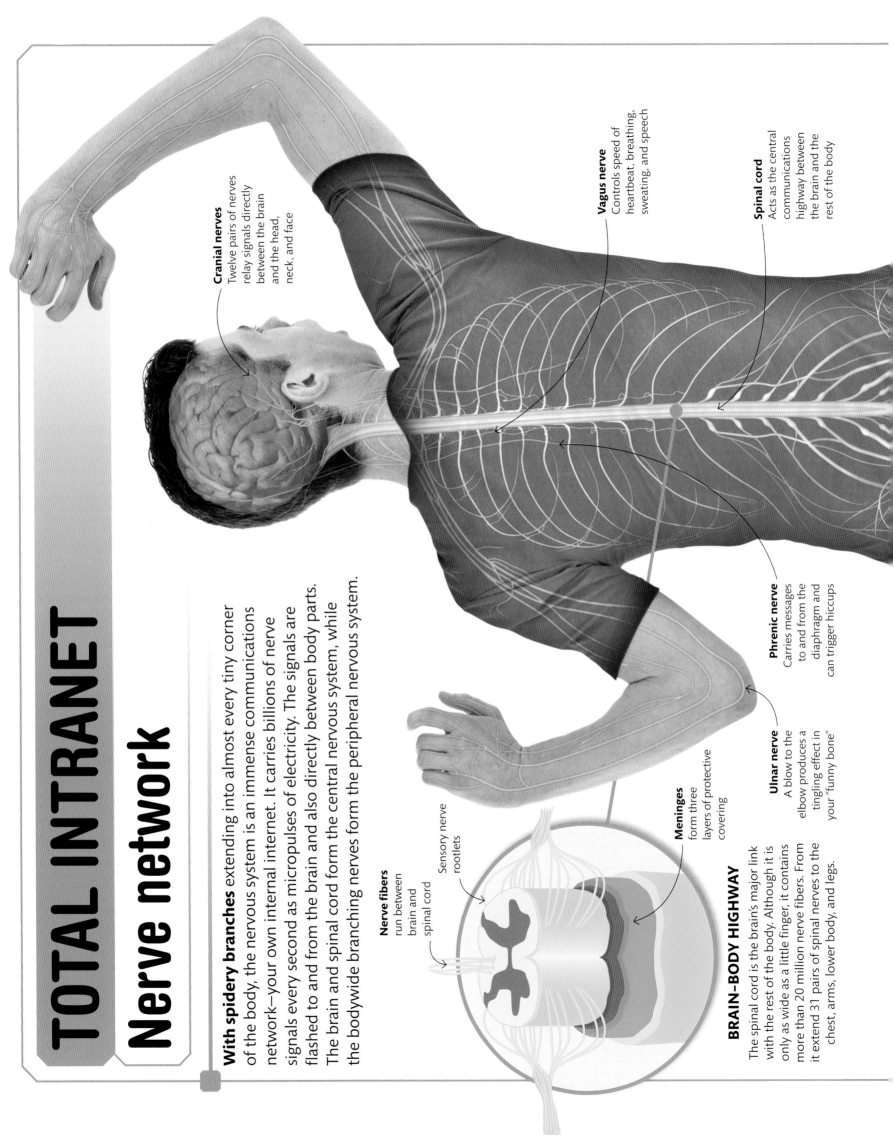

Cranial nerves
Twelve pairs of nerves relay signals directly between the brain and the head, neck, and face

Vagus nerve
Controls speed of heartbeat, breathing, sweating, and speech

Spinal cord
Acts as the central communications highway between the brain and the rest of the body

Phrenic nerve
Carries messages to and from the diaphragm and can trigger hiccups

Ulnar nerve
A blow to the elbow produces a tingling effect in your "funny bone"

Meninges
form three layers of protective covering

Nerve fibers
run between brain and spinal cord

Sensory nerve rootlets

BRAIN–BODY HIGHWAY

The spinal cord is the brain's major link with the rest of the body. Although it is only as wide as a little finger, it contains more than 20 million nerve fibers. From it extend 31 pairs of spinal nerves to the chest, arms, lower body, and legs.

Sacral plexus
Ten nerves merge, link, and separate at this junction

Sciatic nerve
The longest and thickest nerve in the body

Peroneal nerve
Runs down the inside of the thigh

Plantar nerve
Responds to tickling on the sole of the foot

Tibial nerve
Produces pins and needles in the lower leg when squashed

HEAD TO TOE
Nerves stretch throughout your body like electric cables, branching and dividing to reach every part. The distance from the brain to the toe can be more than 6 ft (1.8 m) in an adult, yet messages can travel between the two in $1/100$ of a second.

Adult brains lose 100,000 neurons per day

WHAT A NERVE!
A typical nerve contains thousands of nerve fibers, or axons, wrapped into bundles called fascicles. The whole nerve is contained within a tough, flexible covering that protects the fibers as the body parts around the nerve move, bend, squash, and pull at it.

Protective covering

Bundle of nerve axons

Axons (nerve fibers)

Blood vessels

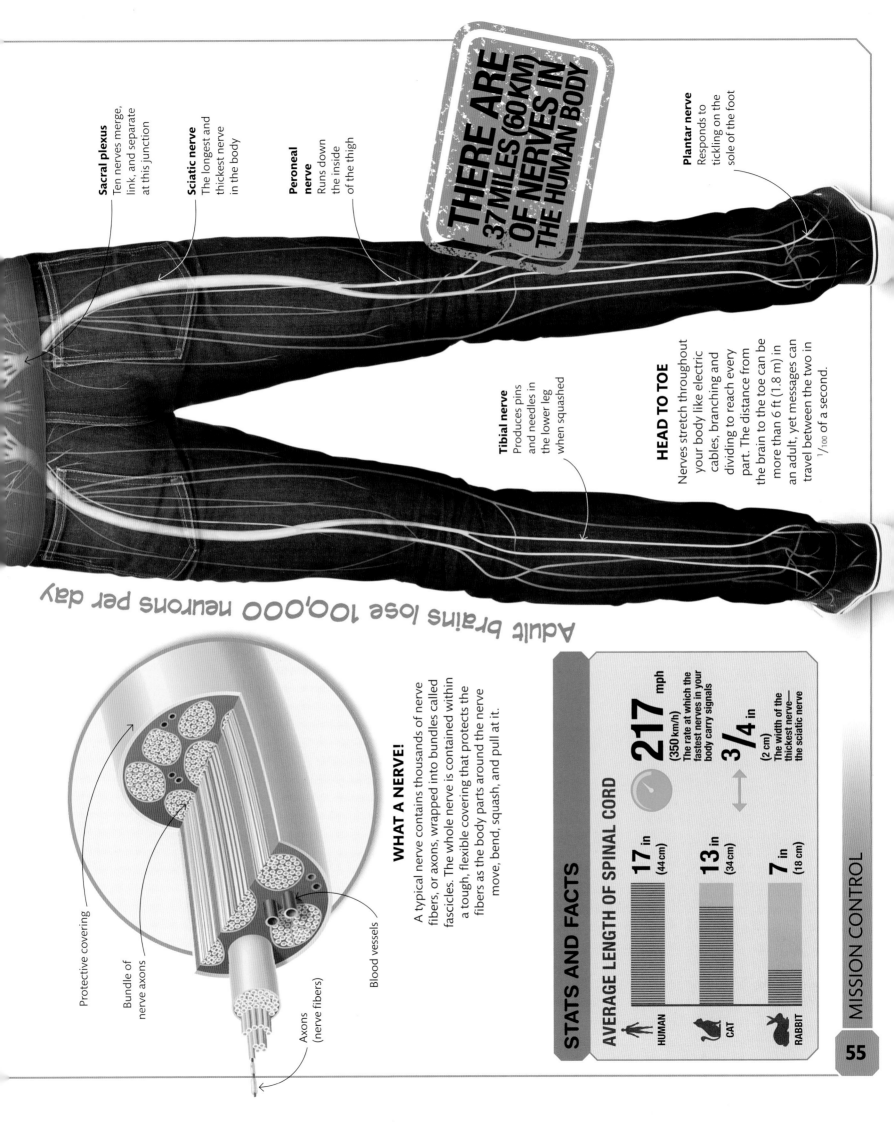

STATS AND FACTS

AVERAGE LENGTH OF SPINAL CORD

217 mph (350 km/h)
The rate at which the fastest nerves in your body carry signals

3/4 in (2 cm)
The width of the thickest nerve—the sciatic nerve

HUMAN: 17 in (44 cm)

CAT: 13 in (34 cm)

RABBIT: 7 in (18 cm)

Split-second decisions

To perform a steep turn, a pilot has to multitask: lower the left hand to descend, feel the nose dip, move the right hand sideways and right foot down, watch the horizon, and monitor balance—all in one second!

"The **brain** can handle **1 billion billion** nerve messages **per second**"

ZK-HZE

56

FLYING HIGH
Multitasking

Action situations put the brain into a state of high alert, turning it into a living supercomputer. Millions of messages, flooding in from all the senses, are sorted and filtered in different parts of the brain, but you only become aware of the most vital pieces of information. Hundreds of decisions, some conscious but many automatic, fire thousands of instructions every second to dozens of body muscles, to produce coordinated reactions to each situation.

STATS AND FACTS

COUNTDOWN TO A COLLISION

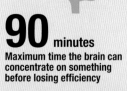

TIMELINE TO AVOID MIDAIR COLLISION

0.1 sec	SEE OBJECT
1.0 sec	RECOGNIZE OBJECT
5.0 sec	BECOME AWARE OF POTENTIAL COLLISION
4.0 sec	DECISION TO TURN OR CLIMB
0.4 sec	MUSCULAR REACTION
2.0 sec	AIRCRAFT RESPONSE TIME
12.5 sec	TOTAL

90 minutes
Maximum time the brain can concentrate on something before losing efficiency

INSIDE THE MEGAWEB
Nerves and nerve cells

Take apart the nerve system, bit by bit, and you reach its smallest parts—nerve cells, or neurons. They are among the most specialized and long-lasting of all cells. Their job is to receive, process, and send on nerve messages, in the form of tiny pulses of electricity. Each neuron has a complex weblike shape and thousands of delicate connections with other neurons. These shapes are not fixed. They change as connections grow or shrink, day by day, year after year.

Star-shaped glial cells

LITTLE HELPERS

In the entire nerve system, fewer than half the cells are neurons. The rest—called glial cells—give neurons physical support, nutrients, and protection from damage and germs.

Bundles of nerve fibers inside nerve

Nerve

Incoming signals from faraway neurons

Electrical signal passes along axon

Axon, or nerve fiber inside protective sheath

NERVE BUNDLE

Incoming signals from nearby neuron

Nearby neuron sending a signal

Nucleus of neuron

NERVE IMPULSES

Each nerve cell, or neuron, receives signals on its short spiderlike arms or its cell body. It constantly combines and processes these incoming signals and sends the resulting messages along a thicker, longer leg—called the nerve fiber, or axon—to other neurons.

End of
sending axon

Neurotransmitters
are chemicals that
cross the gap

MAKING THE LEAP

At a link, called a synapse, between
neurons, the two neurons do not
actually touch. They are separated
by a gap 10,000 times thinner than a
strand of hair. Nerve signals cross this
gap in the form of chemicals, then
carry on as electrical pulses again.

Receptor on
next neuron

Receptor opens its channel
to allow neurotransmitter
through to pass on the signal

Outgoing signals
along axon

Dendrite, one of
the spiderlike arms
on the cell body

**Nerve fiber
endings** connect
with more neurons

Fibers at end of
axon branch out

Myelin sheath
around axon
speeds signals
and stops them
from leaking out

NERVE CELLS
CAN LIVE LONGER
THAN OTHER
BODY CELLS

"If you were a
neuron you
would have
10,000 arms"

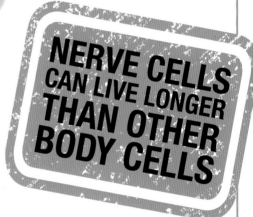

STATS AND FACTS

SURFACE AREA OF ALL
NEURONS
IN BRAIN

4 x SOCCER FIELD

NERVE CONNECTIONS

NEURON CARRYING CAPACITY

500 SIGNALS/ SEC

500 trillion
The number of connections
in the nervous system

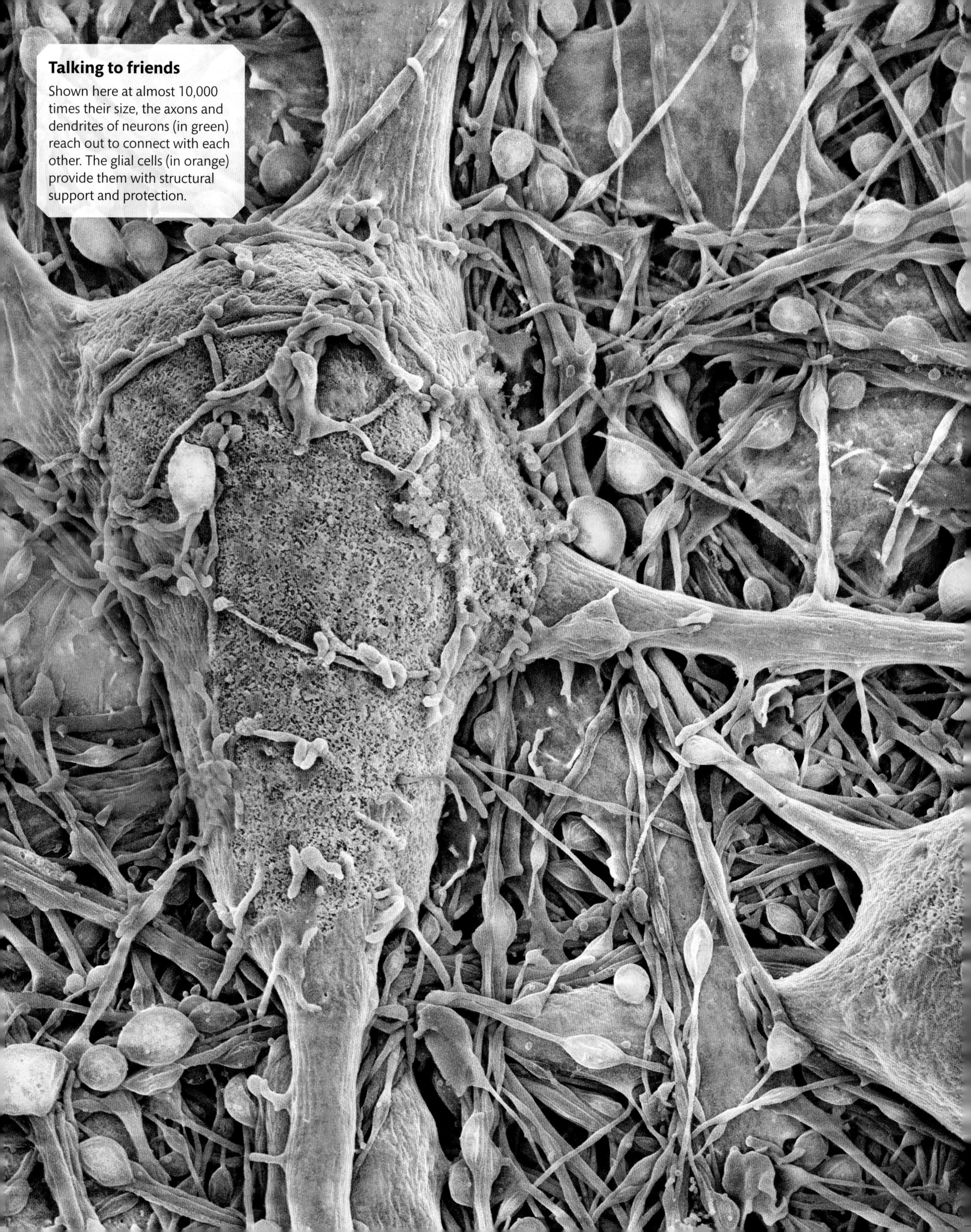

Talking to friends
Shown here at almost 10,000 times their size, the axons and dendrites of neurons (in green) reach out to connect with each other. The glial cells (in orange) provide them with structural support and protection.